Naming Evil, Judging Evil

Naming Evil
Judging Evil

Edited by Ruth W. Grant

With a Foreword by Alasdair MacIntyre

The University of Chicago Press | Chicago & London

Ruth W. Grant is professor of political science and philosophy at Duke University and a senior fellow at the Kenan Institute for Ethics. She is the author of *John Locke's Liberalism* and *Hypocrisy and Integrity,* both published by the University of Chicago Press.

The University of Chicago Press, Chicago 60637
The University of Chicago Press, Ltd., London
© 2006 by The University of Chicago
All rights reserved. Published 2006
Printed in the United States of America

15 14 13 12 11 10 09 08 07 06   1 2 3 4 5

ISBN-13: 978-0-226-30673-5   (cloth)
ISBN-10: 0-226-30673-9   (cloth)

Library of Congress Cataloging-in-Publication Data

Naming evil, judging evil / edited by Ruth W. Grant ; with a foreword by Alasdair MacIntyre.
    p. cm.
  Revisions of papers presented at a conference held Jan. 27–29, 2005 at Duke University. Includes bibliographical references and index.
    ISBN 0-226-30673-9 (cloth : alk. paper)   1. Good and evil—Congresses.
2. Judgment (Ethics)—Congresses.   I. Grant, Ruth Weissbourd, 1951–
  BJ1401.N36 2006
    170—dc22   2006010697

Contents

Foreword

There are these days all too many not quite good enough academic conferences and all too many not quite good enough books manufactured from papers delivered at such conferences. What a pleasure then to be asked to write a foreword to a book of papers from a conference that, unlike most, I wish that I had attended, a book that poses questions as interesting as any that there are! Yet, although I am delighted, I am not surprised. For the papers in this volume are by a group of colleagues at Duke University who have sustained an admirable tradition of collegial friendship among those in Duke's various departments and schools—Political Science, History, Philosophy, the Divinity School—who engage with central issues of political philosophy. They represent a range of viewpoints, and they have different projects and concerns. But over time their work has been informed by their shared reading, by extended interdisciplinary conversations and arguments, and by learning from each other's work. I was privileged to be part of this for a number of years.

This particular conference was the outcome of a set of discussions that had gone on for over two years, and the final versions of the participants' papers, now published in this volume, benefited significantly from comments presented at the conference by scholars from outside Duke. This has been a collective enterprise in a way that has too few parallels, at least in the humanities. It was and is of course important that conversation and enquiry about the subject matter that the participants addressed, which is inexhaustible, first opened up, at least according to the author of Genesis, in words exchanged by God, Adam, Eve, and the serpent, and is still carried on in our own day by Hannah Arendt and her numerous successors. So it would be ludicrous to expect anything like a conclusive treatment of the issues raised, either by our various and often incompatible understandings of the nature of evil or by our confrontations with evil in our own lives. Yet why speak of evil at all? Why is it not enough to speak of good and bad rather than good and evil? The contributors to this volume suggest several possible answers. Let me add to their suggestions one more but begin with a warning of dangers to be avoided. One such arises from the current climate of political incivility in the United States, which permits both liberal and conservative agitators to employ types of rhetoric that debase the linguistic currency and make it easy to use the word "evil" lightly, promiscuously, and irresponsibly. This kind of corruption of speech is itself a great evil.

A second danger derives from what Wittgenstein called an unbalanced diet of examples. By allowing one or two examples to engross not only the mind but also the imagination, we may give to striking features of those particular examples a significance that may obscure the character of evil. It is impossible now to think about evil without thinking about the Holocaust. And part of the horror that thought of the Holocaust elicits is the sheer number of murders. But what made the Holocaust a very great evil was not the number of deaths. With evil, quantity is not the issue. And so it is not the issue either over massacres in Bosnia or in Rwanda. A third very different type of danger arises from putting too great an emphasis upon choice, so that evil is taken to consist in the making of bad choices. But evil can arise from inaction as much as from action, from failures to will as much as from willing. Some evils result from our not having learned what it was our responsibility to learn and from consequent failures to recognize where and when we may have a duty to intervene. A failure by myself or by others to enquire, a lack of any impulse to enquire, about the oppression and exploitation that is occurring close at hand, but in disguised forms—a failure rooted in our desire to go on leading comfortable and undisturbed lives—can be quite as much an evil as oppression and exploitation are.

Yet these warnings, just because they draw our attention to a variety of evils, may themselves point us in the wrong direction, by tempting us to conclude—prematurely—that there is after all no such thing as evil, but only evils, and that evils have no one thing in common but resemble each other in an indefinite variety of ways. After all, we may ask, what *do* the corruption of language, the massacres of innocent people, and the negligent failure to unmask and confront oppression and exploitation have in common? And, looking for an answer, we may follow Susan Neiman's lead and began to think of these examples as members of a very much larger class. Stanley Hauerwas quotes Neiman's remark that "nothing is easier than stating the problem of evil in nontheist terms" (*Evil in Modern Thought* [Princeton: Princeton University Press, 2002], p. 5). She goes on: "Every time we make the judgment *this ought not to have happened* we are stepping onto a path that leads straight to the problem of evil . . . For what most demands explanation is not how moral judgments are justified, but why those that are so clearly justified were disregarded in the past." But this is to confuse the problem of evil with the problem of evils and both with the problem of bads—if I may use a rare, but badly needed word—and they are, so I am going to suggest, not at all the same. The problem of evil is a much narrower and more particular problem.

For evil, as Ruth Grant points out, is one particular kind of badness, yet it differs strikingly from most other kinds. A starting point for enquiring what it is might be by considering further questions that Grant and Nannerl Keohane open up in their essays. Both examine claims advanced by Rousseau, who connects the origin of evil with on the one hand inequality, on the other *amour-propre*. So Keohane in her paper focuses on aspects and types of inequality that are a source of evil. Yet we have to remember—pace Rousseau—that not all inequality is bad, let alone evil. All government, including the best of governments, necessarily involves inequality in respect of authority and power. All military organizations, including the best of armies fighting in the best of causes, requires such inequality. The inequalities that corrupt are of a different kind: inequalities of respect that result in inadequate recognition for someone's qualities as a human being, inequalities that violate the norms of justice in respect of need and desert, inequalities that are arbitrary and imposed for no good end.

Such types of inequality bring us to the threshold of evil, because they are apt to involve just that thought that informs the intentions of an evil will: "*I / we* are going to impose *my / our* will. This may be a matter of *my / our* visiting affliction upon you—whether there is one of you or six million of you—to achieve what it pleases *me / us* to achieve, no matter what the cost in pain, humiliation, and death to you, no matter what norms and values may be violated, and for no sufficient reason except that it is *my / our* will to do so. Or it may be a matter of *my / our* will and pleasure in securing a tranquil and pleasant existence for *me / us*, no matter what evils are being visited upon others. But, either way, let *my / our* will be done, just because it is *mine*, just because it is *ours*." This is the voice of pride. It is a voice that we may fail to recognize because its utterances can be and often are high-minded and moralistic. So it may on occasion speak in the vocabulary of a relentless benevolence, telling those upon whom it visits affliction that it is only doing this for the sake of their own good but omitting to add that what makes the achievement of that good its motivation is just that it is its own will and pleasure to do so, irrespective of what those others may need or desire. It was of course one of Nietzsche's insights that morality can be the mask worn by this kind of pride. And Nietzsche had been anticipated in this by Augustine.

Have we by identifying the part that pride so understood plays in human life also understood the nature of evil? Have we arrived at a unitary core conception of evil? If I am tempted to say "Yes," as I am, then the essays in this book should give me pause. For collectively they present a challenge to any large unitary account. Reading through these essays, I cannot but ask whether the conception of evil that I am inclined to defend can be spelled out in such a way as to take adequate account of the complexities that are so compellingly presented from such different perspectives. And this will be, I predict, the experience of many readers. What should the outcome be? Surely it should be an even more solidly grounded recognition that we have been participating in an unfinished conversation, in an enquiry in which there is a great deal more yet to be said. What matters is to have become part of that conversation so that one's own conclusions have been tempered by one's participation in it.

It is one mark of a university that is flourishing that it is a place where such continuing, fruitfully inconclusive conversations on matters of moral and metaphysical moment are sustained. The contributors to this volume have served not only their university but also their readers well.

Alasdair MacIntyre

Preface

This book is the product of a collaboration among nine faculty members at Duke University. I was prompted to convene the group out of the desire to discuss with my colleagues troubling issues surrounding the 9/11 attacks and the public discussions that had been generated by them. I was interested in exploring questions such as the following: What is the term "evil" good for, if anything? How are the evils that occur in the world affected by the ways in which evil is understood? How does one come to the judgment that some actions are evil, and when one does, should one always say so out loud, or is it sometimes important to bite one's tongue? What is involved in taking a stand? You can well imagine that, as we met, the questions multiplied. And, while the concerns with 9/11 remained present in the conversations, as they do in the essays in this volume, the discussions became quite wide-ranging.

Some of us were primarily concerned with the "problem of evil": is there anything that can be properly called evil, and if so, what are its sources and how can it be understood? Others were more interested in issues involved in making moral judgments and in the political consequences of such judgments. How can we come to sophisticated and nuanced judgments when we confront deep cultural differences? The sense of conviction about one's moral judgments can feed self-righteousness, but abdicating judgment in the face of uncertainties or disagreements has its dangers too. What are the political conditions that support responsible moral judgment? In pluralistic liberal democracies in particular, where is the balance between making judgments (required for democratic action) and forbearance from passing judgment on others (required for liberal toleration). In our conversations, the emphasis shifted back and forth between understanding evil and understanding moral judgment, but these issues finally are not separable. In the essays in this volume, despite the differences in emphasis, the questions raised in thinking about evil and moral judgment are continually intertwined.

In September 2003, we began meeting every few weeks over lunch to discuss readings pertinent to these issues among ourselves, and we continued meeting for three semesters. On January 27–29th, 2005, we held a working conference at Duke University where nine invited guests joined us as commentators on the papers we had prepared, which were draft versions of the essays published here. The commentators were Eleonore Stump (philosophy, St. Louis University), James Wetzel (philosophy and religion, Colgate University), David Wootton (history, University of London), Sanford Levinson (law, University of Texas, Austin), John McGowan (English, University of North Carolina, Chapel Hill), Philip Costanzo (psychology, Duke University), Jerome Levi (sociology and anthropology, Carleton College), Frances Ferguson (English, University of Chicago), and Georgia Warnke (philosophy, University of California, Riverside). They are listed here in the order of the chapters as they are published in this volume: Eleonore Stump commented on Michael Gillespie's chapter, and so on. Also participating in the discussions were Neil DeMarchi (economics, Duke University), Douglas MacLean (philosophy, University of North Carolina, Chapel Hill), Michael Moses (English, Duke University), and Susan Wolf (philosophy, University of North Carolina, Chapel Hill). The commentators could not have done a better job—we are all extremely grateful to them. And the conversation over the course of the conference was a model of what interdisciplinary dialogue should be.

As a result of the process I have just described, from the first lunchtime conversation among the authors to the editing of the papers in response to the conference comments and conversation, the work developed and improved. Moreover, this collection of essays has greater coherence than most. I hope that the reader will find that the chapters speak to each other in a variety of ways and that reading the book is something like entering into our conversation.

None of this would have been possible without the generous support of the Provost's Common Fund at Duke University. Additional funding was supplied by the Kenan Institute for Ethics and the Gerst Program in Political, Economic and Humanistic Studies, also at Duke University. I deeply appreciate their support. To everyone involved with this project, but particularly to my collegial coauthors, I owe a large debt of gratitude.

Ruth W. Grant, 2005

Introduction

Ruth W. Grant

"Hear no evil, see no evil, speak no evil." This familiar proverb, originally associated with the Buddhist god Vadjra, carried the message that those who followed its injunction would not suffer evil themselves. The message implies that there is an intimate connection between the way in which evil is or is not identified, recognized, and communicated, on the one hand, and the way in which evils actually happen in the world, on the other. This is a central insight animating this project.

How we understand evil and how we speak about evil affect the evils that we are likely to suffer or inflict. Acknowledging this connection was the tacit common ground behind opposing American reactions to the terrorist attacks of September 11, 2001. There were some who most feared the dangers of a Manichean response: that "we" would label "them" the "evil" ones and, by implication, see ourselves as entirely "good"—a move that blinds us to the way in which such a response mirrors the Manicheanism of our enemies and that can be used to justify violence. Others feared at least as much the dangers of an abdication of judgment: that the inability to name what had happened properly as "terror" and "evil" would cripple our ability to respond in such a way as to prevent more of the same. A quite similar argument is taking place among psychiatrists about the propriety of using the term "evil" when speaking of killers who are particularly cruel.[1] Which is more dangerous: to speak of evil or not to?

There are many ways in which various conceptions of what evil is and how it works in the world can be implicated in evil action. Ironically, opposing ideas can lead to the same result. Is evil a matter of malicious individual intent? If it is, and evildoers believe themselves to be well intentioned, how can they recognize what they do for what it is? "Precisely the belief that evil actions require evil intentions allowed totalitarian regimes to convince people to override moral objections that might otherwise have functioned."[2] Is evil a product of systemic historical forces and not of malicious individual will? In this case, too, one can overcome the restraints of conscience. The inevitable progress of history becomes a powerful justification. This idea also fueled the terrors of totalitarian regimes. How should we understand evil and how should we speak about it given that when it comes to evil, thought and action cannot be neatly compartmentalized?

We might ask also why it is that these questions seem so pressing today. This is our paradoxical situation:

> [A] gulf has opened up in our culture between the visibility of evil and the intellectual resources available for coping with it. Never before have images of horror been so widely disseminated and so appalling—from organized death camps to children starving in famines that might have been averted . . . The repertoire of evil has never been richer. Yet never have our responses been so weak.[3]

On the one hand, we have witnessed an unending stream of incredible horrors in the last century. "Auschwitz" no longer represents the unique depth and perversity of human evil manifested in the Holocaust; instead, that name can be invoked as *paradigmatic* today. The full impact of that realization also animates this project. On the other hand, and with that realization in mind, we seem to have lost the conceptual resources and the vocabulary with which to understand and communicate about evil. We cannot recognize evil if we cannot speak of it. How do we come to the judgment that some actions are evil? A certain paralysis in the face of this question is surely one of the weaknesses of our intellectual resources today. What are the intellectual resources that we need in order to understand the problem of evil? Is there something about the modern world that has both given it a distinctive visage and exacerbated it?

There are many ways in which the "problem of evil" and the dilemmas of judgment that follow from it might be framed, each suggested by a different fundamental question. Why do the innocent suffer? This question is at the root of the "theodicy problem": how can there be evil in a world ruled by a god who is both good and omnipotent? In the absence of a satisfactory answer to that question, one seems to be left to conclude that God is either not good or not omnipotent, that there is no God, or that the world is fundamentally irrational. Much of what does happen shouldn't happen. Good does not always come from good, nor evil from evil. Some conclude that tragedy is a part of the human condition and evil is, at bottom, inexplicable, beyond comprehension. These are familiar metaphysical and religious formulations of the fundamental problem.

How is it that so often human beings perpetrate evil in the name of the good? This question grounds the psychological formulation of the problem. We want to know, not only how to account for the consciousness of the evildoer, but also how to explain the disjunction between that self-consciousness and the observer's judgment. How can a person who seems perfectly monstrous see himself as perfectly justified? Can well-intentioned people be held responsible for the evil that they do? Is evil a matter of failures of judgment or of something else entirely: failures of empathy or imagination, for example? And, if it is a matter of failures of judgment, are people culpable for those failures? Hannah Arendt, in her famous discussion of the "banality of evil," suggested that Adolf Eichmann, who managed the logistics of Hitler's "final solution," did not send millions of Jews to the death camps with malicious intent. In her view, it was his "thoughtlessness" that allowed him to act as he did.[4] Presumably, thoughtfulness or responsible judgment is an antidote to evil. But what is responsible judgment?

Finally, there is a historical formulation of the problem that revolves around the question, "Is moral progress possible?" Machiavelli wrote that there is always the same amount of evil in the world, a view perfectly compatible with ancient conceptions of history as cyclical.[5] But we moderns have become accustomed to assume that history is progressive and, along with that assumption, to assume that evils are "problems" amenable to "solutions." The history of the last century cannot help but call those assumptions into question. And, taking into account the insight with which we began—that our ideas about evil influence evil action in the world—we are compelled to take seriously the possibility that the faith in progress itself has played a role in modern horrors. The temptation is to rethink the idea of progress; but this too implies that getting the ideas "right" might provide some sort of solution. Perhaps *that* is the dangerous fantasy to be avoided. How do we confront the likelihood that evil is permanently with us?

Each of the three fundamental questions that I have identified—theological / metaphysical, psychological, and historical—have been raised everywhere and always. But the "problem of evil," as I have already suggested, also has a peculiarly modern cast. This book is a collection of reflections on evil, on judgment, and on the intimate relations between them. Making moral judgments at all seems to be particularly problematic today. The ability to judge has been disarmed in part by the fact of permanent and deep disagreements over moral issues. But, the fact of disagreement certainly is not news. What is problematic today is the frequent inference from disagreement to the conclusion that argument, and even judgment, are impossible. The essays in this volume presuppose that this inference is not correct. There are many ways to explain the permanence of moral disagreement that do not entail rejecting the possibility either of dialogue between those who disagree or of better and worse moral judgments.

And in fact, the contributors to this volume would insist on the necessity of moral judgment whatever position is taken on the question of moral truth. If there are universal moral truths, at the very least, we must judge among them when they come in conflict. We might need to decide, for example, whether the demands of loyalty or the demands of justice are greater in a given case. If all values are relative to the specific cultures that generate them, we are no less obliged to judge. No culture is univocal; cultural practices are continually contested and change over time. For many reasons and in either case, judgment is simply inescapable.[6]

But there are both powerful pressures and powerful temptations to try to escape judgment nonetheless. Democratic sensibilities pull in two directions on the matter. Democracy depends on the notion that sound judgment is a real possibility. But it also tends to erode the sources of authoritative judgment.[7] "Who are you to judge?" is a disarming question, one that should be followed by, "Whom do I have to be?" The reluctance to sit in judgment can be the consequence of appropriate humility, but it can also be the consequence of a corrosive lack of confidence in one's judgment. And that reluctance, along with the temptations to denial, to rationalization, and to the avoidance of conflict, also contributes to the evils of the world. This is one way of talking about Arendt's "thoughtlessness." If we shirk our responsibility to judge, we lose the capacity to hold others responsible as well. Judgment and evil are linked through the concept of responsibility. Taking a stand in resistance to evil requires not only making a judgment but passing judgment on others.

But now we move from the Scylla to the Charybdis of this matter. When passing judgment becomes fanatical righteousness, it too becomes a source of evil. The dangers of fanaticism and the dangers of abdication are equally real. Thus, if we are concerned about the relations between evil and judgment, we need to attend, not only to making good judgments, but also to how the moral commitments that follow from those judgments are brought into public life. And in taking up these issues, we need to keep in mind the most sobering of the issues that have been raised here. We need to take very seriously the permanence of evil in human history, the question of the possibility of moral progress, and the limitations on any project that focuses on improving thinking and speaking about evil as a way of addressing evil itself.

The reader may wish to know, before turning the page and embarking on the substance of this book, what we mean by "evil." I owe the reader a word or two on this question. Starting with a dictionary definition helps some, but not much: "The suffering which results from morally wrong human choices." Of course, now we will want to ask what "morally wrong human choices" are. The definition is certainly insufficient in this respect. But it does tell us some things. Evil can be distinguished from natural disasters, like floods or earthquakes,[8] and also from wrongs that do not necessarily cause suffering, like lies or cheating. Evil is one kind of wrong or badness, often used to suggest a particularly intense wrong, probably on account of the association with suffering. The definition implies that cruelty is a primary form of evil: suffering caused by human choice.[9]

But there are aspects of this definition that have produced vigorous debates among the authors of the chapters in this book. Foremost among them is what might be meant by "human choice." If the phrase implies deliberate action, we have excluded the whole class of evils due to negligence or "sins of omission." If the phrase locates the problem of evil in individual agency, we have excluded consideration of systemic evils of the kind that are the consequences of the way in which individual choices are organized and delimited.[10] Systemic evils may not be caused by human choices in quite the same way that individual evil actions are, but many would argue that they are evils for which human beings must take responsibility in a way that we do not take responsibility for floods and earthquakes.[11] If the phrase implies malicious intent, we have excluded evils that are perpetrated in the name of the good, which is a very large class of evils indeed.

Perhaps, though, this conclusion depends upon what is meant by "malicious intent." The worst sorts of crimes against humanity—the cruelties that have accompanied modern political movements—can be seen as perpetrated both in the name of the good *and* with malicious intent.

The perpetrators know that murder, rape, torture, and so forth are bad things to do. They do not do them to their family and friends. But they believe that there are certain circumstances that justify doing these admittedly cruel things to certain people. In fact, they often deliberately choose to subject their victims to what they know to be the worst evils—rape or torturing children in front of their parents, for example—precisely because they know that such actions are dehumanizing and effectively serve to terrorize others. Or, sometimes they engage in what they know to be horrific acts in order to show their loyalty to a cause by their willingness to overcome their scruples in its service—not unlike a gang initiation ritual that requires doing something terrible to someone else. The whole point would be lost if the action were not universally recognized as evil. In these situations, people justify their malicious intention to treat someone cruelly with some belief that their cruelty serves a greater good or is morally required of them.

This is very different from the sort of practices that raise the "cultural relativism" question, practices that some might consider evil that are not intended maliciously by the practitioners at all. In some cultures, foot binding or female genital mutilation are considered good things to do—people do them precisely to the people whom they love. In other cultures, these practices are considered abhorrent. Are we entitled to judge such practices as "evils," regardless of the intentions behind them? Should we speak of "female genital cutting," so as to avoid implying by our very choice of words that it is an evil? Is it the degree of suffering and not the character of the will that matters, so that polygamy might be considered a wrong while female genital mutilation can properly be considered an evil? These are the sorts of questions that have engaged us.

I have employed the term "we" in a general sense throughout this introduction. In attempting to explain his similar use of the word, Bernard Williams wrote:

> Obviously, it can't mean everybody in the world . . . I hope it does not mean only people who already think as I do. The best I can say is that "we" operates, not through a fixed designation, but through invitation . . . It is not a matter of "I" telling "you" what I and others think, but of my asking you to consider to what extent you and I think some things and perhaps need to think others.[12]

We, the contributors to this volume, invite you to join us in our conversation in the pages that follow.

To make that venture a little bit easier, I will briefly preview each of the book's chapters, and then I will explain why they are ordered in the way that they are and identify some of the common threads that make a whole of these nine parts. Michael Gillespie begins by tracing the history of conceptions of evil in the West from the Middle Ages to the present in order to explain why the contemporary understanding of evil is so impoverished. We are unable to speak about quotidian forms of evil, recognizing only horrendous, demonic evil of the sort represented by Hitler. Evil thus appears both inhuman and incomprehensible to us. Gillespie takes the heterodox view that our difficulties in this regard stem not from the death of God, but rather from a view of his omnipotence that dates back to William of Ockham.

Stanley Hauerwas also addresses the destructive features of a modern morality whose only moral touchstone is ultimate evil. Modernity is characterized by a fascination with evil coupled with skepticism about the good. Hauerwas turns to Augustine for a critical alternative. Augustine views evil as nothing other than a privation of the good. Thus, moral reflection must begin with a conception of the good. Building on Augustine, Hauerwas argues for a conception of the good shared by a particular community, one which is humble in the knowledge of its own propensity for sin and, in particular, for perpetrating evil in the name of the good.

The next chapter, by Ruth Grant, begins with a discussion of Jean-Jacques Rousseau's pivotal argument that evil is the product of systemic forces; without particular evil individuals, evil can arise nonetheless. Rousseau provides an alternative both to Christian doctrines of original sin and to Enlightenment hopes for moral progress based on the advancement of reason. The French revolutionaries joined his beliefs in the natural goodness of man and the systemic origins of evil to the idea that a complete break with the past and a progressive history were possible. This conjunction of ideas contributed to the Terror. In contrast, the American revolutionaries held that the sources of injustice and civil strife are "sown in the nature of man" and therefore that these evils are a permanent possibility. Grant uses these examples to show how different "logics of evil" can be used to justify different sorts of evils and to argue that, though the systemic view is often advanced as a positive alternative to Manicheanism, it can easily become indistinguishable from it.

Nannerl Keohane's chapter explores the relation between inequality and evil in all of its dimensions. Her argument proceeds through an analysis and critique of Rousseau's understanding of the origins and the impact of social, political, and economic inequalities. Inequalities of wealth and power set the conditions for evildoing and themselves can be the motivation for severe mistreatment. Moreover, inequality can undermine the natural impulses of compassion that temper injustice and evil in human relations. In Keohane's view, inequality is not just an incidental accompaniment of evil but central to it. Keohane thus concludes that a sincere attempt to confront the problem of evil must begin by attending to inequality.

In the next chapter, Peter Euben takes the novel *The Remains of the Day* as a template to discuss the strategies of evading moral judgment that allow people to be complicitous in the evils of their time. The novel's protagonist, a butler named Stevens, runs one of England's pre–World War Two "great houses" with consummate efficiency. While Stevens displays many admirable characteristics—professionalism, dedication to larger purposes, loyalty, and refusal to give in to emotion—his ethical and political judgment is cauterized by an absolute dedication to his master, Lord Darlington (a naive and dangerous man who attempts to push England into an alliance with Nazi Germany). Euben's analysis of the butler raises many of the same issues raised by Hannah Arendt's portrait of Eichmann. His discussion helps us to recognize the dynamics of moral evasion and its relation to "professionalism" but also to see in Stevens's development the grounds for the claim that taking responsibility for moral and political judgment is an essential component of human dignity.

From the psychology of moral evasion, the next chapter turns to the psychology of moral conviction. How does the sense of conviction loosen constraints and allow people to perpetrate evil in the name of opposing it? Evil is often committed by those convinced of their own righteousness. David Wong's analysis considers in particular those occasions where this simplifying and polarizing "morality of conviction" is entangled with ignorance of other cultures. His primary illustrative case is the current conflict between Islamicism and the United States. While nuanced appreciation of the truth in one's opponents position can lead to paralysis and while decisive action is served by oversimplification, Wong maintains that, in the best case, we must act decisively with our eyes wide open, in honest acknowledgment of the moral ambiguities of the conflict.

Elizabeth Kiss tackles the matter of judgment in the face of cross-cultural complexity by examining two controversial cases—female genital mutilation and suicide bombings. She constructs a model of good judgment that combines a commitment to core substantive norms with a capacity to make layered judgments that distinguish between moral assessments of (a) an action or practice, (b) the social contexts that shape, sustain, and give meaning to the practice, (c) the motivations and interests of those who engage in or defend it, (d) our own moral standing in relation to it, and (e) appropriate and effective responses to it. Kiss argues that a layered model of moral judgment avoids two extreme responses to situations where judgments must be made cross-culturally: clarity purchased at the price of cultural sensitivity and complexity that undermines the capacity to judge altogether.

Finally, the last two chapters address problems of moral and political judgment as they appear in the particular context of pluralistic, liberal democracies. Malachi Hacohen argues that there is little historical evidence to support the concern that liberals will abdicate or evade the responsibility to pass judgment. Historically, the problem has been one of political mobilization; and this is a problem that arises from within liberalism itself. From Benjamin Constant to Alexis de Tocqueville to Raymond Aron, liberals have struggled with the political question of how to mobilize a public to defend liberty and then assure that it does not abuse its power and endanger liberty; how to form consensus while protecting pluralism; how to encourage commitment yet avoid fanaticism. In other words, liberalism has always been ambivalent: the people is either the sovereign public or the mob. Hacohen argues that this ambivalence cannot be resolved without destroying liberalism itself; the cure would be worse than the disease. But he suggests that the situation can be ameliorated by improving the conditions enabling responsible moral judgment through religious, educational, and voluntary organizations, the sites liberals traditionally have recommended.

In the final chapter, Thomas Spragens, Jr., examines the tension between the norms of tolerance and mutual respect, on the one hand, and the virtue of being a person of good judgment and sound conviction, on the other, particularly in the context of democratic citizenship. The exercise of good moral judgment is a problematic virtue in itself. The tension between the necessity of passing judgment and the necessity of forbearing from it is present in the biblical tradition, for example. But it is particularly problematic in pluralistic democracies where people with different moral vocabularies must reach collective judgments. Spragens concludes that the tension between candor and civility, between taking a stand on principle and biting one's tongue in the name of mutual respect, is not wholly resolvable. But he offers the hope that a combination of empathy and judgment can lead us to recognize "that human plurality is not simply an obstacle to moral judgment but also a dialectical resource for achieving it."

There are many synergies between these nine essays, and consequently, more than one logical way that they might have been arranged. I could have used the three approaches to the problem of evil explored earlier in this introduction: theological / metaphysical (Gillespie and Hauerwas); historical (Grant and Hacohen); psychological (Euben and Wong). I could have grouped the first three essays together as treatments of various ways of thinking about what evil is and their implications. The next three deal broadly with the moral psychology of evil. The last three focus on the difficulties of making judgments within a liberal frame of reference that requires appreciating different points of view. In the end, I made a simple division between the first four essays, which are primarily concerned with the problem of evil, and the last five essays, which concentrate on moral judgment.

Much more important than this broad division, however, is that the chapters are arranged so that each one is quite closely related to the one that precedes it and the one that follows it. For example, Keohane's chapter stands between Grant's and Euben's. Like Grant, she explores Rousseau's understanding of evil. But she focuses on inequalities of wealth and power as sources of evil and thus shares common ground with Euben's discussion of the butler in *The Remains of the Day*. Because the chapters are arranged in this way, the reader will profit from reading the book start to finish. There is a kind of natural progression from one essay to the next. At the same time, the reader will doubtless find common questions and issues scattered throughout. For example, Euben and Hacohen both ask what sort of politics supports the capacity for moral judgment and political action. Gillespie explains the paradox with which Grant begins; that in the modern world, we continue to expect moral progress at the same time as we experience horrendous evils on a grand scale. Examples could be multiplied, but I will leave them to the reader to discover.

Finally, there are certain commonalities that unite these essays. It is most striking that nobody has a good word to say about Manicheanism in any of its many forms.[13] Most of the authors identify some sort of tension between alternatives, which are polar opposites, and seek either a complex middle ground or a third alternative, with varying degrees of optimism about the possibilities for success. For Kiss, the poles are "clarity" and "complexity." Wong's corresponding categories are a kind of blind, self-righteous decisiveness in contrast to thoughtful paralysis. Hacohen sees the dilemmas of liberal politics as irresolvable, though that is not particularly troubling to him. Spragens finds the tension between "bigotry" and "nihilism" irresolvable and is more troubled by it. Many of these essays struggle to surmount one "either / or" or another.

"Evil" itself is a term that suggests polar opposites. It is one half of a binary, a pair. It indicates an extreme, and one expects a corresponding extreme at the other end of some imaginary line; like hot or cold, black or white, all or nothing—good or evil. The temptation to speak of evil in this way is very deeply rooted. It is a temptation to be vigorously resisted. If this volume shows nothing else, it shows that speaking about evil is far more complicated than that.

NOTES

1. Benedict Carey, "For the Worst of Us, the Diagnosis May Be 'Evil,'" *New York Times*, February 8, 2005.

2. Susan Neiman, *Evil in Modern Thought: An Alternative History of Philosophy* (Princeton: Princeton University Press, 2002), p. 275.

3. Andrew Delbanco, *The Death of Satan: How Americans Have Lost the Sense of Evil* (New York: Farrar, Strauss and Giroux, 1995), p. 3. See Richard J. Bernstein, *Radical Evil: A Philosophical Interrogation* (Cambridge: Polity Press, 2002); and George Kateb, "The Adequacy of the Canon," *Political Theory* 30, no. 4 (2002): 482–505.

4. Hannah Arendt, *Eichmann in Jerusalem: A Report on the Banality of Evil* (New York: Penguin, 1963, 2d ed., 1964), p. 287. See George Kateb, *Hannah Arendt: Politics, Conscience, Evil* (Totowa, NJ: Rowman and Allanheld, 1984), pp. 73–74; see also pp. 93–96 for a strong critique of Arendt on the relation of pity and cruelty.

5. Niccolò Machiavelli, *The Prince and The Discourses* [1517], introduction by Max Lerner (New York: Modern Library, 1950), pp. 115, 117, 216.

6. Ruth W. Grant, "Political Theory, Political Science and Politics," *Political Theory* 30, no. 4 (2002): 577–595, pp. 582–83.

7. Alexis de Tocqueville, *Democracy in America* [1835], introduction by Sanford Kessler, trans. by Stephen D. Grant (Indianapolis: Hackett, 2000), vol. 2, pt. 1, chap. 2.

8. It was not always so. These have been seen as expressions of divine will and often as punishments for human evil. They were considered "physical evils," as opposed to "moral evils." The difference between the reaction to the Lisbon earthquake of 1755 and the tsunami of 2004 is indicative of the degree to which evil has come to be seen as an exclusively human problem in modern times. See Neiman, *Evil in Modern Thought*, pp. 3–5; and Judith Shklar, *The Faces of Injustice* (reprint; New Haven: Yale University Press, 1992), pp. 51–54.

9. See Judith Shklar, "Putting Cruelty First," in *Ordinary Vices* (reprint; Cambridge, MA: Belknap Press, 1985).

10. Kenneth Waltz makes a similar distinction between individual agency and systemic analysis as alternative ways of understanding the causes of war in *Man, the State and War: A Theoretical Analysis* (New York: Columbia University Press, 1954, 1959), see especially p. 80.

11. Shklar, *Faces of Injustice*, explores the distinction between injustice and misfortune.

12. Bernard Williams, *Shame and Necessity* (Berkeley: University of California Press, 1993), p. 171.

13. Manicheanism, founded in Persia in the third century, holds the dualistic view that good and evil, associated with the spiritual and the material, respectively, were created by different gods and that they are in eternal conflict with one another. Man should thus attempt to purify himself through asceticism from the evil associated with the material part of his nature. "Manicheanism" has come to signify any approach to moral issues that posits a bright line between good and evil and the possibility of any individual or group standing entirely on one side or the other of it.

PART 1

Speaking About Evil

Where Did All the Evils Go?

From a fading photo on the title page of Ron Rosenbaum's recent book, *Hitler: The Search for the Origins of His Evil*,[1] a small child peers out at us. Who is this child? A victim of the Holocaust? An image of all that was lost? Or perhaps a shattered survivor who lived on haunted by the ghosts of those who died? No, it is something worse, a photo of baby Adolf, as innocent as any child who has "not yet bitten of the apple." There is no hair combed carefully into place, no steely glint in his eye, no narrow mustache above an unsmiling lip, no arm extended in salute, and no indication of future deeds so horrible as to beggar the imagination. Just a small child, filled with all the promise that youth has to offer. The question at the heart of the book is captured in this photo. It is a question posed not merely by the victims of the Holocaust or the millions killed in Hitler's war, but by our very humanity. Is there a humanly comprehensible path from that small child to the gray and brooding figure searing his course across our history? And if there is, how can we ever use the word "humane" again? How can we look at ourselves in the mirror and not wonder if that unspeakable something that was in him is not also in us?

Rosenbaum's personal search takes him not only to piles of crumbling newspapers and letters, to distant towns and lost places in all corners of Europe, Israel, and North America, but also into the pages and the living rooms of nearly all the world's most famous Hitler scholars. What he discovers there is quite disturbing. Although they are all ardent foes of Hitler and everything he stood for, they fundamentally disagree about his moral character. For some, such as Emile Fackenheim, Hitler is evil incarnate, utterly inhuman, the epitome of absolute evil. In stark contrast, others such as H. R. Trevor-Roper (author of *The Last Days of Hitler*), argue not only that he was not evil but that he was in fact an idealist, horribly misguided, to be sure, but an idealist nonetheless, who sought to do good. There was no evil will at work in Hitler, they maintain, only (terribly) faulty reasoning. There are some, such as Robert Waite, who try to steer a middle course between these two extremes, but this proves difficult, for while they describe a path from here to there, they are almost all forced to admit that at some point that path is profoundly ruptured, that it passes through an unfathomable abyss, an anomaly of such magnitude that it is difficult to say how the human being who entered it is related to the inhuman being who comes out the other side.

If we accept Rosenbaum's account, we seem compelled to choose between one of two impossible alternatives: either Hitler was not evil or Hitler was not human. This dilemma is particularly troubling because for many years Hitler has been the only absolute in our relativistic moral universe, the one point on our moral map that always flashed "Forbidden! Do not enter here!" And our certainty of his evil has been just about the only thing that has given us the resolve to defend the cause of humanity. Apartheid, ethnic cleansing, and the like evoke not merely disapprobation but action because, at some level, we see in them the reappearance of that malignant spirit we imagine to have possessed Hitler. If we doubt that Hitler was evil, how can we sustain any notion of evil or find any ground for moral judgment or action? And if we are left with only silence in the face of this question, how can we not conclude that we are lost on an infinite moral sea, beyond good and evil?

Nietzsche believed that such a fate was inevitable, for the death of God and the collapse of everything built upon that God were already well underway, even if most Europeans had not yet recognized that fact.[2] He was equally convinced that the consequence of this "greatest event" would be the collapse of European morality, centuries of brutal war, and the advent of a world in which everything is permitted. Was he right? Is this the source of the difficulty we face when we consider the question of evil? Are we at heart already entertaining that "uncanniest of all guests," nihilism? While it is tempting to leap to such a conclusion, it might behoove us to ask a preliminary question, not whether the absence of a point of absolute evil on our moral map is the result of a creeping atheism and nihilism, but how it came about that all the lesser points of evil were effaced. Might our difficulty in coming to terms with the possibility of "radical" or "ultimate" evil not be connected to our difficulty in believing in evil in all of its lesser forms?

The existence and variety of evil was certainly not a question for the High Middle Ages. Aquinas and Dante, for example, knew what evil was, described its forms and degrees, and laid out the appropriate punishments and remediations. Judas, the medieval moral equivalent of Hitler, was in this way clearly connected to the baby who, according to Augustine, concupiscently sucked at its mother's breast. For these thinkers, there is no problem with how we get from the child to the monster. Medieval Christianity had a moral map that was complex, rooted in reason and revelation, reflected in civil and canon law, and embedded in creation. Yet by the middle of the seventeenth century, the points on this map had largely been erased. Indeed, Descartes and Hobbes, the two great pillars of modern thought, proclaimed that good is what pleases me and evil what causes me pain or opposes my will. Where, then, did all the evils go?

This is the question I address in this essay. I believe that the answer helps to explain the mysterious ambiguity of evil in modern times. In what follows, I argue that the answer to this question lies in the theological and philosophical transformations that mark the passage from the late medieval to the early modern world. Descartes and Hobbes are not the source of this change. They articulate a radically subjective, quasi-utilitarian view of morality. However, they do so not because they clearly prefer it but because the alternative they see in front of them is so much worse. They turn away from a notion of evil so vast and a notion of good so compelling that it had become easy on moral grounds to justify not merely casuistic equivocation but the slaughter of whole populations. To understand how morality came to this pass and why our moral map has become so useless to us, we thus need to examine not Nietzsche, or even Descartes and Hobbes, but the tremendous theological and moral transformation of the fourteenth, fifteenth, and sixteenth centuries. In doing so, I believe we can see that our inability to sustain a notion of evil arises not from the death of God but from the proclamation of his omnipotence, thus not from atheism but from a particular kind of theism.

The Scholastic Idea of Evil

From its inception, Christianity was deeply concerned with questions of evil. This concern crystallized in two questions that have remained central to the Christian tradition. Where did evil come from, and what can be done about it? If the world and everything in it were created by God, was God the source of evil, as the Manicheans and others argued, or was evil the result of Adam's disobedience, a sinful turning away from God, as Augustine maintained? This question was bound up with the role of Christ and his sacrifice. Was he one with God or was he only the highest of the creatures and therefore closer to human beings, as Arius suggested? What was the meaning of his life and death? Does morality consist in emulating his example or in praying for his assistance? This question was also bound up with a further question: can human beings overcome sin on their own or are they finally dependent on divine grace? The answer to this question too turns on the meaning of Christ's life and death. Did his sacrifice wipe away sin and restore human beings to their prelapsarian state, or did it only make evident the power of God to graciously save those whom he had already chosen? Pelagius argued that humans have the capacity to act virtuously and secure salvation through their own efforts, while Augustine maintained that grace was decisive.

The history of Christianity is characterized by a series of attempts to answer these questions while avoiding the extremes of Manicheanism, which sees God as the source not merely of all good but also of all evil, and Pelagianism, which attributes to man the power to win salvation by his own powers and without grace. In seeking such answers, Christianity has repeatedly struggled with the question of Christ's dual nature. The contention among Christian fathers over this question had a great deal to do with the extreme difficulty of reconciling divine omnipotence and divine humanity. In attempting to do so they drew heavily on the philosophical teachings of the ancient world and particularly the work of the neo-Platonists, and while the Platonic notion of participation, for example, gave them some purchase on answers to these questions, it also opened up a whole host of other problems that were difficult to reconcile with scripture.

Scholasticism, which arose in the eleventh and twelfth centuries, tried to develop a more consistent theology for Christianity, drawing on an Aristotelianism that had recently come to Europe through Islamic scholars such as Averroës. Christians had known of Aristotle's work through Boethius, but the Aristotle that came to Christianity through Islam played a new and important role. At its core, scholasticism was an attempt to reconcile reason and revelation, to show that Aristotelian rationalism was compatible with the biblical notion of divine omnipotence. This task was not easy, for the two traditions differed in their understanding of theology, cosmology, and anthropology. The Aristotelian notion of a demiourgos as an autonomous and indifferent "thinking of thinking" bears little resemblance to the notion of a wrathful God in the Old Testament or the notion of a more merciful God in the New

Testament, both of whom take an active interest in human affairs. The Aristotelian notion of the eternity of the world also stands in sharp contrast to the relatively recent Creation and looming destruction of the world envisioned by Christianity. Finally, while Aristotle suggested that an ethical life could be achieved for all but the most brutish human beings by rational laws and the proper habituation of desire, Christianity believed that all human beings were tainted by an original sin that only Christ's sacrifice could overcome. These differences were exacerbated not merely by Aristotle's paganism but by the fact that his writings came to Europe through an Islam that was both a theological and a military threat to Christendom.

Despite these difficulties and suspicions, Aristotle offered a coherent means for coming to terms with a world that showed no signs of ending any time soon. We see this in the scholastic treatment of *metaphysica generalis* (i.e., ontology and logic). God may have created the world out of nothing by means of his absolute power, but in doing so his will was guided by his reason. What is ontologically real are not the individual things but species or universals that inform these things. This was the scholastic doctrine of realism. Within this context, the world can be understood by means of a syllogistic logic that describes the relationship between these universals. The mutuality of divine reason and divine will thus makes the connection of Christianity and pagan philosophy a possibility. This is even more evident in scholasticism's *metaphysica specialis* (theology, cosmology, and anthropology). Theologically, we have access to God not merely through revelation but also (at least analogically) through our reason. There is thus not merely revealed theology but also natural theology. Cosmologically, we can understand the world as a rationally ordered whole. Everything has its natural place and course, moving toward the actualization of its intrinsic rational essence or end. The meaning and purpose of things is thus a reflection of the beneficent action of the divine will guided by divine reason. Anthropologically, human beings are creatures created in God's own image as rational animals. As such, they seek the good, that is, they seek to realize their potential, to be human in an essential way. Unfortunately, each of them is also a child of Adam and his sin. This sin, which damaged (though it did not destroy) human reason, makes it difficult for humans to find their way. God, however, sent Christ to redeem them from their sins. This God achieves by Christ's sacrifice but also by the continuing action of the Holy Spirit that was imparted to the Apostles and embodied in the Church. The Church is thus God's agent on earth, distributing sacraments and performing the rites necessary for salvation. Moreover, it is the teacher of morality and the overseer of the secular realm in which laws are established to further direct people toward the good.

Creation is good, and evil therefore cannot be a part of it. It is nothing. This does not mean, however, that it is an illusion. Rather, evil is not and cannot be a real substance, that is, it cannot be a universal. Evil comes about not because God wills it but because individual human beings at times seek not their natural and supernatural end but rather their own momentary individual advantage. Evil is ontologically an accident in an Aristotelian sense, but an accident that arises inevitably out of human individuality. Original sin is bound up with our finitude and the passions that inevitably accompany it. These passions are rooted in a self-love that obscures our universal nature and end. While humans are tainted by sin, they are not totally blinded by it. Indeed, even in their fallen state they are sometimes moved by charitable impulses that, if properly habituated, can impel them toward virtue and goodness.

Evil can be measured by the extent to which individual will is directed toward or away from reason and thus toward or away from God. We see this magnificently portrayed in Dante's *Divine Comedy*. The most heinous evil is the result of turning against God or against the moral order as a whole. Thus, Judas, who betrayed Christ, and Brutus and Cassius, who betrayed Caesar (the founder of the universal empire), are in the lowest circle of hell, caught in the mouths of Satan. Such men can never love God and consequently cannot be saved. Their sins are mortal, not venial. Venial sins are typically evil directed against another person or his property that do not necessarily separate one from God. They thus do not merit eternal damnation, but they do require remediation, both on earth and in purgatory. The gravity of the sin and the harshness of its punishment are thus commensurate with the excellence of the good that it rejects or damages.

Insofar as it is possible to classify evil, to recognize its severity, and to determine what kind of disorder it is, it is possible to develop remedies to lessen its occurrence and to redeem those who have sinned. Indeed, it is an obligation of Christian charity to do so. The principal question for scholasticism thus becomes not the nature, variety, and degree of evil but what is needed to overcome it, in particular, how much the individual can do on his own, how much depends on grace, and how much falls to the Church. Good and evil are not a question—the moral laws are written in nature and manifest to human reason. They are also spelled out in Scripture and in the practices of the Church. Reason, revelation, and nature all teach a single lesson that is reinforced and enjoined by secular and canon law.

This scholastic view avoids both Manicheanism and Pelagianism. Evil does not come from God but from human beings. It is a disorder in their nature that otherwise seeks God and the good. Moreover, while individuals on their own cannot wholly overcome it, they have an obligation to do what they can. Central to the entire process is the Church, which plays a decisive role in bringing people back to their rational ends.

Divine Indifference and the Uncertainty of Good and Evil

Aquinas and Dante developed a detailed moral map that allowed people to understand where they stood with respect to good and evil, which direction they should go, and which they should avoid. Moreover, this map stretched beyond this world to the next, making explicit what individuals could do to improve their chances of attaining salvation. What happened to the moral universe that made this map obsolete?

The end of all moral striving in Dante's view is beatitude, the supernal joy of seeing God face to face. All human choice and action is oriented and evaluated in terms of this goal. Good actions move us toward God and evil actions away from him. The usefulness of such a map, however, depends on the certainty of the destination. Many in our time have come to believe that God is dead and that the idea of beatitude was always merely an illusion. The thirteenth century came to an opposite but equally debilitating conclusion—not that God was dead but that God was so much greater than anyone had ever imagined that it was impossible to understand him except through his own revelation and that even this revelation was subject to unexpected revision.

This transformation of the moral universe was the result of the nominalist revolution carried out by William of Ockham and his followers. Ockham drew on the protonominalism of Roscelin and Abelard as well as the voluntarism of Henry of Ghent and Duns Scotus but combined these in a new synthesis that radically transformed Christianity. From the beginning, Ockham was opposed to the Averroist reading of Aristotelianism that was essential to realism. In this respect he joined a movement of thought that began in the later thirteenth century. Indeed, Aristotelianism had been condemned at Paris and Oxford, first in 1270 and then more comprehensively in 1277. This condemnation was certainly a reaction to the growth of secular philosophy and Averroism, but it was also a consequence of the collapse of the delicate balance of contradictory elements in scholasticism. In its attempts to incorporate Aristotelianism, scholasticism gave great weight to reason in God, nature, and human beings. In so doing, however, it limited God's omnipotence, for God was bound to act according to the laws of reason. Many Christians, however, were convinced that if God were God, he could not be subjected to anything other than his own will.

This was an article of faith that separated nominalism from realism. God is God, and he is no man's debtor. He acts as he acts for no reason other than his own will. The consequences of this view are earthshaking. Ontologically, radical omnipotence obliterates realism. God cannot create real universals without limiting his own power. Every being must thus be created uniquely by God. Moreover, if there are no real universals, then there can be no syllogistic logic that delineates the relationships among these universals. Words then do not point to real things but are merely tools or fictions that we use to make sense of the world. Since they are fictions, however, we should use as few of them as possible. Hence, the principle that governs reasoning is not the principle of noncontradiction but Ockham's razor: "Do not multiply universals needlessly."

We see a similar change in *metaphysica specialis*. The world created by God is not a necessary but a contingent order. Here nominalists distinguish between two forms of divine will, *potentia dei absoluta* and *potentia dei ordinata*. The former is God's absolute power, which is limited only in the sense that he cannot do what is contradictory. The latter is his ordained power that consists of the choices he has actually made. For nominalism, there is nothing that can bind God's will. That he chooses one thing rather than another is not the result of the fact that such a choice is more rational or better in any way. God is, to use the technical theological term, indifferent. His choices are groundless, hence unknowable, and therefore unpredictable. As a result, we cannot know the order of the world without looking at what is there. Similarly, we cannot understand what God demands of us without looking at what he actually says.

The consequences of this doctrine for religious practice are profound. The Church has only an ordained and not an absolute power to make or fulfill promises on God's behalf. God saves and damns whom he will. The ordained order he establishes is thus radically contingent. There are no rational ends to either natural or human motion, thus no highest good or any standards of good and evil that can be deduced by reason. Thus, there can be no rational theology and no natural law governing morality. Only revelation can tell us what God has ordained that we do, and even revelation is not definitive because, by his absolute power, God can change whatever he ordains. He may destroy the world at any moment or recreate it from the very beginning according to radically different laws.

Today he may save the saints and damn the sinners, but tomorrow he may do the reverse. He could even reverse the Decalogue without contradiction. The order of good and evil is thus radically contingent.

The harshness of this vision of God is mitigated by two factors. First, while God could overturn the ordained order, nominalists generally believed that he probably would not do so. In this sense they were probablists. Second, as a practical matter, many of them believed that God would save anyone who did everything that it was in him to do (*Facientibus quod in se est Deus non denegat gratiam*). This is the so-called *Facientibus* principle.

Nominalism after Ockham developed in two different directions, one laying great weight on divine omnipotence and arbitrariness, the other building on this *Facientibus* principle. The former tended toward Manicheanism, the latter toward Pelagianism. The former emphasized God the father as a terrifying and unpredictable being who could not be propitiated in any way and who thus had to be feared rather than loved. The second emphasized the generosity of the Son in forgiving human weakness. However, even the assurances of this latter path are problematic. While I need only do all I can do, how much is that? How can I know whether I have satisfied God? The more Manichean strain of nominalism recognizes objective (although arbitrary) standards of good and evil. From this point of view, God for them appears to be more an irrational despot than a kind redeemer. The more Pelagian view, by contrast, grants a greater role to divine charity but also puts a greater burden on the individual's own introspection to determine whether he has been good or evil. This God may seem kinder, but he is also more inscrutable.

For the scholastics, reason, revelation, nature, and law taught the same thing. For the nominalists neither reason nor nature gives us any guidance about good or evil. Moreover, while revelation provides us with an indication of what God demands of us, it is only an expression of God's ordained power that can be superseded by his absolute power. Finally, even if we know the standards of good and evil, we cannot know whether we are living up to them.

The role of the Church in sustaining standards of good and evil was also in decline. There were multiple reasons for this. Most important was the growing power of the secular states that began first to rival and then to dominate both the papacy and the empire. The relocation of the papal court to Avignon, the Great Schism, and the growing separation of the Church and the empire were bound up with this political transformation. There was also deep disagreement within the Church about standards of good and evil, especially between the Franciscans, who thought that a pious life should be a life of poverty on the model of Christ, and the clerical hierarchy, which saw the Church as the kingdom of God and themselves as its aristocracy. This disagreement was at the core of the famous poverty dispute between Pope John XXII and the Franciscans. The Franciscans, led by Michael of Caesna and William of Ockham, argued that a true Christian life was led in emulation of Christ. This challenged the established order of the Church that Pope John XXII argued was ordained and hence immutable. This seemed to deny God's absolute power and led Ockham to declare the pope the Antichrist. The pope's reaction was swift and Ockham had to flee for his life, settling in the court of Emperor Ludwig of Bavaria, where he worked with Marsilius of Padua developing arguments against papal supremacy. The medieval Church was torn asunder, not merely by outside forces but also by its own internal contradictions that came to the fore in the nominalist revolution.

While the nominalist view of divine omnipotence and unpredictability might have been unbelievable a century earlier, the disruptions within the Church, the Hundred Years' War, and the Black Death gave it great credibility. As a result, nominalism had a tremendous impact, especially on the Christian understanding of good and evil, rendering the moral map of Dante and Aquinas unreliable. At the core of this transformation was an understanding of God and man as principally willing beings. The harmony of God and man under scholasticism was made possible by the supremacy of reason. In this context, freely willing but fundamentally rational human beings were imagined to will the good by nature, habituation, and education. The willfulness of God and man that nominalism imagined made it much more difficult to achieve harmony because there were no fixed ends or goals. The resulting opposition between divine and human will could be resolved in one of two ways: either by emphasizing human freedom at the expense of divine power or by eliminating human freedom in favor of divine supremacy. The question, in essence, is whether it is possible for the human will to act independently of God. Augustine had raised this question in his debate with the Manicheans, granting free will but only in order to show that man, and not God, is the source of evil. However, while humans can freely turn away from God, according to Augustine, they cannot turn back to him on their own accord. Original sin makes it impossible for humans to simply will the good. In opposition to the Pelagians, he thus argued that there could be no redemption without grace.

To say that God is supreme, however, does not necessarily rule out human freedom, if we reconceive freedom as action in and through God. I can thus freely will the good only if God wills the good through me.

Such a deterministic view of the relation of divine and human will does, however, seem to eliminate the possibility of human moral choice and action and to leave humans in the unenviable position of Abraham confronted with God's demand that he sacrifice his son, not knowing whether to hope for the graciously given strength to do so or the sinful weakness to refuse. In the world that nominalism brings into existence, Christians are thus confronted with the choice between a moral but only half-pious Pelagianism and an amoral but radically pious Manicheanism. The choice of the former leads to humanism, the choice of the latter to the Reformation

Making Oneself Good: Humanist Individualism

Like nominalism, humanism rejects realism in favor of ontological individualism. In contrast to both nominalism and realism, however, it abandons metaphysical disputation for a discussion of human possibilities in concrete historical situations. It turns away from Aristotelianism toward the rhetorical eclecticism of Roman moralists such as Cicero and Seneca, and then to the neo-Platonism of Plotinus, Proclus, and Origen. Despite this secular beginning, humanism was not antireligious and from the time of Petrarch was explicitly Christian in most of its incarnations.

The central concern of humanism, however, was not God but human being. Like nominalism it sees humans not as a species with an inherent telos, but as unique individuals in particular historical contexts willing their own idiosyncratic ends. Indeed, to be human for humanism is to be an individual and not just a member of the crowd. Each person, Petrarch argues in *The Solitary Life,* must find his own virtue. In this pursuit, a study of various human types is essential. Hence, biographical works such as Plutarch's *Lives* played a central role in humanist education. Such lives are not intended as models for slavish imitation but as exemplars that inspire one's own efforts at self-making. Petrarch, for example, wrote his *Illustrative Lives* (which eventually contained twenty-three biographies of noble Romans), and *Africa* (the epic depiction of Scipio Africanus) to serve as a stimulus and guide to his own and other's self-creation. He and other humanists such as Bruni and later Montaigne also presented themselves as exemplars. These works offered a new way to think about good and evil in concrete ways.

In this context, becoming human does not mean realizing one's universal potential as a rational animal but becoming an individual. For humanism, there is thus no one true or good way of life or even a hierarchy of ways of living that stretches from good to evil. The good life is the life that the individual constructs to fit his own peculiar nature, in which he discovers and perfects his own virtue. The variety of human paths to the good is thus as great as the variety of individual human beings. There are also multiple forms of evil as well, but again they are not hierarchically or systematically related to one another. There are undoubtedly some elements of the medieval tradition left even in a thinker such as Machiavelli, who distinguishes those who come to power through *virtu* from those who come to power through crime, but they are losing their significance, for the comprehensive account of goods and evils that made the distinction of crime and *virtu* meaningful has disappeared.

Scholasticism drew an analogy between divine and human reason and asserted that both aimed at the good. Humanism draws an analogy between divine and human will and, at its most extreme, imagines that both God and man are indifferent to what is good and evil. On the model of the willful God, humanists thus imagine that willful human beings can lay out their own visions of good and evil. There are two problems with this approach. First, humans exist not in a vacuum but in a world with others and always find themselves competing with these other individuals to achieve their individual goals. The world in this sense seems to be governed not by reason but by *fortuna* and political life seems to be a struggle for individual preeminence.

Humanists also struggle to sustain a notion of human will in conjunction with a notion of divine will. Drawing on neo-Platonism, Ficino, for example, argues that our will or desire is itself a manifestation of divine grace acting through nature, which causes us to desire and love things in such a way that we are naturally directed toward the good. In developing and laying out this argument in *On Love,* he draws heavily on the idea of the ladder of love spelled out in Plato's *Symposium.* Love in all its forms draws us upward and leads us to God. We can freely will the good because the good is pleasant, noble, beautiful, and awe-inspiring. In contrast to Plato, however, Ficino argues that there are multiple ways to God.

Pico offers another alternative in his *Dignity of Man.* According to Pico, when God created the creatures, he gave a specific nature to each, but by the time he came to man, all the existing natures had been distributed. As a result, he gave humans the ability to choose their own nature, to imitate any other creature, or even to imitate God himself. Human beings thus have a free will that knows no bounds. While this notion of will owes something to Augustine, it is much more Pelagian for it sees the will not merely as the source of evil but also of human dignity. While God may not thereby become irrelevant, he certainly plays a smaller role in human life.

Erasmus presents a third possibility. He accepts the fact of the free will and sees it as intrinsic to human dignity and moral life, but recognizes that it cannot be absolute, since God's will is supreme. In this world, humans can will freely, but they cannot will their own salvation or obligate God to save them. Salvation depends on the initial action of divine will, but importantly, humans have the freedom to accept or reject the proffered grace. Charitable works also play an important role, demonstrating that one's will is governed by a charitable and not a concupiscent love. Erasmus thus tries to steer a moderate course between humanists like Valla and Pico on one hand and Augustine and the nominalists on the other. In contrast to scholasticism, which imagined that divine and human will could act in perfect harmony because both were guided by reason, Erasmus believes that human will is drawn toward the good, not by reason, but by love. In this respect, he agrees with Ficino in seeing nature as a form of divine grace but also places great weight on the inspiration afforded by both scripture and ancient literary examples. Erasmus thus seeks a moderate path between the nominalist notion of divine omnipotence and the humanist notion of self-making. Despite his great fame and influence, however, this effort was, at least in the short run, a failure, for instead of reconciling all parties, it cast into sharp relief the threat humanism posed for Christianity. Indeed, it was more this semi-Pelagianism of Erasmus than the manifest Pelagianism of Pico that provoked the Manichean reaction of Luther.

Evil, Evil Everywhere: The Subjective Manicheanism of the Reformation

There was perhaps no one who experienced the contradictions of Christianity with greater intensity than Martin Luther. Like his nominalist and humanist predecessors, Luther was an ontological individualist. His early philosophical training at Erfuhrt was nominalist, and he described himself as an Ockhamist. When he took orders and entered the monastery, he joined the Augustinian Hermits whose theology was also deeply nominalistic. Luther was thus intimately acquainted with the nominalist assertion of divine omnipotence and the *Facientibus* principle. He was also steeped in the humanist tradition and considered Cicero his favorite author.

The problem that tormented Luther grew out of the radical uncertainty generated by the nominalist idea of God. How can I know if I am saved and among the elect? This problem was always important to Christianity but took on great significance in the fifteenth and sixteenth centuries. We see indications of this, for example, in the striking growth in the number of religious paintings focusing on the torments of hell. The practical answer to this anxiety was the *Facientibus* principle, but this did not satisfy everyone. How can I judge myself, if I only have myself to judge by? How can I know when I have given my all, unless I know what my all is? For the truly conscientious, the *Facientibus* principle is not a source of relief, but of agony, stimulating a hyperbolic sense of sinfulness. This seems to have been Luther's fate.

In attempting to ameliorate his suffering, Luther followed the advice of his spiritual mentor, Staupitz, and focused his attention not on the omnipotent God enthroned in glory, the final and objective judge who generated such anxiety in him, but on Christ crucified, the incarnate redeemer, who took pity on him. This new focus was the basis for his transformation of Christianity. Luther came to see that God was omnipotent not in an objective sense but in and through me, that is, that God was all wise, etcetera, always through me. This insight provided a solution to the contradiction of the human and divine wills. Evil is not my fault but the result of the fact that my soul is ruled by Satan rather than God. It is the satanic presence in me that leads me to believe that I can will or make myself. Only when God comes to dwell in me through grace can I have faith and thus the certainty that my will is good. My own will and choice thus play no role in the matter.

In this way, Luther develops a notion of divine omnipotence and possession that obliterates all freedom of the human will. Indeed, he goes further than Augustine, asserting not only that we are incapable of willing the good, but also that we are incapable of willing evil. If God does not rule in our soul, we are the slaves of Satan. For Luther, human power and, above all, human reason are thus tools of the devil. Nature may be God's creation and it may be governed by divine love, but in us this nature has been completely corrupted by sin. Our self-will (and our pursuit of our self-interest) is always a repetition of Adam's original act of disobedience in which we claim to be God, and the reason that justifies our action is also just another expression of satanic pride. In this way, Luther decisively rejects the core moral contention of the humanist enterprise.

Luther also denies that the institutions and practices of the Church can secure our salvation. This was, of course, part of his argument against indulgences, but it goes deeper than this, turning against not only rites and ceremonies but against the idea of law itself as a means of directing humans to justice and righteousness. In his view, the Law and the Commandments exist only to humble us by demonstrating our inability to live in accordance with them on our own. Everything that comes from man without God, whether that man is a vicious criminal or a moral exemplar, is thus evil.

The incapacity of the human will is perhaps most evident in the fact that we cannot even choose to love God. Man, according to Luther, is saved by faith alone, but faith comes only through grace. Moreover, even after receiving justifying grace, humans often still act in evil ways because the "Old Adam," as Luther calls him, still lives within them. This Adam must be constantly confronted and controlled. Therefore, justification must be followed by sanctification, by a purification of the will and the elimination of all thought of oneself. To be and to do good we must learn to will only God's will.

Humanism imagined a divine will that drew us toward God. Our reason had been damaged but not obliterated by sin, and Christ's example showed us how to become moral beings. Luther, by contrast, suggests that sin has rendered us incapable of moral action, because it has subjected us to Satan. For Luther everything that does not come directly from God's will is evil. Moreover, it is all more or less equally evil—the actions of Socrates or Cato are no different in this respect from those of Judas. This teaching thus expands, homogenizes, and subjectivizes the notion of evil. It also decouples the goodness or evil-ness of an act from its content. The same act motivated by self-will and divine will has a radically different status. Action that would be considered morally good is evil if it is not also pious, and action that might otherwise be evil can be good if inspired by God. This is a recipe for disaster.

Luther was reluctant to accept this conclusion, but it was painfully driven home by the Peasants' War and the radical Anabaptist movement. If the goodness of actions are entirely dependent on the subjective certainty of divine inspiration, it is very difficult to determine their rectitude because it is impossible to distinguish divine possession from madness. The radical Reformation moved inevitably in such a subjective direction, and while Luther tried to place limits on the radically individualized interpretation of scripture, individual prophecy, and antinomianism, his attempts were incompatible with the theological position he himself had articulated.

In his attempt to avoid the semi-Pelagianism of humanism, Luther is driven toward Manicheanism. This becomes evident in his debate with Erasmus over the nature of the will. Erasmus argued that to deny the efficacy of the will was to make God the source of evil. Luther did not like this conclusion, insisting that there is a struggle between God and Satan, but he finally admitted that this struggle is ultimately a sham, since Satan is also a creature of God and thus subject to divine will. Behind both Satan and Christ stands an ominous and omnipotent figure that Luther refers to as the "hidden God," a God whom he believes we should not think about because it might shatter our faith. He urges Christians to focus instead on Christ crucified. Luther thus deploys not a theology of glory but a theology of the Cross, focusing not on an omnipotent God who pulls all the strings but on a God who sacrifices himself on our behalf. And yet, this theology does not eliminate the all-powerful God, it only conceals and thus, in many ways, empowers him.

To overcome his unendurable sense of sinfulness, Luther thus gives himself over to divine will. In rejecting the spiritually destructive *Facientibus* principle, he leaves no room at all for human effort, and in rejecting the primacy of law and rites, he eliminates the Church as the mediating agency between God and man. Every human stands alone before God, and God speaks to each directly through scripture. In Luther and in the Reformation period generally we see the transformation of Christianity from a religion of practice into a religion of faith. The great danger in this transformation is the content of faith. What does it mean to will as God wills? To have our will be God's will? How do we know that this supposedly divine will is not the expression of subliminal passions and prejudices? What cannot be justified by such a notion? What cannot be motivated by such enthusiasm? And, to turn the matter around, how much that we previously considered morally good must now be accounted sin, pride, prepossession, and evil? And how much of what was hitherto considered evil, can now be called virtue when practiced by the soldiers of light?

Nominalism created an indifferent God who laid out particular standards of good and evil in an almost whimsical fashion; humanism argued that humans have the capacity to discover and will their own good and evil: Luther and the Reformation denied this capacity but at the same time magnified it enormously by conjoining the divine will of nominalism with the creative will of humanism. Humanism recognized that individuals existed in a world with others and that there was always a clash of wills that had to be resolved. Luther suggests that the will of God manifests itself in and through chosen individuals who must struggle against the satanic will that governs the world. What cannot be done by such a will in the name of such a God?

The wars of religion that raged across Europe in the sixteenth and seventeenth centuries had many causes, but their brutality was at the very least enabled and legitimated by this Manichean notion that the children of God were at war with the children of darkness. Modernity as it crystallizes in the thought of Descartes and Hobbes struggles to find a way out of this Manichean abyss.

The Pursuit of Goods

The moral ideas of Descartes and Hobbes develop in reaction to the chaos unleashed by the Manicheanism of the Reformation. Like their predecessors, they are ontological individualists. In contrast to the humanists, who focus on individual human beings, and Luther, who focuses on God, Descartes and Hobbes turn their attention to nature. They accept the antischolastic view of their predecessors that nature is nonteleological, merely matter in motion. In contrast to those humanists who saw this motion as governed by a kind of love or eros embedded in the natural order of things, Descartes and Hobbes take a much more mechanical view of things. Moreover, they abandon the humanist notion of *fortuna* and adopt a position closer to the Reformers, arguing that everything happens through necessity. The key to understanding this necessity for them, however, is not scripture but method. This idea of method comes in part from humanist neo-Platonism (especially the hermeticism of Ficino, Bruno, and others) but principally from Bacon's revolutionary idea of science. They move beyond Bacon's idea of an inductive science to a much more powerful understanding of causality. Here they draw on Galileo's great insight that motion can be analyzed mathematically in formulating their method. With this mathematical method, they believe they can realize Bacon's dream of understanding the hidden laws of motion and making man master and possessor of nature. To put this theologically, Descartes and Hobbes came to believe that mathematical reasoning, if properly and comprehensively employed, can reveal the hidden order of Creation, that is, the hidden will of God that determines the motion of all matter. In contrast to nominalism, humanism, and the Reformation, they thus come to believe that divine will is not arbitrary but lawful—lawful, however, in a new way. At the heart of Creation they see no universals and therefore no teleological reason. Instead, they discern efficient causes that determine the motions of all particulars. This motion, however, is not chaotic but is governed by laws that can be mathematically discovered. Once we have understood the laws that govern the motion of matter, we will be able to use them to immensely improve our lives.

But what does it mean to improve our lives? In order to know this we need to know what is good for us. In a world without natural ends, however, this is difficult to determine. Should we follow the humanist dictum and each try to discover our own virtue and thus our own ends? And if so, what is to prevent the collision of our various individual projects with one another? Scripture might provide guidance, but it is open to varying interpretations, and the disagreements over such interpretations in Descartes's and Hobbes's view had led to disaster. They thus aim in a different direction, seeking to maximize not what is *supernaturally* good for us but rather what is *naturally* good—what is good, in other words, for our bodies rather than for our souls. They understand this to mean avoiding violent death, prolonging life, diminishing suffering, and increasing prosperity. These are not ends as they were traditionally understood, but the conditions or means for the pursuit of individually chosen ends. Rather than developing a specific argument about the good, Descartes and Hobbes seek to maximize our capacities for pursuing whatever goods we individually desire. The good, by default, thus becomes whatever makes an individual happy without injuring another. Goods in this way are subjectively determined, and the general good as a result comes to be nothing more than the maximization of individual satisfaction or aggregate utility.

Descartes and Hobbes agree with the humanists that our passions or loves are good, and they reject Luther's notion that everything not done by the will of God is evil. To defend this position they must then show that God's will is irrelevant for our moral decisions. Descartes and Hobbes do so in different ways. Descartes demonstrates that even a radically omnipotent God could never deceive me about the fact that I am whenever I think I am, and then shows that such a God could not be a deceiver at all. Even in the face of the hidden Manichean God of Luther, Descartes thus believes that it is possible for those guided by the light of (mathematical) reason to gain everything worthwhile in life. Mathematical science gives us the power to transform this world into a paradise and to infinitely prolong our stay in it. Under such circumstances the question of salvation becomes less pressing.

Hobbes takes a different approach. He accepts Wycliffe's and Luther's assertion that everything happens as a result of strict necessity but shows that this very fact renders religion unimportant for our moral choices. If everything is preordained, we can do nothing to gain or lose salvation. Thus, we need only be concerned with what we can control, which is our well-being in this world. Or to put this in the language of scholasticism, we need only be concerned with secondary causes and not with the primary cause, that is, not with God himself. What matters is security from violent death (not death per se), the prolongation of human life, and the maximization of commodious living, that is, the production and acquisition of as many goods or commodities as possible. Moreover, scripture, properly interpreted, leads to the same conclusion.

Descartes and Hobbes thus avoid the profound questions about good and evil that troubled the earlier tradition. Their argument, however, rests on an unarticulated and indemonstrable assumption, that in coming to understand the laws that govern motion, we come to understand the true and unchanging will of God. To us today, this seems to be an odd way of thinking about the laws of nature, but it was essential to Galileo and Newton, to take only the two most famous examples. The eternity of the laws of nature and the dependability of science rests on God's will being inalterable. We cannot know, of course, that this is the case. Einstein himself thus felt compelled to assert (because he could not prove) that God does not play dice with the universe. Modern science in this way rests upon the assumption that God acts always only *potentia ordinata* and that he cannot or at least will not act *potentia absoluta,* that the laws of nature, in other words, do not change. Modern science in this sense is a form of probablism, even if it does not recognize this fact.

As deeply rooted as this rationalist faith is, it is not universally convincing, because on its own grounds science cannot give a definitive account of the origins of motion. Modern science in theological terms is thus a radically Pelagian enterprise, but it is an enterprise that does not and cannot eliminate the possible resurgence of Manicheanism. The historical world is understood in Pelagian fashion as the consequence of the multiple interactions of conflicting and cooperating human wills, but it is also seen from a Manichean perspective as the product of a universal good or evil will. Thus, history on one hand seems to be progressive, governed by a universal causality (Turgot), or a hidden hand (Smith) or the cunning of reason (Hegel), while on the other it appears to be the degeneration of human innocence (Rousseau), the unfolding of a demonic will (Schopenhauer), the dialectical development of the means of production (Marx), the unfolding of global technology (Heidegger), or even the tyranny of reason itself (Adorno and Horkheimer). In a similar vein, the failure of progress or modernity is attributed to the evil influence of nationalism, cosmopolitanism, fundamentalism, imperialism, and so on. Radical evil thus lurks just beneath the surface of the scientifically interpreted and formed world, but when it appears, it is understood not as intrinsic to the world but in opposition to it. It is thus not a relative evil, but always only absolute evil, whether it lies in "the system" or in some "rough beast slouching toward Bethlehem to be born."

Beyond Banality and the Demonic

In the development of modernity, this notion of good and evil as individual utilities comes to predominate. As a result, the very terms themselves are transformed. We continue to talk about evil in the abstract, but it is typically identified with the absence or maldistribution of goods, that is, with poverty and its concomitant notion, inequality. For the most part, evil is not seen as the result of free actions by individual willing beings but as the (unintended) result of the operation of a system. Under such circumstances, we are less concerned with individual moral training to produce virtue and eliminate vice and more concerned with how we can maximize our ability to obtain the goods we desire. The chief debate then becomes whether the market or the state is best able to achieve such an end. Moreover, individual moral failure is attributed not to an evil will but to an improper upbringing, illness, or some other involuntary cause, and is treated therapeutically.

We thus find it difficult to conceive of evil in everyday terms as something intrinsic to the human will. Evil is something demonic and incomprehensible. To put this in theological terms, we find it difficult to understand anything as evil from our dominant Pelagian perspective, and equally difficult to understand evil as in any way human from a Manichean perspective. The Hitlers of the world thus remain unintelligible to us as long as we continue to think within the conceptual framework we have inherited. Whether we can come to terms with the problem of evil thus depends on our ability to develop a vocabulary and a framework to confront these questions. This in turn depends upon our coming to understand that there is a path from baby Adolf to the grown Hitler and thus that there is something in us that is capable of such evil. Evil is not just demonic and it is also not just banal, and we are not entirely children of light and our adversaries are not merely the children of darkness. We are in the end all human, even if at times all too terribly, all too abysmally human.

NOTES

1. Ron Rosenbaum, *Hitler: The Search for the Origins of His Evil* (New York: HarperCollins, 1999).
2. Friedrich Nietzsche, *The Gay Science with a Prelude in Rhymes and an Appendix of Songs*, trans. Walter Kaufmann (New York: Random House, 1974), 343.

Seeing Darkness, Hearing Silence

Augustine's Account of Evil

The question of why evil exists is not a theological question, for it assumes that it is possible to go behind the existence forced upon us as sinners. If we could answer it then *we* would not be sinners. We could make something else responsible. Therefore the "question of why" can always only be answered with the "that," which burdens man completely.

The theological question does not arise about the origin of evil but about the real overcoming of evil on the Cross; it asks for the forgiveness of guilt, for the reconciliation of the fallen world.

Dietrich Bonhoeffer[1]

The Attraction of Evil

"After one of my many presentations following my return from Rwanda, a Canadian Forces padre asked me how, after all I had seen and experienced, I could still believe in God. I answered that I know there is a God because in Rwanda I shook hands with the devil. I have seen him, I have smelled him and I have touched him. I know that the devil exists, and therefore I know there is a God. *Peux ce que veux. Allons-y.*"[2] Lieutenant General Romeo Dallaire, a French Canadian Roman Catholic who was the force commander of the UN Assistance Mission for Rwanda, discovered the significance of his faith in Rwanda. Prior to Rwanda he was a conventional Catholic, but in Rwanda he found that without his Catholicism he could not comprehend the evil he saw there.

Lieutenant General Dallaire's story of his attempt to contain the genocide in Rwanda is a sad and tragic tale. That he thinks he "shook hands with the devil" in Rwanda is understandable but theologically a mistake. Christians do not believe in God because Christian belief states that God is necessary for comprehending the reality of evil. Rather the Christian belief in God requires that one does not believe in the reality of evil or the devil.[3] Robert Jenson observes that Karl Barth, the theologian in modernity who is usually credited with restoring Christian "orthodoxy," puzzled ordinary minds by saying the devil was a myth. Jenson notes that "Barth's point was that *not* believing in the devil is the appropriate relation to the devil's mode of existence. That the devil is a myth does not mean, in Barth's thinking, that the devil does not exist; it means that he exists in a particular way, as the ordained object of denial."[4]

That many, Christian and non-Christian alike, find the traditional Christian denial of the existence of evil unintelligible is but an indication of the pathos of Christianity in modernity. Many, like Lietenant General Dallaire, think that if Christianity is intelligible it is so because it helps us name what has gone wrong with our world. Christian and non-Christian now believe that, even if we do not share a common belief in God, we can at least agree about actions that are evil. Accordingly, modern accounts of morality are determined by agreements about what constitutes inhumanity. But ironically, just to the extent that Christians underwrite the high humanism that sustains the confidence that, in spite of our differences, we share common intuitions about evil, the Christian faith in God becomes unintelligible.

I have argued elsewhere that the question "Why does a good God allow bad things to happen to good people?" is not a question that those whose lives have been formed by the Psalms have any reason to ask.[5] Suffering, even the suffering occasioned by the death of a child, does not constitute for Christians a theodical problem. Kenneth Surin rightly argues that theodicy is a peculiar modern development that unfortunately shapes how many now read the Psalms as well as the book of Job.[6] The realism of the Psalms and the book of Job depends on the presumption that God is God and we are not. When Christians think theodical justifications are needed to justify the ways of God at the bar of a justice determined by us, you can be sure that the god Christians now worship is not the God of Israel and Jesus Christ.

The very presumption that a crisis of faith is created when "bad things happen to good people" indicates that the God whom Christians are alleged to believe has been confused with a god whose task is primarily to put human beings on the winning side of history. In modernity

> a mechanistic metaphysic is combined with a sentimental account of God; in this way the pagan assumption that god or the gods are to be judged by how well it or they insure the successful outcome of human purposes is underwritten in the name of Christianity. It is assumed that the attributes of such a god or gods can be known and characterized abstractly. But the God of Abraham, Isaac, and Jacob is not the god that creates something called the "problem of evil"; rather, that problem is created by a god about which the most important facts seem to be that it exists and is morally perfect as well as all-powerful—that is, the kind of god that emperors need to legitimate the "necessity" of their rule.[7]

Terrence Tilley suggests that those who engage in the theodical project "participate in the practice of legitimating the coercive and marginalizing ecclesiopolitical structure which is the heritage of Constantinian Christianity."[8] Once Christianity had become the established religion of the empire, Christians had a stake in justifying that the way things are is the way things are meant to be. But that project has now decisively come to an end. So it is not God that is the subject of theodicy but the human. That is why the crucial theodical question today is not "Why does a good god allow bad things to happen to good people?" but rather "Why has medicine not cured cancer?" Medicine has become the institution in modernity dedicated to saving the appearances; that is, we look to medicine to create a world in which we can entertain the illusion that it may be possible to get out of life alive.[9] That is why one of the legitimating functions of modern states is to promise to provide the best medical care available.

If, as Tilley suggests, theodicy is a project of established orders, it may seem strange to turn to Augustine as the representative figure who taught Christians how to think about evil. Augustine is often credited with providing the theological rationale for the development of Constantinian Christianity.[10] However, I hope to show that Augustine's understanding of the nonexistence of evil is not only how Christians should think about evil, but also, in the world we currently inhabit, represents a challenge to those who would rule the world in the name of human "progress." Such a rule, that is, the rule in the name of securing a future free from suffering in the name of humanity, is a secular version of what Constantinianism was for Christians.[11] Accordingly Augustine's understanding of evil cannot help but be a political challenge to secular forms of Constantinianisms.

Augustine on Evil

In the *Enchiridion*, a text Augustine wrote around 423 at the request of a layman, Laurentius, for a handbook that would sum up essential Christian teachings, Augustine provides his most considered judgment on evil. According to Augustine there can be no evil

> where there is no good. This leads us to the surprising conclusion: that since every being, in so far as it is a being, is good, if we then say that a defective thing is bad, it would seem to mean that we are saying that evil is good, that only what is good is ever evil and that there is no evil apart from something good. This is because every actual entity is good (*omnia natura bonum est.*) Nothing evil exists *in itself*, but only as an evil aspect of some actual entity. Therefore, there can be nothing evil except something is good. Absurd as this sounds, nevertheless the logical connections of the argument compel us to it as inevitable.[12]

In his *Confessions,* written soon after Augustine became a bishop (397), he anticipated this passage from the *Enchiridion* when he suggested that evil simply does not exist. He argues that

> we must conclude that if things are deprived of all good, they cease altogether to be; and this means that as long as they are, they are good. Therefore, whatever is, is good; and evil, the origin of which I was trying to find, is not a substance, because if it were a substance, it would be good. For either it would be an incorruptible substance of the supreme order of good-ness, or it would be a corruptible substance which would not be corruptible unless it were good. So it became obvious to me that all that you have made is good, and that there are no substances whatsoever that were not made by you. And because you did not make them all equal, each single thing is good and collectively they are very good, for our God made his whole creation *very good.*[13]

I am convinced that Augustine has rightly said what any Christian should say about evil: ontologically evil does not exist. Such a view, however, many find counterintuitive. How can you say evil does not exist when, like Lieutenant General Dallaire, you have witnessed a genocide? I think Augustine has a very persuasive response to such a query, but to understand his response we need to appreciate how he came to his conclusion, a conclusion he says was forced on him by logic, that is, that evil is always parasitical on the good. I have no doubt that Augustine found himself driven to this conclusion by "logic," but Augustine's logic requires a narrative that takes the form of the story, that is, the "confession," of his sin. This means, I think, you cannot understand Augustine's account of evil without following his account in the *Confessions* of how he came, through his involvement with the Manichees as well as the Platonists, to the conclusion that evil is nothing.

It is not accidental that the only way Augustine has to display how he came to understand that evil is nothing was by providing a narrative of how he arrived at that judgment.[14] That a narrative was required rightly suggests that to understand properly why evil does not exist requires a transformation of the self that takes the form of a story. Moreover, that a narrative is required to rightly understand the parasitical character of evil is not only true of our individual lives but is also required if we are to make sense of our collective existence as well as the cosmos. Christians believe the recognition of evil is possible because God never leaves us without hope. That is, hope makes possible the ability to take the next step necessary to discover that we are not condemned to live out our past. We discover that we are only able to name our sins on our way to being free from them. This means we are only able to give an account of our lives retrospectively.

By attending to Augustine's *Confessions* I hope to show that his account of evil as privation is keyed to his understanding of scripture and, in particular, how scripture is only rightly read as prayer (worship). In other words, Augustine's understanding of evil as privation is necessary to make sense of the Bible's story of Creation, Fall, and redemption. All that he says about evil is disciplined by that theological project, which means for Augustine there is no freestanding "problem of evil," but rather, whatever Christians have to say about evil must reflect their convictions that humans are creatures of a God who has created and redeemed.[15]

The *Confessions* is a complex prayer Augustine prays in an effort to discover how God has made his life possible. He unsparingly confesses his sins, his unwillingness to acknowledge the One who is his creator, because the *Confessions* are not about Augustine but rather about the God who makes Augustine Augustine. Moreover, he makes clear that it is his inability to understand God that makes it impossible for him to rightly understand the nature of evil. He confesses that

[my] own specious reasoning induced me to give in to the sly arguments of
fools who asked me what was the origin of evil, whether God was confined
to the limits of a bodily shape, whether he had hair and nails, and
whether men could be called just if they had more than one wife at the
same time, or killed other men, or sacrificed living animals. My ignorance
was so great that these questions troubled me, and while I thought I was
approaching the truth, I was only departing the further from it. I did not
know that evil is nothing but the removal of good until finally no good
remains.[16]

The "fools" were the Manichees, a religious sect to which Augustine
belonged for nine years, because he believed that they offered him a compelling account of the cosmos and, in particular, of evil. In her wonderful book, *Augustine on Evil*, G. R. Evans suggests that what attracted
Augustine to the Manichees was what he took to be the explanatory
power of their position.[17] According to the Manichees, the world is constituted by a god who is supremely good and by an evil principle that is
identified with materiality, and in particular, the body. Therefore the
Manichees did not try to avoid the problem of evil, but rather they
"explained" evil by finding a place for evil in the ontological character of
the universe.[18] Such an explanation appealed to Augustine because he
had a passion to know the truth about his and the world's existence. In
short, the Manichees seemed to offer Augustine a "scientific" account of
the way things are. Such an explanation appealed to Augustine, he confesses, because when he was at that stage of his life he was readier to
believe that the universe was out of joint than that there was anything
wrong with himself.[19]

Evans also suggests that the Manichees might have been attractive
to Augustine because their position seemed to share some aspects of what
Augustine had learned from his mother about Christianity. Christians,
like the Manichees, claimed God is completely good and the human task
is to seek that good. Accordingly the *Manichean Psalm-Book* seemed to echo
the Christian desire for illumination gained through being freed from
bodily desire. Augustine, who certainly knew about bodily desire, was
attracted to the spiritual discipline of the Manichees because they
offered him a discipline by which he could join the spiritual elite. No
doubt one of the reasons the Manichees appealed to Augustine, a reason
he suggests in the *Confessions*, is because they confirmed his high opinion
of himself. The Manichees played to what Augustine was to learn was his
deepest enemy, his pride, by providing him with knowledge befitting his
intelligence. He was freed from the Manichees only when he was forced

to conclude that "the very attempt to search for the cause of evil in the way he did was itself an evil thing."[20]

That the Manichees seemed to provide Augustine with the best account of the cosmos is crucial to understanding his break with them. Augustine tells us he often asked questions that his fellow Manichees could not answer, but they assured him that when the great Manichean scholar, Faustus, came, he would be able to answer Augustine's worries. When Faustus came, however, though Augustine found him a man of "agreeable personality," he also discovered that Faustus "was quite uninformed about the subjects in which I had expected him to be an expert."[21] In particular, Augustine thought the Manichean books were full of "tedious fictions about the sky and the stars, the sun and the moon" and their mathematical calculations simply did not square with what he had studied in other books.[22]

That the Manichean "science" proved to be false was one of the crucial reasons Augustine had for leaving the Manichees, but just as important was his discovery that his most fundamental mistake was assuming that God could be understood as part of the metaphysical furniture of the universe. Augustine confesses he "could not free himself from the thought that you (God) were some kind of bodily substance extended in space, either permeating the world or diffused in infinity beyond it."[23] It was by reading the neo-Platonist that Augustine was freed of the presumption that, metaphysically, that which is a substance must have a body. Moreover, it was the neo-Platonist who helped him see that "all other things that are of a lower order than yourself, and I saw that they have not absolute being in themselves, nor are they entirely without being. They are real in so far as they have their being from you, but unreal in the sense that they are not what you are."[24]

It was from the Platonists, therefore, that Augustine began to imagine that evil is a privation, which means it is a mistake to try to understand how, as Evans puts it, "evil can have a bodily place in the universe." For Augustine, this meant that he was beginning to realize it is a mistake to ask from whence evil comes or where evil may be. Now Augustine understands for God

evil does not exist, and not only for you for the whole of your creation as well, because there is nothing outside it which could invade it and break down the order which you have imposed on it. Yet in separate parts of your creation there are some things which we think of as evil because they are at variance with other things. But there are other things again with which they are in accord, and they are good. In themselves, too, they are good. And all these

things which are at variance with one another are in accord with the lower
part of creation which we call the earth. The sky, which is cloudy and windy,
suits the earth to which it belongs. So it would be wrong for me to wish that
these earthly things did not exist, for even if I saw nothing but them, I might
wish for something better, but still I ought to praise you for them alone . . .
And since this is so, I no longer wished for a better world, because I was thinking of the whole of creation and in the light of this clearer discernment I had
come to see that though the higher things are better than the lower, the sum
of all creation is better than the higher things alone.[25]

There can be no question of the significance of the Platonists for
Augustine, but this passage in praise of God's creation indicates that, for
Augustine, Platonism was a way station on the way for Augustine to
become a Christian. Augustine never left his Platonism behind, though I
think the assumption that he remained more Platonist than Christian is
clearly wrong. He understood that he could not remain a Platonist,
because to be a Christian requires that you believe that all that is, is as it
is because it has been created. Augustine tells us that "by reading these
books of the Platonists I had been prompted to look for truth as something incorporeal, and I 'caught sight of your invisible nature, as it is
known through your creatures,'"[26] but what he could not find in the
Platonist books was "the mien of the true love of God. They make no mention of the tears of confession or of the sacrifice that you will never dis-
dain, a broken spirit, a heart that is humbled and contrite (Psalm 50:19),
nor do they speak of the salvation of your people, the city adorned like a
bride (Revelation 21:2), the foretaste of your spirit (II Corinthians 1:22), or
the chalice of your redemption."[27]

From Augustine's perspective, the Platonists, as helpful as they had
been, did nothing for his besetting problem that he came to understand
was his pride. Through his encounter with the stories of Victorinus and
Anthony and how those stories led him to face the humiliation of the
cross of Christ, Augustine was finally able to confess that evil was "not
out there" but rather resided in his will.[28] Augustine confesses

I began to search for a means of gaining the strength I needed to enjoy you,
but I could not find this means until I embraced the mediator between God
and men, Jesus Christ, who is man, like them (I Timothy 2:5) and also rules
as God over all things, blessed for ever (Romans 9:5). He it was who united
with our flesh that food which I was too weak to take. For I was not humble
enough to conceive of the humble Jesus Christ as my God, nor had I learnt
what lesson his human weakness was meant to teach.[29]

That lesson quite simply is that we are cured of our pride only through following the Word, the Truth, which surpasses even the highest parts of creation by becoming one of us.

The *Confessions* is Augustine's testimony to God and God's grace as necessary for the healing of his pride. We can only know our sin in the light of God's grace.[30] This means we cannot will our way out of our pride, but rather God's grace can only be appropriated through recollection.[31] Commentators on Augustine's *Confessions* often find his descriptions of being a sinner as a young child, that is, his greedy desire for his mother's breast, to be exaggerated. Yet Augustine is not trying to make us think that, even as a child, he was the most sinful of sinners. To engage in that project would be another form of pride. Rather, he is trying to help us see the disorder that grips our most basic desires, as well as our ability to reason which is shaped by those desires, which cannot help but lead to the destruction of ourselves and others. To appreciate a child's disordered desire is part and parcel of Augustine's rejection of the Manichees.

Augustine's famous account of the stealing of the pears is his paradigmatic example of what it means to discover that we do not so much choose to sin but rather we are sin. Crucial for Augustine is that he stole that for which he had no need. He and his friends threw the pears to the pigs. To be sure, Augustine joined in this petty crime because he desired the good opinion of his friends, but that he did so is not a sufficient explanation for his sin.[32] He did what he did for no purpose other than his love of mischief. So acting, he sought to gain from the world what he learned he could only gain from loving the One alone worthy to be loved. In short he was trying to be more than he could be. Thus he confesses "all who desert you and set themselves up against you merely copy you in a perverse way: but by this very act of imitation they only show that you are the Creator of all nature and, consequently, that there is no place whatever where man may hide away from you."[33]

Evans notes that Augustine's observations about his early boyhood sins are meant to help us see that one of the distinguishing marks of an evil action is its unprofitableness.[34] That seems just right to me and helps us understand why Augustine thought we have no ability to will our way out of sin. We cannot will our way out of sin because we seldom pursue sin to sin, but rather our sins are done in the name of "great goods." We learn of the unprofitable character of sin only retrospectively. Indeed, too often attempts to avoid sin rely on alternatives that are themselves sinful but fail to be acknowledged as such only because they seem different than the sin we think we have clearly identified. For Augustine, evil cannot be defeated by evil.[35] Rather, our only hope is that we are offered an

alternative community and correlative way of life that make it possible
for us to locate the extraordinary power of the evil we are and do in the
name of the good. For all of its ambiguity, Augustine thought he had discovered that alternative community by being made a member of the
church.[36]

Where Has This Gotten Us or Why I Am Not a Nazi

I do not pretend that I have provided an adequate account of Augustine's
understanding of evil, but hopefully, my attempt to show how Augustine
thought about these matters can help us gain some perspective on where
we are today. If Susan Neiman is right that "the problem of evil is the
guiding force of modern thought" and that "nothing is easier than stating the problem of evil in nontheist terms," then we clearly have some
indication that "modernity" names a development that stands at a great
distance, and the distance is not simply determined by time, from
Augustine.[37] With all due respect to Neiman, I suspect, for example, she
has no idea that Augustine's understanding of evil was not "theistic" but
trinitarian.[38] Yet I fear that Neiman represents the kind of misunderstanding of Christianity in modernity most determinatively found
among Christians.

Yet from Neiman's perspective, the Augustinian account of evil I have
developed here cannot help but seem intellectually obscurantist, if not
dangerous. The problem quite simply is that the account I have provided
is so Christian, so particularistic. Why should anyone who is not a
Christian take it seriously? Moreover, appeals to particular traditions
seem to reproduce the problem many assume is at the heart of the challenge facing modernity; that is, how to counter the violence perpetrated
in the name of a god or tradition. In short, does not my vigorous defense
of Augustine's understanding of evil play into the hands of the most
destructive form of politics in our time? I fear that I cannot provide the
kind of answer to such a question that many desire because such answers
undercut the contribution Christians have to make.

It has been the sad fate of Christianity in our time to be that form of
life that tries to "bind up the wounds" of our existence. As a result,
Christians have tried to offer explanations of evil that do not implicate
God. As I suggested at the beginning of this essay, you can be sure that
when Christians attempt to justify the ways of God before the bar of
human experience they no longer believe in the God that animates the
work of Augustine.[39] Even worse, I suspect that Christians today do not

know what it would mean to believe in Augustine's God, precisely because we have no idea what practices are required to make our worship of the God of Abraham, Jacob, and Isaac and Jesus Christ intelligible, not only to those who do not share our faith, but even to ourselves.

I need to be clear, however, that it would be a mistake to think the geno-cide in Rwanda is somehow better understood if we see what happened there as "sin." That would make "sin" exactly what Augustine suggests sin cannot be—an explanation. To say "sin" explains nothing.[40] Rather, sin is a confession that holds out the hope that, even in the face of a terror like Rwanda, redemption is possible. To say that there is hope suggests that evil cannot overwhelm the good that is God's creation. Yet honesty demands that often we have nothing to say in the face of events like Rwanda. Nevertheless silence, at least the honest silence that can be a form of pres-ence, can be a way not to let the darkness overwhelm us. Indeed, Christians believe that God would have his people be such a presence.

Silence, moreover, is required when words like "sin" and "evil" are used, in Terry Eagleton's words, "to shut down thought."[41] Eagleton notes that the use of the word "evil" in the so-called war against terrorism really means:

> Don't look for a political explanation. It is a wonderfully time-saving device.
> If terrorists are simply Satanic, then you do not need to investigate what
> lies behind their atrocious acts of violence. You can ignore the plight of the
> Palestinian people, or of those Arabs who have suffered under squalid right-
> wing autocracies supported by the West for its own selfish, oil-hungry pur-
> poses. The word "evil" transfers the question from this mundane realm to
> a sinisterly metaphysical one. You cannot acknowledge that the terrible cri-
> mes which terrorists commit have a purpose behind them, since to ascribe
> purposes to such people is to recognize them as rational creatures, however
> desperately wrong headed.[42]

To describe enemies as evil ironically has the effect of creating the Manichean world that Augustine was intent on defeating.[43] If Augustine teaches us anything it is that the Christian confession of sin is a first-person activity. Christians, of course, think it important to be able to name their sins as well as confess their sins to one another.[44] We are obli-gated to reveal our sins so that we may have some hope of being freed from sin through the work of the Holy Spirit. Our ability to name our sins comes through the mutual responsibility we share with other Christians exemplified by lives such as Augustine's life.[45] By attending to lives like Augustine's life, Christians hope to be able to discover in what ways they are possessed by sin. If sin is attributed to others, it is done out of the recognition of the sin in one's own life.

But what could such a confession mean when faced by a Rwanda? I think if we are thinking with Augustine, it might mean that to be a Christian requires that one believe that even a Rwanda someday might be a memory capable of being healed. What it would mean for such a memory to be healed I think would mean that a story can be told about such senseless killing that offers those killed as well as those that killed reconciliation.[46] I confess I cannot imagine what such a reconciliation might mean, but that is why God is God and I am not.

This finally brings me back to politics. In the preface to her important book, *The Nazi Conscience*, Claudia Koonz observes that we may find it repugnant to think that mass murderers understood themselves to be acting morally. But according to Koonz that is exactly what they did. She observes:

> The popularizers of anti-Semitism and the planners of genocide followed a coherent set of severe ethical maxims derived from broad philosophical concepts. As modern secularists, they denied the existence of either a divinely inspired moral law or an innate ethical imperative. Because they believed that concepts of virtue and vice had evolved according to the needs of particular ethnic communities, they denied the existence of universal moral values and instead promoted moral maxims they saw as appropriate to their Aryan community. Unlike the early twentieth-century moral philosophers who saw cultural relativism as an argument for tolerance, Nazi theorists drew the opposite conclusion. Assuming that cultural diversity breeds antagonism, they asserted the superiority of their own communitarian values above all others.[47]

I suspect many will find my judgment that Augustine provides how Christians should think about evil far too close to what Koonz describes as the Nazi exaltation of their particular community's values. We, that is, we who are modern, think the only way to defeat the kind of evil we associate with the Nazis is to have at our disposal a universal ethic, that is, an ethic on which all agree. Christians are often thought to represent such an ethic. However, Augustine thought that virtue and vice were correlative to a particular community. According to Augustine, God's law is a law for anyone, but he also thought that law would differ from age to age and place to place. "What may be done at one time of day is not allowed at the next, and what may be done, or must be done, in one room is forbidden and punished in another. This does not mean that justice is erratic or variable, but that the times over which it presides are not always the same, for it is the nature of time to change."[48] The variable character of ethics does not mean justice is arbitrary, but Augustine argued that for justice to be rightly understood requires the right worship of the true God. Absent that worship, Augustine assumes that there can be no alternative to what we know as "relativism" or what James Edwards calls normal nihilism.[49]

Does the loss of common worship mean, however, that there is no alternative, that there is no defense, against the "Nazi conscience"?[50] I do not think such a conclusion follows, but such an alternative will depend on whether communities exist capable of discerning their own propensities for the evil so often done in the name of good.[51] It would be tempting to put Christians on the side of those who advocate "universal moral values" as a bulwark against "relativism." That strategy, however, fails to see that "relativism" is the creation of the assumption that "universal values" can be known apart from formation in a community capable of recognizing the evil it does in the name of those same "values." Ironically, too often, as I suggested above, those who try to sustain accounts of morality in the language of universal rights or values are but secular versions of Constantinian Christianity that pridefully assume they know what is wrong with the world. That such is the case should not be surprising, because the philosophical developments that gave original impetus to these now-widespread political movements intended, if possible, to defeat or replace Christianity in the name of the human or, failing that, at least to render Christian convictions at best "private" having no role for the public discernment of evil or good.

But if we cannot rely on "universal values," does that not mean we live in a very dangerous world? That is exactly what it means. That world, moreover, has been made all the more dangerous by attempts to save the world from danger by appealing to "universal values" that result in justifications to coerce those who do not share what some consider universal. If Christians have any contribution to make for helping us survive the world as we know it, it is because God has "brought us low," forcing humility on us by humiliation. Such humility hopefully might help Christians refrain from identifying or comforting themselves with the sentimentalities of reigning humanisms. Christians do not believe in the "human." Christians believe in a God who requires that we be able to recognize as well as confess our sins. Exactly because Christians are in lifelong training necessary to be a sinner, it is our hope that we might be able to discern the evil that so often is expressed in idealistic terms. So what Christians have to offer is not an explanation of evil, but rather a story, and a community formed by that story, that we believe saves us from the idols of the world. That I think is what Augustine might say today.

ACKNOWLEDGMENT

I am grateful to Charlie Collier, Greg Jones, and David Aers for their criticisms and suggestions.

NOTES

1. Dietrich Bonhoeffer, *Creation and Fall: A Theological Interpretation of Genesis 1–3* (London: SCM Press, 1962), p. 78. I am indebted to Charles Mathewes for calling attention to this passage in Bonhoeffer. See Mathewes, *Evil and the Augustinian Tradition* (Cambridge: Cambridge University Press, 2001), p. 201.

2. Romeo Dallaire, *Shake Hands with the Devil: The Failure of Humanity in Rwanda* (New York: Carroll and Graf, 2004), p. xviii.

3. In *The Death of Satan: How Americans Have Lost the Sense of Evil* (New York: Farrar, Straus, and Giroux, 1995), Andrew Delbanco notes John Wesley's remark that because there is "no devil" there is "no God." Delbanco then observes that "we want Satan back because God depends on him. This is because the essence of religious faith is the idea of transcendence, a concept that contains within itself the idea of its opposite—as in its two Latin elements (*trans-*, beyond or over, and *scandere*, to climb or to scale): limitation, boundedness, the thing to be transcended. As an American evangelical put it a few decades after Wesley, 'in all . . . instances of God's permitting sin, he had a view to the manifestation of himself'" (pp. 228–229). I greatly admire Delbanco's book, but I think that he has allowed himself to be misled by bad Christian theology. Wesley (if he said what Delbanco attributes to him) was "wrong," as is the evangelical quoted by Delbanco who suggests that God permits sin to manifest himself. To believe that sin can determine the character of God is to make sin more interesting than God—a problem Milton knew well. Just to the extent you let the devil become a major character in a play, the devil threatens to become the main character. The assumption that sin precedes salvation mimics the Protestant revival tradition that assumed that people would only "come to Christ" by first being convinced of their sin. As a result, sin determined the character of grace, resulting in quite distorted views of what the Crucifixion is about. Sacrificial theories of the atonement often betray a quite crass understanding of the trinity. That is why, moreover, it is very important not to let abstract notions of "transcendence" become an attribute of God in and of itself. You know you are on your way to deism when the most important thing you can say about God is that God is transcendent.

4. Robert Jenson, "Nihilism: Sin, Death, and the Devil," *Newsletter: Report from the Center for Catholic and Evangelical Theology* (summer 1998): 4.

5. Stanley Hauerwas, *Naming the Silences: God, Medicine, and the Problem of Suffering* (Grand Rapids, MI: Eardmans, 1990).

6. Kenneth Surin, *Theology and the Problem of Evil* (Oxford: Basil Blackwell, 1986).

7. Hauerwas, *Naming the Silences*, pp. 56–58.

8. Terrence Tilley, *The Evils of Theodicy* (Washington, DC: Georgetown University Press). p. 136.

9. Ernest Becker argues that theodicy in modernity is not about the justification of God in the face of evil but rather an attempt to explain why evil continues to exist in the absence of God. Becker names the latter effort "anthropodicy." See his *The Structure of Evil* (New York: George Braziller, 1968), p. 18.

10. See, for example, Alasdair MacIntyre's account of the relation of Augustine's theology to the papacy of Gregory VII in his *Whose Justice? Which Rationality?* (Notre Dame:

University of Notre Dame Press, 1988), pp. 152–163. Constantianism is usually associated with the legalization of Christianity.

11. In *With the Grain of the Universe: The Church's Witness and Natural Theology* (Grand Rapids: Brazos Press, 2001), I argued that William James rightly understood that the implication of a Darwinian world is that our lives are but the reflection of chance. It was only after I read Louis Menand's *The Metaphysical Club: A Story of Ideas in America* (New York: Farrar, Straus, and Giroux, 2001) that I began to understand the significance of the Civil War for why James (and Oliver Wendell Holmes) would find Darwin but a confirmation of what the war meant for them. In *The Death of Satan*, Delbanco also calls attention to the significance of the Civil War for underwriting the conviction that our lives are constituted by "dumb luck." (pp. 144–153) Delbanco also thinks William James to be the American who quite clearly articulated the "pervasive pathology of modern life: the fear of annihilation." p. 163.

12. Augustine, *Confessions and Enchiridion*, translated and edited by Albert Outler (Philadelphia: Westminster Press, 1955, p. 344), 4, 4.

13. Augustine, *Confessions*, translated with an introduction by R. S. Pine-Coffin (Baltimore: Penguin Books, 1961, p. 148), 7, 12.

14. Some years ago I wrote an article with David Burrell in which we used Augustine's *Confessions* as a paradigm for arguments concerning the traditional character of rationality. That essay, "From System to Story: An Alternative Pattern for Rationality in Ethics," now appears in Stanley Hauerwas, *Truthfulness and Tragedy: Further Investigations into Christian Ethics* (Notre Dame: University of Notre Dame Press, 1977), pp. 15–39.

15. I am indebted to Professor John Bowlin for helping me see how Augustine's account of privation is theologically determined.

16. Augustine, *Confessions,* translated by Henry Bettenson (Harmondsworth: Penguin, 1977), pp. 62–63, 63, 67.

17. G. R. Evans, *Augustine on Evil* (Cambridge: Cambridge University Press, 1994), pp. 12–14. I am indebted to David Aers for calling Evans's book to my attention.

18. Evans, *Augustine on Evil*, p. 8.

19. Augustine, *Confessions* (ed. Pine-Coffin, p. 136), 7, 3. Evans observes that Augustine was more inclined to believe "that God could be affected by evil, rather than admit that he himself was the agent of evil. He tried every way his wit could devise to avoid the conclusion that he himself might be the source of evil he was seeking, ensnarer of his own soul, gaoler of the prison." Evans, *Augustine on Evil*, p. 13. If Becker is right about the development of "anthropodicy" then it is no surprise that we are ready to see evil "out there" in others rather than in ourselves.

20. Evans, *Augustine on Evil*, p. 5.

21. Augustine, *Confessions* (ed. Pine-Coffin, p. 98), 5, 7. Augustine's concern that what he believed should be tested by the best science of the day is often not appreciated. His early attraction to astrology, for example, ended because he rightly tested whether people born at the same moment had the same subsequent history. Platonist though he may have become, he always thought that what he thought should be tested by empirical methods. See, for example, his wonderful account of Firminus's birth in *Confessions* (ed. Pine-Coffin, p. 141), 7, 6.

22. Augustine, *Confessions*, (ed. Pine-Coffin, p. 98), 5, 7. Evans observes that one of the attractions of Christianity for Augustine was that he was never able to exhaust, as he did after nine years with the Manichees, the intellectual depth of the Bible and Christian doctrine. Augustine, of course, would not have become a Christian if Ambrose had not introduced him to how the Bible should be read.

23. Augustine, *Confessions* (ed. Pine-Coffin, p. 133), 7, 1.

24. Augustine, *Confessions* (ed. Pine-Coffin, p. 147), 7, 11.

25. Augustine, *Confessions* (ed. Pine-Coffin, pp. 148–149), 7, 12. Augustine's understanding of the interrelation and hierarchy between God's creatures is extremely important for his account of what goes wrong in particular circumstances.

26. Augustine, *Confessions* (ed. Pine-Coffin, p. 154), 7, 21.

27. Augustine, *Confessions* (ed. Pine-Coffin, p. 156), 7, 21.

28. Augustine's discovery as well as understanding of the will is as important as it is often times misunderstood. It would simply take me too far afield to try to "explain" what Augustine was about with the introduction of the will, but suffice it to say that I think James Wetzel is right to suggest that Augustine was developing an alternative to "classical psychology's distinction between the rational decisions of the mind and the irrational impulses of the emotions or the appetites." *Augustine and the Limits of Virtue* (Cambridge: Cambridge University Press, 1992), p. 86.

29. Augustine, *Confessions* (ed. Pine-Coffin, p. 152), 7, 18.

30. This point is often misunderstood particularly by conservative and liberal Christians. Both, for different reasons, assume that sin can be known independently of what God has done in Christ. As a result, salvation is determined by a prior understanding of sin that is not Christologically disciplined. As a result, sin controls what God has done in a manner that makes God subject to human desires. Augustine knew better, so his account of his sinfulness is always dependent on grace. No theologian in modernity has done more than Karl Barth to challenge the presumption that sin is more intelligible than what God has done through Christ. In contrast to the view that our knowledge of sin is more or less self-evident in contrast to our knowledge of God, Barth maintains that "only when we know Jesus Christ do we really know that man is the man of sin, and what sin is, and what it means for man." *Church Dogmatics*, vol. 4, part 1, trans. by G. W. Bromiley (New York: Scribner's Sons, 1956), p. 389. From Barth's perspective, sin is simply absurd. We have no reason to sin, but when confronted by the Gospel, we discover we are sinners—which means we can only know our sins on our way out of sin.

31. Wetzel wonderfully shows how it is only through recollection that "we are able to effect the gradual convergence of virtue and self-determination." *Augustine and the Limits of Virtue*, p. 124.

32. In *The City of God*, trans. by Henry Bettenson (Harmondsworth: Penguin, 1977), 480, Augustine argues that "one should not try to find an efficient cause for a wrong choice. It is not a matter of efficiency, but of deficiency; the evil will itself is not effective but defective. For to defect from him who is the Supreme Existence, to something of less reality, this is to begin to have an evil will. To try to discover the causes of such defection—deficient, not efficient causes—is like trying to see darkness or to hear silence. Yet we are familiar with darkness and silence, and we can only be aware of them by means of eyes and ears, but this is not by perception but by absence of perception. No one therefore must try to get to know from me what I know, unless, it may be, in order to learn not to know what must be known to be incapable of being known." p. 480.

33. Augustine, *Confessions* (p. 50), 2, 6.

34. Evans, *Augustine on Evil*, p. 3.

35. Charles Mathewes rightly criticizes Reinhold Niebuhr—who is often credited with reclaiming the significance of Augustine's understanding of sin to illuminate modern political life—for "naturalizing" evil by positing evil "as a preexisting and primordial force which we meet in interpreting our world, and so undermines our confidence that God is wholly good." *Evil and the Augustinian Tradition*, p. 8. Niebuhr made the mistake of thinking evil, or at least the effects of evil, can be defeated by being confronted by alternatives that are "less evil." Yet, as Mathewes observes, "given the sheer negativity of evil, we cannot respond to it directly; we must respond to it through its manifestations as a perversion of our loves. But our loves are also the source of our every attempt at a response; that is, the problem is essentially with *us*, and not directly with anything 'external' to us. So our loves are simultaneously the root of the problem and the source of any possible response to the problem" (p. 233). Niebuhr, like many Protestant liberals, wanted Augustine's account of sin without Augustine's Christology, but that is exactly what cannot be done, or at least cannot be done if we are trying to be faithful to Augustine. In *The Death of Satan*, Delbanco takes Niebuhr (and Melville) to be one of the last representatives of an Augustinian understanding of the world, but such a view Delbanco judges, not happily I think, to be anachronistic having been lost through the development of a culture of irony (pp. 192–208). It is quite understandable that Delbanco so reads Niebuhr, but I think Niebuhr's reputation as

a recovery of Augustine can fail to understand that Niebuhr's work stands in the tradition of Protestant liberalism. For my understanding of Niebuhr see *With The Grain of the Universe*, pp. 87–140.

36. Much is made of Augustine's refusal to identify the church with the city of God. There can be no question that Augustine understood that the church, like his own life, was still under the power of sin. Yet the very ability of the church to confess its sinfulness meant for Augustine that the church was an alternative to the world. Rowan Williams argues that Augustine's politics presumes that the church has a distinctive character in his "Politics and the Soul: A Reading of the *City of God*," *Milltown Studies* 19–20 (1987): 55–72. This is the article on which John Milbank draws in his robust account of the significance of the church as an alternative civitas in his *Theology and Social Theory: Beyond Secular Reason (Signposts in Theology)* (Oxford: Blackwell, 1990, 1993), pp. 380–438.

37. Susan Neiman, *Evil in Modern Thought: An Alternative History of Philosophy* (Princeton: Princeton University Press, 2002), quotations on pp. 2, 5. Kant's account of "radical evil" in *Religion within the Limits of Reason Alone* can be interpreted as fundamentally "Augustinian" just to the extent that radical evil names what should not be, but is. For Kant, evil is radical because evil resides in the will which is also the source of our ability to live according to the moral law. See Kant, *Religion within the Limits of Reason Alone*, trans. by Theodore Greene and Hoyt Hudson (New York: Harper and Brothers, 1960), pp. 15–39.

38. For the significance of Augustine's understanding of the trinity see Michael Hanby, *Augustine and Modernity* (London: Routledge, 2003). In particular, Hanby's account of Augustine's *De Trinitate* emphasizes the importance of beauty and delight for understanding the relations of the three persons of the trinity. Accordingly sin and evil are rightly understood as that which is profoundly ugly.

39. However, for a wonderful "defense" of God from the charge that God unjustly allows evil, see Herbert McCabe's chapter "Evil" in his *God Matters* (Springfield, IL: Templegate Press, 1991), pp. 25–38. McCabe argues that if you accept the principle that you are innocent until proven guilty, then any account of God's responsibility for evil will show he cannot be proved innocent, but "it will remain a mystery to you why God has done what he has done; but you will at least agree that what he has done does not prove his guilt" (p. 26).

40. Terry Eagleton notes that this Wittgensteinian point is to know when justifications have come to an end; that is, that there is a point when we must simply say, "This is simply what I do." That does not mean that, if what I do is defraud the elderly of life savings, an account does not need to be given. But Wittgenstein, according to Eagleton, is "thinking of more fundamental matters than that. He has in mind the very cultural forms which allow us to think what we think and do what we do." *After Theory* (New York: Basic Books, 2003), p. 192.

41. Eagleton, *After Theory*, p. 223.

42. Eagleton, *After Theory*, p. 141.

43. Delbanco calls attention to Joseph Goebbels "blood freezing candor" when he confessed, "Oh, I can hate, and I don't want to forget how. Oh, how wonderful it is to be able to hate." Delbanco observes that to listen to Goebbels is to realize again what Augustine and Melville knew, "that the crusader who construes evil as a malignant, external thing—a thing alien to himself—is by far the worst kind of barbarian. The struggle of the twentieth century was to keep this proficient hater from seizing the world." *The Death of Satan*, p. 183. Our problem may be even more complex because now those who express such hatred are assumed legitimate just because they are representatives of "democratic" societies. In his wonderful response to this paper, "Labored Knowledge: Reflections on Hauerwas on Augustine on Evil," James Wetzel challenges Augustine's avowal to have left Manicheanism behind. Wetzel does so by suggesting that Augustine's very depiction of the unintelligibility of his sin is connected to his sense of his self-created destructiveness. Wetzel argues Augustine struggled to live acknowledging that God's forgiveness is ahead of our reactions, thus freeing us from "having to be the selves we imagine ourselves to be." As Wetzel recognizes, this is an Augustinian criticism of Augustine.

44. Some may wonder if sin and evil are equivalent expressions. Evil is often associated with events that seem to have no agency, which has led some to assume that evil is a more

inclusive description than sin. However, the suggestion that evil is a broader category than sin can lead to the assumption that sin is intelligible because it is something we have done. Yet Augustine thinks sin and evil equally without explanation.

45. The first-person character of the confession of sin does not mean that the whole church cannot confess our sins as the church. So prayers of confession often use "we." For example, consider the prayer from the *Book of Common Prayer* (p. 79):

> Most merciful God,
> we confess that we have sinned against you
> in thought, word, and deed,
> by what we have done,
> and by what we have left undone.
> We have not loved you with our whole heart;
> we have not loved our neighbors as ourselves.
> We are truly sorry and we humbly repent.
> For the sake of your Son Jesus Christ,
> have mercy on us and forgive us;
> that we may delight in your will,
> and walk in your ways,
> to the glory of your Name. Amen.

46. I have tried to make a beginning to think through what it might mean to narrate a wrong so wrong there is nothing one can do to make it right in "Why Time Cannot and Should Not Heal the Wounds of History, But Time Has Been and Can Be Redeemed," in *A Better Hope: Resources for a Church Confronting Capitalism, Democracy, and Postmodernity* (Grand Rapids: Brazos Press, 2000), pp. 139–154.

47. Claudia Koonz, *The Nazi Conscience* (Cambridge, MA: Harvard University Press, 2003), p. 1.

48. Augustine, *Confessions* (ed. Pine-Coffin, p. 64), 3, 8.

49. James Edwards, *The Plain Sense of Things: The Fate of Religion in an Age of Normal Nihilism* (University Park: Pennsylvania State University Press, 1997).

50. This way of putting the matter is misleading because "loss of common worship" suggests that at one time in the past Christians "got it right." On Augustine's grounds, Christians can never assume they ever get it right, but the past can serve as a spur for the imagination to save us from current alternatives.

51. For my attempt to begin to think through what it would mean for Christians to remember the Holocaust, see my "Remembering as a Moral Task: The Challenge of the Holocaust," in my *Against the Nations: War and Survival in a Liberal Society* (Notre Dame: University of Notre Dame Press, 1992), pp. 61–90.

Chapter 3

Ruth W. Grant

The Rousseauan Revolution and the Problem of Evil

The starting point for these reflections is the observation that evil is permanently with us. Consider *Candide.* In Voltaire's improbable tale, the characters experience every possible form of evil: rape, slavery, religious persecution, torture, and on and on. It is fiction, of course. Yet the device of this fiction resembles the device of soap opera. All of these things do happen; there is nothing improbable about them. The improbable fiction is only that all of these things are unlikely to happen to the same three or four people in a single lifetime or a single television episode. Most of the events in Voltaire's story are real and documented.[1] And, of course, all of these things are still happening. Considering the history of the world, there is very little reason to believe that there could come a time when no woman is ever raped, no child ever abused, no person ever tortured or murdered for political reasons.

Yet the permanence of evil is a difficult notion to accept, particularly for those who were raised in the immediate postwar period in the United States. Many at that time were optimistic that a new and better world would emerge from the ashes of World War Two. "Never again" did not have the hollow ring that it has today after Cambodia, Bosnia, and Rwanda, to name only a few.[2] It seemed then that the progress of history would surely include moral progress.[3] Today, such a perspective seems dreamy; it has been called "the great illusion of the twentieth century."[4] The degree, variety, and constancy of political evil and its presence across the globe in the years since the defeat of Hitler should provoke, at the very least, a deep skepticism about the possibility of moral progress.

This skepticism elicits the following question: what is it that you have to believe about evil—about what it is and where it comes from—in order to believe that it is the sort of thing that could be eradicated or overcome? Clearly, you could not believe, as Leibniz and Pope did, that evil is part of the divine plan, a necessary element of an ordered world that contributes to the goodness of the whole, however inexplicably.[5] Similarly, belief in original sin is inseparable from the idea of the permanence of evil in the world as we know it. Any system of beliefs that locates the source of evil in the human passions or in human nature (Freudianism, for example) also supports skepticism about moral progress. In short, the belief that evil can be eradicated entails the idea that the source of evil is something that is subject to change.

One possibility, then, for those who see evil as contingent and eliminable is to conceive of evil as the product of systemic forces. Evil comes about as human beings react and adapt to particular cultural and institutional conditions. Consider, for example, the famous Stanford prison experiments.[6] College students were arbitrarily assigned to roles as either prisoners or guards in a mock prison. After a very short time, the behavior of the guards became sufficiently brutal that the experiment had to be prematurely terminated. The implication of the experiment was that assigned roles determined behavior. This implication is perfectly compatible, of course, with the idea that there are permanent natural human passions that tend toward evil, which are enabled by certain systemic conditions. The pessimistic conclusion is that each and every one of us is capable of perpetrating the worst evils under the "right" circumstances. A more hopeful conclusion would be that well-structured institutions could contain and direct our worst impulses, though it would always be an uphill battle. The most optimistic interpretation of the Stanford experiments would be that, given the right systems, all of us are capable of leading our lives in accordance with the good. The optimistic alternative couples the idea that evil is systemic with the idea that human beings are naturally good or at least, not naturally evil. According to this view, it is *only* our social relationships that corrupt us, and, in principle, these are subject to change. Evil results from the historical development of social institutions that have led humanity astray and perverted our natural goodness.

This is the view that originated with Rousseau.[7] It might be seen as the reverse of the well-known Kantian view that, with the proper institutional structure, a nation of devils can be well governed.[8] In a Rousseauan world, even a nation of angels will be badly governed, given the institutional systems of inequality and oppression that have developed historically. Men born angels will not long remain so in corrupted societies. Rousseau's view has had a powerful impact on modern thinking about the character of evil and particularly about moral responsibility. Rousseau opens up the possibility that there is sometimes evil in the world without evil people; without individual agents who are responsible for it. His view is reflected in the ease with which we speak of "oppression," "exploitation" or "injustice," rather than speaking of "evil." The former are conceived as systemic, often impersonal, forces, whereas the language of "evil" immediately implicates individual "evildoers." If the problem is identified as one of "injustice" or "exploitation," we are not necessarily called upon to hate or to punish particular individuals as perpetrators. One can indulge righteous anger against the system without the bad conscience that might accompany hatred and vengeance toward real people. Or, put positively, one can work to correct evils while holding out a hand to those who otherwise might be dismissed as enemies when evils are understood to be systemic.

Rousseau joins the idea of systems as a determining source of behavior with the idea of natural goodness. He does not, however, take the final step and join these ideas to the idea of progress. In Rousseau's view, once human beings have been corrupted, there is no going back.[9] But Robespierre took this final step. If people are good and evil is systemic, revolutionary change can produce a new world purged of evil; a Republic of Virtue. Paradoxically, the Terror was the evil that was justified by these very ideas about the possibility of eliminating evil.[10] This is one of the reasons that the French Revolution is often deemed the first modern revolution, despite the fact that the American Revolution preceded it: the purge is characteristic for modern revolutionary movements, particularly Communist ones.[11]

In this respect, the Communists ought to be distinguished from the Nazis. Each represents a different view of the nature and sources of evil, which justifies different responses to it. The Communists embrace a version of the idea that evil is systemic. As a result, in addition to the revolutionary overthrow of the system and the elimination of its supporters, forced reeducation appears as a reasonable approach to counter the corrupting effects of the system. For the Nazis, reeducation of the Jews would have been senseless. The Nazis were driven by a kind of Manichean vision. They themselves represented all that was noble and good, while evil was personified in the Jewish people and other non-Aryan peoples and could be eradicated only by their physical elimination. The label "totalitarian" conflates this distinction between the Nazi's Manicheanism and the Communist understanding of evil as systemic.

Each of these modern movements represents an alternative set of beliefs about evil that includes the belief that evil can be eradicated. And this belief itself drives a considerable amount of evil in the world. As Isaiah Berlin wrote:

> One belief, more than any other, is responsible for the slaughter of individuals on the altars of the great historical ideals . . . This is the belief that somewhere, in the past or in the future, in divine revelation or in the mind of an individual thinker, in the pronouncements of history or science or in the simple heart of an uncorrupted good man, there is a final solution.[12]

If Berlin is right, the importance of understanding the answer to my initial question is evident: what do you have to believe about evil to conceive of it as something that could be eliminated? Both Manicheanism and the systemic view can fuel the impulse to seek a final solution.

Interestingly, these were the alternative views that divided reactions in the United States to the terrorist attacks of 9/11. The poles are represented by a headline in a Tennessee newspaper announcing "Bush Vows to Eliminate Evil,"[13] on the one hand, and the frequently repeated phrase, "We have to understand where they are coming from," on the other. For some, the very act of calling the suicide bombers "evil" was a critically important part of the proper moral response to the attack. Others, while condemning the bombing, could not bring themselves to use that word in speaking of the bombers, in part for fear of the evils that might be prompted by a Manichean response. But the systemic view, though it seems immeasurably "softer" and more sophisticated in its understanding of evil, certainly is no guarantee against political violence employed in the name of eradicating evil; witness the examples of the French Revolution and of Communist revolutions. Under the right circumstances, the systemic view too can be used to justify evil. It is this horn of the dilemma that is the subject of this essay.

My aim is to explore one modern "logic of evil": the combination of the belief in the goodness of man, the systemic nature of evil, and the possibility of progress. I return to Rousseau and the French Revolution and develop the contrast with the American Revolution in order to explore both the ways in which responsibility is reconceived and the consequences of that reconceptualization for politics where this "logic of evil" has been accepted. The investigation bears on the question of how so much evil can be perpetrated in the name of the good. It is an opportunity to investigate how ideas about evil can themselves contribute to justifying certain sorts of evil. Given that my starting point is the premise of the permanence of evil, the investigation raises two central questions. First, how can we recognize the importance of ideas about evil for the actual practice of evil in the world without succumbing to the fantasy that getting the ideas right could ever put an end to evil? And second, how can we give their due to the truths contained in the proposition that evil is systemic without generating the false hope that a change in systems would be sufficient to overcome it?

Rousseau and the Problem of Evil

> Everything is good as it leaves the hands of the Author of nature; everything degenerates in the hands of men.
>
> Jean-Jacques Rousseau, *Emile*[14]

Rousseau is clear that we cannot look to God as the source of the evils in the world. In his famous exchange with Voltaire in the wake of the devastating earthquake at Lisbon, Rousseau laid out his position: God is omnipotent and God is good. There must be another source of the evils man suffers, and that can only be man himself.

> "You must acknowledge," Rousseau declared, "that it was not nature that piled up there [Lisbon] twenty thousand houses of six or seven floors each; and that if the inhabitants of this great city had been spread out more evenly . . . the destruction would have been a lot less, and perhaps insignificant . . . How many poor creatures died in this disaster because one wanted to go back for his clothes, another for his papers, a third for his money?"[15]

Evil, in this case, was the result of human corruption but not of malicious will: Rousseau does not imply that anyone intended to murder the residents of Lisbon. While the evil of the Lisbon disaster was manmade, it was not made by evil men.

Rousseau faces what looks like a particularly knotty problem in trying to explain the sources of evil. God is not its source: "Everything is good as it leaves the hands of the Author of nature." But "everything" includes man: the natural goodness of man is the unifying premise of Rousseau's work.[16] Rousseau emphatically rejects the doctrine of original sin. If neither God nor man is the source of evil, where does it come from? Rousseau insists that men are good by nature *and* that evil is manmade. How can men be responsible for evil when they are naturally good? This is the "anthropodicy" problem that replaces the theodicy problem in Rousseau's work.

Rousseau's response to this problem is a complex story of human corruption. Evil arises through the interaction between accidental changes in man's natural circumstances, the historical development of the species, and individual human psychology. We *become* evil as we come to inhabit the artificial world of human society. This is the process Rousseau describes in the *Second Discourse* with respect to the species. In the *Confessions,* he tells a similar tale of the corruption of a single individual: himself.[17] Both works leave the reader with a great deal of sympathy for human beings as victims of external social and historical forces beyond their control; forces that make them vicious but also miserable. Masters as well as slaves, history's winners as well as its losers, they are all to be pitied as they lose both their natural purity and the possibility of happiness.

The *Second Discourse* traces the development of corruption and misery as the effects of inequality.[18] Corruption is born of inequality because inequality produces a system of personal dependence, and dependence, in turn, produces vice. Rousseau describes the moral impact of economic dependence:

> [B]ehold man, due to a multitude of new needs, subjected so to speak to
> all of nature and especially to his fellow men, whose slave he becomes in
> a sense even in becoming their master; rich, he needs their services; poor,
> he needs their help; and mediocrity cannot enable him to do without them.
> He must therefore incessantly seek to interest them in his fate, and to make
> them find their own profit, in fact or in appearance, in working for his. This
> makes him deceitful and sly with some, imperious and harsh with others . . .
> Finally, consuming ambition, the fervor to raise one's relative fortune less
> out of true need than in order to place oneself above others, inspires in all
> men a base inclination to harm each other, a secret jealousy all the more
> dangerous because, in order to strike its blow in greater safety, it often
> assumes the mask of benevolence.[19]

Social, economic, and political inequalities that develop historically transform man's passions and inclinations. Human beings are naturally independent and self-sufficient, and their only sentiment toward others is a kind of primitive pity. The development of dependency relationships replaces that sentiment "in all men" with "a base inclination to harm each other."[20]

The key psychological factor in this transformation is *amour-propre;* the desire to be preferred or the desire for distinction. It is, in a sense, a desire for inequality and particularly for the recognition of inequality. The satisfaction of this desire thus depends both on the existence of a hierarchy of value and on the opinion of others. *Amour-propre* can take a variety of forms including ambition, envy, jealousy, vengeance, vanity, and pride. It is this passion that explains why people often react more strongly to insult than to injury. As we saw, systems of unequal relationships inflame *amour-propre*. At the same time, this desire sustains systems of inequality:

> [C]itizens let themselves be oppressed only insofar as they are carried away by blind ambition; and looking more below than above them, domination becomes dearer to them than independence, and they consent to wear chains in order to give them to others in turn.[21]

Unequal and unjust relations of dependence develop over time as the human species progresses technologically and culturally. This dependence corrupts the human soul. Finally, dependence and the passions it produces come to reinforce one another. Structural or systemic inequality, with its attendant *amour-propre,* is the root of all evil; "it is the spirit of society alone and the inequality it engenders, which thus change and alter all our natural inclinations."[22] In reference to his letter to Voltaire, Rousseau wrote, "I proved to him that out of all [the evils of human life], there was not one from which providence was not exculpated, and which did not have its source more in the *abuse* that man has made of his faculties than in nature itself."[23] Rousseau thus solves his "anthropodicy" problem.

According to Rousseau, none of the motivating emotions associated with *amour-propre* (envy, ambition, jealousy, and so forth) are natural in human beings in the sense that they are not part of what human beings are originally, if for no other reason than that Rousseau depicts man as originally living in isolation, and these are necessarily social passions. Yet, *amour-propre* seems to arise inescapably once human beings are brought into sustained contact with their fellows, particularly because *amour-propre* is tied to sexual preference (though not to sexuality simply). Once a person comes to prefer a particular sexual partner, that person wishes to be preferred in turn. This is the context in which *amour-propre* first appears in Rousseau's story of the development of the species, and it is very early in the story.[24] In the case of an individual living in society, its appearance cannot be delayed beyond the onset of adolescence.[25] It seems that, while Rousseau insists that *amour-propre* is not natural, it might as well be. The species cannot return to the original condition of individual isolation even if that were desirable, and *amour-propre* will inevitably appear even in the most primitive social conditions. The passions that lead men to wish to harm others will always be with us.

At this point, it might seem that in Rousseau's account *amour-propre* is simply a functional equivalent of original sin. Human beings have fallen from an original state of innocence, and henceforth each of us carries in our soul a predisposition to sin or evildoing. But I think this view is mistaken, first, because *amour-propre* can be the source of the best in men, as well as of great evils, and second, because it becomes predominantly destructive only under certain historical conditions that are not inevitable. *Amour-propre* is inseparable from conjugal love, for example, which Rousseau calls one of "the sweetest sentiments known to men."[26] Rousseau describes the primitive stage of human society where people live in groups of self-sufficient family units as the "happiest and most durable epoch" even though *amour-propre* has become a feature of human psychology by this time.[27] It is only after a series of accidents that lead to the discovery of metallurgy, the development of agriculture, the division of labor, and finally the institution of unequal property that *amour-propre* produces far more evils than it does good for human beings. Moreover, Rousseau's ideal egalitarian communities seek to satisfy the desire for distinction by awarding honors according to merit. Under these conditions, where there is no personal dependence and status inequalities are both limited and justified by merit, *amour-propre* supports virtue, for example, civic spirit and excellence in public service.[28] In short, despite the psychological dimension of Rousseau's account of the origins of evil, the structure of social institutions, which are not natural but arise historically, remains the critical determining factor. Consequently, we are led to view corrupted humanity with sympathy; perpetrators of evils to be sure, but only because we are all also victims of our circumstances.

This view emerges also from an analysis of Rousseau's depiction of his own corruption in the *Confessions*. Rousseau portrays himself in many ways as a victim of circumstances, and while he has much to confess, he views himself as corrupted in a qualified sense. He does bad things, but he retains a purity of sentiment. In almost every case, Rousseau explains his transgressions in such a way that it is easy for him to forgive himself and to lead the reader to do the same. Most of the other people in the book are treated in similar fashion. People do bad things largely out of errors of judgment and weakness of will; very rarely out of true wickedness or malicious will. And only the latter is considered truly evil by

Rousseau. Purity of intention can even excuse Rousseau's decision to abandon his children at birth to a foundling home. Again, while evil is manmade, most of it is not made by evil men.

Rousseau's first experience of injustice can serve as an example. As a child, Rousseau was falsely accused of breaking a comb. All appearances indicated that only he could have been the culprit. Consequently his protestations of innocence were treated as barefaced lies. He was punished along with his cousin who had also been unjustly accused of a serious transgression. This incident marks a turning point in Roussseau's development; it is the equivalent of the Fall.

> There was the end of the serenity of my childlike life. From that moment, I ceased to enjoy a pure happiness . . . We remained at Bossey for several months. We were there as the first man is represented to us in the terrestrial paradise, but we had ceased to enjoy it. . . . Attachment, respect, intimacy, confidence no longer tied the students to their guides; we no longer regarded them as Gods who read in our hearts: we were less ashamed of doing wrong, and more fearful of being accused: we began to hide ourselves, to mutiny, to lie. All the vices of our age corrupted our innocence and disfigured our games. . . . We ceased to cultivate our little gardens, our herbs, our flowers . . .[29]

What is the cause of the vices? Unjust treatment at the hands of others. And are those others evil? On the contrary, they are well-meaning adults who are merely mistaken in their judgment. What is the source of their error? They are misled by the evidence of their senses and their misplaced faith in reason: it seemed that only Rousseau had the opportunity to break the comb. They would have done better had they trusted the judgment of their hearts, saying, "We know Jean-Jacques. He would never have done such a thing."

Errors of judgment coupled with pure intentions account for the immoral behavior of Mme de Warens as well: "[A]ll her faults came to her from her errors, never from her passions." "[S]he could do evil while deceiving herself, but she could not want anything that was evil." She had been led into error and self-deception by her "philosophy teacher," and "the principles he gave her were the ones he needed to seduce her."[30] She too was misled by a misplaced faith in reason. Both examples demonstrate that while errors of judgment cause many of the evils in the world, enlightenment rationalism is hardly the solution to this problem.

Weakness of will is a second major source of evil. Rousseau affirms a practical maxim of morality in response to this problem.

[A]void situations that put our duties in opposition with our interests, and which show us our good in the harm of someone else; certain that whatever love of virtue one brings to such situations, sooner or later one weakens without being aware of it, and one becomes unjust and bad in fact, without having ceased to be just and good in the soul.[31]

The structure of society puts men in situations where interest and duty conflict. The only way to remain pure would be to remove oneself from society. Otherwise, one becomes bad "without being aware of it"; "bad in fact," while remaining "good in the soul." It is striking how little culpability Rousseau attaches to weakness of will and how the soul can remain pure despite bad actions in his view.

Rousseau "confesses" his own weakness of will, illustrating these attitudes with an important example. When he was young and employed in a large household, he stole a fancy ribbon intending to give it to a servant girl. When he was caught, he swore that it was the servant girl who had stolen it. Rousseau refers to this false and unjust accusation as a "heinous crime" and one for which he has suffered the greatest remorse. He knows the seriousness of the consequences for a servant girl who is dismissed from her position for stealing. Yet, after making this confession, Rousseau immediately turns to examine his "internal inclinations" and finds that "never has wickedness been farther from me than in that cruel moment." It was only fear of the shame of a public confession (a form of *amour-propre*) that led him to lie, not any hostility towards the girl. Had he been given the opportunity to confess in private, he surely would have. Instead, "they only intimidated me when it was necessary to give me courage." Finally, "in youth, genuinely heinous acts are even more criminal than in maturity; but what is only weakness is much less so, and at bottom my fault was hardly anything else."[32]

"Genuinely heinous acts," or "wickedness," are motivated by the desire to do harm to others or to use them to aggrandize oneself. It is beginning to appear that a great deal of harm in the world is done without wickedness. Most people are not consciously cruel, callous, and manipulative. There are some, of course, and M. Grimm is the model for this type in the *Confessions*. He is a man of letters who is vain (he uses cosmetics) and proud, and he succeeds because others are too good or too innocent to see his true nature. To try to deal with him fairly and gently only makes matters worse: "the hatred of the wicked . . . becomes further enlivened by the impossibility of finding anything to base it on, and the feeling of their own injustice is only an additional grievance against the person who is its object."[33] The wicked few are fully responsible for the evils that they commit and entirely undeserving of sympathy. But these are the rare exceptions. Most of the evils in the world are caused by people who, with good hearts and pure souls, have been led astray by errors of judgment or weakness of will.

Rousseau offers a new perspective on the problem of evil in contrast both to the Christian doctrine of original sin and the Enlightenment philosophes' analysis of evil as the result of ignorance and superstition. People are naturally innocent and pure, and morality is more a matter of the heart than the head. In fact, the development of the rational faculties is certainly no proof against wickedness (e.g., Grimm); reason becomes rationalization more often than not (e.g., the case of Mme de Warens); and errors of judgment can follow from an excessive reliance on empirical evidence and a distrust of sentiment (e.g. the "fall" at Bossey). Rousseau's new alternative position is illustrated in the *Letter to D'Alembert* where he argues against instituting a theater in Geneva. With the Calvinist ministers of that town, he sees this project, supported by Voltaire and Diderot, as exemplary of the cultural sophistication that breeds corruption of various kinds. But distinguishing himself from the ministers' austerity, he recommends alternative healthy forms of public pleasures: simple, egalitarian festivals directed toward cultivating sentiments of brotherhood in the community and purified of negative competitive rivalries.

In Rousseau's account, purity of feeling is the key to moral goodness; it seems to excuse almost anything. And such feeling is very difficult to preserve in people who live within institutionalized structures of inequality and dependence where *amour-propre* is fully operative. Rousseau was extremely pessimistic as to the practical possibilities for establishing communities like his idealized depiction of Geneva, but the depictions were meant to be moving and inspiring. Robespierre was among those inspired. Rousseau had explained how evil could arise in human communities without emanating either from God or from the nature of man. Artificial institutional systems of inequality, often arising in response to historical accidents, transform people. Some become outright wicked. Many others do bad things as a result of the injustices they suffer, of mistakes, or of weakness in the face of conflicts created by the system in which they live. But they remain good at heart. Rousseau combines the principle of natural goodness with the principle of systemic evil. It remains to be seen how these principles operated in the justification of the Terror.

Rousseau and the French Revolution

> The first thing the legislator must know is that the people is good.
>
> Robespierre[34]

That Rousseau had a profound influence on the revolution of 1789 is well established. What the Revolutionaries found in Rousseau was both a model of virtue and a compelling indictment of society as the source of the degradation of mankind. He was admired at least as much for his persona as for his writings, and of his writings, the *Confessions* was more influential than the *Social Contract*. Rousseau was admired for preserving his integrity in spite of the injustices he suffered. He was a primary source for the language of virtue, corruption, and purity that permeated revolutionary discourse. In short, his analysis of the origins of evil, what I have been calling the systemic approach, had a powerful effect on the Revolution.[35]

There is a puzzle here. In Rousseau's own work, as we have seen, his analysis tends to be exculpatory. Individuals are rarely to blame for the evils of the world; even the masters are portrayed as victims of the system; purity of intention is sufficient to justify forgiveness. How, then, does the analysis of evil as systemic become transformed in the hands of the Revolutionaries into a justification for the brutality of the Terror? I concentrate here on three components of the Revolutionaries' analysis, only the first two of which are Rousseauan: (1) the premise of natural goodness; (2) the claim that systemic hierarchies are corrupting; and (3) the belief in the possibility of a complete break with the old regime.[36] I might have included the Rousseauan concepts of the unity of the people's will and of compassion, which were also important in Revolutionary discourse.[37] But my purpose is not to give a complete accounting of Rousseau's influence on the French Revolution. It is to show how the understanding of evil as systemic and eradicable can itself become a justification for evil.

It was axiomatic for the Revolutionaries that the people is always good.[38] This meant that whenever popular counterrevolutionary activity took place, an explanation had to be found that was compatible with the axiom. There were two possibilities: either the people had been contaminated by some external influence or these particular people had to be excluded from "the people." The first logic was applied to peasant and worker revolts outside of Paris in the Vendee and elsewhere. France's foreign enemies were blamed for corrupting the people and turning them against the fatherland.[39] The second logic was applied to mobs of poor Parisians who responded to food shortages with riots and looting. "What is there in common between the people of Paris and a mob of women, led by valets of the aristocracy" Robespierre asked.[40] "The people" could remain pure as an abstraction whose will was always good and was represented by the leadership of the Revolution, while actual people in revolt against that leadership could be demonized as foreign enemies or internal enemies of "the people." The premise of natural goodness is transformed into a Manichean dichotomy of good and evil forces justifying extreme measures against the latter.

The premise of the natural goodness of man played a role in the justification of the purges as well. We have seen how, in Rousseau's thought, the idea that essentially good people are corrupted by the pressures of the system in which they live leads to the view that purity of intention is the crucial factor in moral goodness. And contrariwise, the only real crime is a corrupted heart. Trials during the Terror were not examinations of evidence of criminal activity. They were judgments by a patriotic jury of the purity of sentiment of the accused. The only real question was, "Is the accused an enemy of the people?" This is the vision of justice explicitly codified in the law of 22 Prairial.[41] Purity of intention as a moral principle operated in other ways to enable the Terror as well. The perpetrators of the Terror, fully conscious of the purity of their own intentions, could compliment themselves for their willingness to be cruel for the sake of the Revolution. Devotion to the Revolution, that is, purity of intention, becomes the only moral desideratum. And lastly, the imperative of preserving the purity of the Revolution itself as the expression of the unified will of a people who is always good justifies crushing dissent.[42]

The idea of evil as systemic also shaped the ideal of Revolutionary justice. It too tended to eliminate the importance of evidence of individual guilt for particular criminal deeds. This is nowhere more evident than in Saint Juste's speeches to the Convention advocating death for Louis XVI. His position was not that the king had ruled badly or abused his power; such considerations were utterly irrelevant. Louis XVI was guilty of being a king. Just as the people are virtuous because of their position in the system, Louis XVI was guilty because of his.[43] In Rousseau's hands, the idea of systemic evil leads to a general sympathy for people on the top as well as on the bottom of the social hierarchy. Occupying positions of dependence in an unnatural hierarchical system deforms all souls and creates universal misery. In the hands of the Revolutionaries, the same basic thought justifies an automatic determination of guilt or innocence on the basis of social position. This is a logic that has justified, not only the decapitation of a French king, but the attempt to eliminate whole classes of people in the name of revolutionary justice in many places around the globe.

The final factor in the development of this fatal revolutionary logic is the belief in the possibility of a thoroughly radical break with the past. The old system, the ancien régime, had caused the degeneration of mankind. The Revolution would destroy it and begin anew by instituting a new system that would create a new man. Both destruction and renovation rest on the notion that it is governmental systems that form the people. The Revolutionary project thus joined the Terror with reeducation proposals and festivals for cultural renewal.[44] The "Great Terror" that resulted in the deaths of about 1,300 purported aristocrats began just a few days after the Festival of the Supreme Being. The attempt to eradicate the old and replace it with a new order was not simply an attempt to redirect the course of history. It was an attempt to overcome history itself. It should not be forgotten that the Revolutionaries instituted a new calendar beginning with the year one. Henceforth, history would no longer be a process of degeneration and decay. François Furet wrote: "No sentiment was more intense at that moment than the feeling that a breach had opened up in time . . . The past was the ancien regime, the epoch of man corrupted by society, and in destroying it the Revolution opened up the way to regeneration."[45] The Revolutionaries seemed to believe that evil itself could become a thing of the past. To purify society once and for all is a powerful justification for destruction.

Rousseau argued that naturally good men are corrupted by unjust institutionalized systems of power relations that arise historically. This systemic explanation for the origins of evil appears in his work as benign, particularly in comparison to Manichean visions that identify good and evil as powerful competing forces. But it now appears that the systemic view can become effectively indistinguishable from Manicheanism when coupled with the idea that social systems can be radically altered so as to recover natural goodness. This is what the example of the French Revolution demonstrates. The idea of systemic evil generated dichotomies between the good people on the one hand and the evil mob, or foreign elements, or ruling class on the other. It generated dichotomies between pure patriots and traitors, virtuous citizens and vicious enemies of the people. And it generated the dichotomy between everything evil associated with the old regime and the purity of the new, revolutionary order. The systemic understanding of evil, along with the idea that evil could be eradicated, permitted and encouraged immense injustices and cruelties in just these surprisingly Manichean terms.

There are alternatives to the systemic view and the Manichean view. One of them is exemplified in the public rhetoric of the American Revolution. The understanding of evil deployed during that period has two important distinguishing aspects: that evil is permanently with us and that its source is not something external to each of us, but rather internal to each individual human being. In these particular respects, it resembles the doctrine of original sin. This view dominates the logic of justification during the period of the American Revolution, to which I now turn.[46]

The Idea of Evil in the American Revolution

> The latent causes of faction are thus sown in the nature of man; and we see them everywhere brought into different degrees of activity, according to the different circumstances of civil society.
>
> *The Federalist Papers*, no. 10

Among the Americans of the founding period, the language of evil follows an entirely different logic than the Rousseauan logic just described.[47] Interestingly, there is plenty of talk of virtue, vice, and corruption, but, of purity, none at all. Passions with malignant possibilities are part of the human constitution. People are dangerous to one another unless their passions are regulated, internally and externally. The most politically important of these passions are ambition and acquisitiveness, which are often described as predominating more in the elite ranks of society than among "the middling classes."[48] Self-interestedness, however, is found in every social class. The preference for oneself is both natural and ubiquitous, and it necessarily produces partiality. Partiality or bias is not only unjust in itself but also the source of political conflict and of the domination of one part of the society over another.[49]

To the extent that partiality is the source of evil, reasonableness is the antidote. To act reasonably is to consider a question impartially, judge accordingly, and guide one's action by that judgment.[50] Each of us can be held responsible for the extent to which our conduct is reasonable in this sense. When the consequences of our conduct are manifestly unfair or unjust, there can be no appeal to purity of intention or a core of natural goodness. Both the passions that give rise to evil and the rational faculty that can control them are inherent internal capacities. Hence, responsibility lies with each individual.

Nonetheless, institutional systems and social circumstances vary in the extent to which they either enable or constrain the negative consequences of the passions and appetites of individuals. Madison famously argues that "[a]mbition must be made to counteract ambition"[51] and that such a goal can be achieved through institutional design. But even institutions well designed to constrain the passions can never do so permanently.[52] Ambition and partiality are a constant threat. In contrast to the Rousseauan view according to which good people are corrupted by bad institutions, Madison and Jefferson fear that good institutions will be corrupted by bad people.

This understanding of the relation between the sources of evils and social systems contains within itself both conservative and revolutionary tendencies. It is conservative in that it would condemn any project as hopeless that aimed at eradicating evil and creating the conditions for the regeneration of humanity. On the other hand, it contains a logic that justifies the overthrow of systems that institutionalize partiality and privilege, such as monarchy and aristocracy. And since corruption and factional conflict constantly threaten, vigilance on the part of the public is always called for. The people must be jealous guardians of their rights, ready to take up arms to defend them if need be.

But this sort of revolution is unlikely to produce a terror. It is resistant to the Manichean transformation to which the systemic view of evil is so susceptible. The absence of moral purity as a possibility, the centrality of the notion of personal responsibility, and the absence of messianic hopes provide some protection against those sorts of revolutionary excesses. In the United States, political opponents were not conceived as the personification of evil and subjected to a cataclysmic extermination meant to usher in a new historical era.

This is not to say that the dominant understanding of evil in the American case cannot and has not been used to justify enormous evils; on the contrary. By classifying groups of people as incapable of the internal constraint of reason, their subjection to external domination could be justified. Those thought to be lacking full rationality were classified as childlike or subhuman, and their oppression was characteristically blended with paternalism and institutionalized.[53] The point is that different understandings of what evil is and where it comes from facilitate the practice of evil in different ways.

It would be hard to imagine a set of ideas about evil that could not be employed as justifications for it. Moreover, there are many evils in every society that are perpetrated in spite of and not because of the dominant ideas of the time. These observations in themselves provide some confirmation of the view according to which evil finds its source in permanent human characteristics.

Conclusions

This analysis has focused on what I have called the "systemic view" of evil: a cluster of concepts including the premise of man's natural goodness and the claim that corruption is caused by impersonal structural forces and social relations, formal and informal, that develop historically. I have juxtaposed this view, first, with "Manicheanism," according to which pure forces of good and evil with independent sources contend with one another in the world, and, finally, with an alternative view that maintains that the source of evil resides in each and every one of us and always will.

At first glance, the systemic view and Manicheanism confront one another as opposing alternatives in responding to evil. The Manichean searches for the evildoers and seeks to eliminate them. The advocates of a systemic view focus, not on individual perpetrators, but on the general conditions producing injustice and oppression. In doing so, they believe that they are combating the dangers of Manicheanism; that their approach will produce a more humane politics. Yet, I have tried to show that these two views are not as opposed as they first appear. The systemic view can generate the same sorts of dichotomies as Manicheanism does. The crucial element that the two views share is the idea of evil as the result of external forces; in other words, they both hold out the possibility of the purity of the self. One points to the pure and innocent victims of the forces of evil at loose in the world while the other points to the pure and innocent victims of historical circumstances. But history has shown that this idea of purity, along with the idea that evil can be overcome or eradicated, is potent and dangerous. The dangers are those long recognized as the dangers of self-righteousness.[54]

Unlike the systemic and Manichean views, the third alternative, illustrated here by the American Revolution, entails an inherent suspicion of self-righteousness. Its tendencies are toward bad conscience and permanent vigilance. Self-righteousness is limited by the consciousness of sinfulness, or malevolent passions, or selfish appetites within ourselves. Vigilance is required because those forces can never be entirely overcome, only contained. This view produces a concern with limits.

The separation of powers is a perfect expression of these sensibilities in the American case. And similarly, it is not accidental that the idea of the purity of the people in France was coupled with the idea of an unfettered state as the instrument of the people's will. Moreover, the idea that evil is permanently with us, like the idea that its sources are internal, is a moderating idea as well because it is incompatible with utopian attempts to overcome evil and usher in a new and purified age. While avoiding this Scylla, the Charybdis to fear here is complacency or complicity; these would be the characteristic pitfalls of this perspective. Finally, this perspective encourages introspection and self-examination. In place of the conviction of one's own purity is the conviction that none of us are above reproach. This is a powerful impetus toward self-correction. For these reasons, and in spite of the ways in which it too has been used to justify evil, on balance, it is to be preferred to the alternatives.

But is it not only less dangerous, but also more true than the systemic view? Let us return to my central example and compare Edmund Burke's approach to explaining the French Revolution with Alexis de Tocqueville's. In Burke's view, "History consists for the greater part in the miseries brought upon the world by pride, ambition, avarice, revenge, lust, sedition, hypocrisy, ungoverned zeal, and all the train of disorderly appetites."[55] He puts great emphasis on the kind of men selected for the National Assembly, saying that, after he had read the list of representatives, "Nothing that they afterwards did could appear astonishing."[56] By contrast, Tocqueville, in the *Ancien Regime,* traces the development of political institutions, social relations, economic systems and so forth, sometimes back to the Middle Ages, in order to show how the old order had already been significantly undermined by the time the Revolution took place. Tocqueville's systemic analysis has great explanatory force. While Burke has a point, to explain historical and political events on a large scale, whether or not those events are characterized as "evils," we cannot rely on individual psychology alone.

Moreover, Rousseau's systemic explanation draws attention to the fact that many of the evil deeds in the world are done by people who are not wicked. This is an insight that rings true. Without some explanation for this phenomenon, it would be very difficult to explain the prevalence of evil. Surely one part of the explanation is to be found in the effects of the set of relationships within which individuals find themselves such that the results of their well-intentioned actions may be inadvertently harmful or the pressures of their situation may either lead them to rationalize behavior they know is wrong or thoroughly corrupt their moral sense, and so forth. To return to the Stanford prison experiments, there is strong evidence that systemic power relationships do affect morality and behavior.[57]

The systemic perspective must be given its due, but now grounded in and made compatible with a non-Rousseauan premise. The bedrock premise would be, not the natural goodness of man, but rather the recognition of ineradicable destructive human passions that are constitutive of our being. In this view, there is no possibility of an escape from personal responsibility, no possibility of attributing moral purity to any individual or group, and no possibility of moral progress of the sort that would make evil a thing of the past. Such a view would avoid the Rousseauan dangers.

But it would not and could not avoid all dangers. All moral ideas are dangerous ideas—just not to the same degree or in the same way. Different ideas about what evil is and where it comes from lead people to commit different evils in the name of the good. It follows that getting the ideas right about evil is enormously important for moral progress. But "getting the ideas right" cannot eliminate evil. In fact, the idea that evil can be eliminated is itself one of those dangerous ideas that lead people to commit evils. This is our paradoxical situation. It matters a great deal how we speak about evil, but it bears emphasizing that we cannot eliminate evil by finally understanding it correctly.

NOTES

1. Voltaire, *Candide and Related Writings*, trans. and with an intro. by David Wootton (Indianapolis: Hackett, 2000), pp.viii–ix.

2. Not to mention the persistence in the modern world of virulent forms of anti-Semitism that date back to medieval times.

3. For a theoretical statement of this sort of optimism, see Immanuel Kant, "Idea for a Universal History with a Cosmopolitan Intent" in *Perpetual Peace and Other Essays*, trans. by Ted Humphrey (Indianapolis: Hackett Publishing, 1983), pp. 29–40.

4. Barrington Moore, Jr., *Moral Purity and Persecution in History* (Princeton: Princeton University Press, 2000), p. 133.

5. Gottfried Leibniz, "Metaphysics Summarized," and Alexander Pope, "Essay on Man," in Voltaire, *Candide and Related Writings*.

6. Craig Haney, Curtis Banks, and Philip Zimbardo, "Interpersonal Dynamics in a Simulated Prison," *International Journal of Criminology and Penology* 1 (1973): 69–97.

7. It is encapsulated in Jacques's remark in *Candide*: "It must be the case . . . that human beings have corrupted the natural order of things somewhat; for they are not born wolves, and they have become wolves." Voltaire, *Candide and Related Writings*, pp. 9–10.

8. Kant, "To Perpetual Peace: A Philosophical Sketch," in *Perpetual Peace*, pp. 107–43.

9. But see Bernard Manin, in *A Critical Dictionary of the French Revolution*, ed. François Furet and Mona Ozouf, trans. by Arthur Goldhammer (Cambridge, MA: Belknap Press, 1989), s.v. "Rousseau." "*Emile* lent credibility to the idea of radical change." According to

Manin, the idea that "it is possible to reject custom, break with convention, and construct a new order more truly in harmony with nature" is also part of Rousseau's legacy.

10. I do not say "caused by." The question of the causes of the Terror is far more complex. I am interested here in the self-understanding of the Revolutionaries. The question of the causal relation between Enlightenment ideas and the French Revolution is a contentious one. For a discussion of various approaches, see Robert Darnton, *The Forbidden Best-Sellers of Pre-Revolutionary France* (New York: W. W. Norton and Co., 1995), chapter 6. Darnton's position is that illegal "low" forms of literature were more important than the works of the philosophes in undermining the legitimacy of the regime. But what he finds in this material has been characterized as a "Rousseauian critique" and a "watered down Enlightenment." See David A. Bell, "Why Books Caused a Revolution: A Reading of Robert Darnton," and Jeremy D. Popkin, "Robert Darnton's alternative (to the) Enlightenment," in *The Darnton Debate: Books and Revolution in the Eighteenth Century*, ed. Haydn T. Mason (Oxford: Voltaire Foundation, 1998), pp. 121, 186.

11. Arthur Koestler draws the parallel between the French Terror and Stalin's purges in *Darkness at Noon*, trans. by Daphne Hardy (New York: Modern Library, 1941). Hannah Arendt distinguishes them in *On Revolution* (London: Penguin Books, 1963, 1965), p. 100.

12. "Two Concepts of Liberty," in *The Proper Study of Mankind* (New York: Farrar, Straus and Giroux, 1997) p. 237.

13. Note also the title of David Frum and Richard Perle's book, *An End to Evil: How to Win the War on Terror* (New York: Balantine Books, 2004).

14. This is the opening line of the work. *Emile*, trans. by Allan Bloom (New York: Basic Books, 1979).

15. Voltaire, *Candide and Related Works*, pp. 110–111.

16. Arthur Melzer, *The Natural Goodness of Man: On the System of Rousseau's Thought* (Chicago: University of Chicago Press, 1990).

17. *Emile* is the counterpoint to the *Confessions*. In that work, Rousseau imagines how a child might be raised apart from the influences of society in a manner that preserves his natural goodness from the forces of corruption.

18. See Nannerl O. Keohane, "Inequality and the Problem of Evil," in this volume.

19. Jean-Jacques Rousseau, *The First and Second Discourses*, Roger D. Masters ed., *Discourse on the Origin and Foundation of Inequality (Second Discourse)* (New York: St. Martin's Press, 1964), p. 156.

20. In *Emile*, the child must not experience his dependence on the will of another human being. It would cripple and distort the child's exercise of his own will (p. 66). Dependence on things does not have the same corrupting effect.

21. Rousseau, *Second Discourse*, p. 173.

22. Ibid., p. 180.

23. Emphasis added. Jean-Jacques Rousseau, *The Confessions and Correspondence Including the Letters to Malesherbes*, ed. Christopher Kelly, Roger D. Masters, and Peter G. Stillman, trans. by Christopher Kelly (Hanover, NH: University Press of New England, 1995), p. 361.

24. Rousseau, *Second Discourse*, pp. 134–35, 148–49. For extended discussions of *amour-propre*, see Laurence D. Cooper, *Rousseau, Nature and the Problem of the Good Life* (University Park: Pennsylvania State University Press, 1999); and Ruth W. Grant, *Hypocrisy and Integrity: Machiavelli, Rousseau and the Ethics of Politics* (Chicago: University of Chicago Press, 1997), pp. 155–161.

25. See Rousseau, *Emile*, 213–15.

26. Rousseau, *Second Discourse*, pp. 146–147.

27. Rousseau, *Second Discourse*, p. 151.

28. See, for example, Jean-Jacques Rousseau, *The Government of Poland*, trans. Willmoore Kendall (Indianapolis: Bobbs-Merrill Co., 1972), chap. 13.

29. Rousseau, *Confessions*, p. 18.

30. Ibid., pp. 165, 167.

31. Ibid., p. 47. See n. 30.

32. Ibid., pp. 71–73.

33. Ibid., p. 396. See pp. 390–97.

34. Quoted in Carol Blum, *Rousseau and the Republic of Virtue: The Language of Politics in the French Revolution* (Ithaca: Cornell University Press, 1986), p. 159. Robespierre wrote that he learned this from Rousseau. See Manin, "Rousseau," p. 840.

35. See Blum, *Republic of Virtue*; and François Furet, "Rousseau and the French Revolution," in *The Legacy of Rousseau*, ed. Clifford Orwin and Nathan Tarcov (Chicago: University of Chicago Press, 1997). See also Manin, "Rousseau," for an excellent treatment of the complexities of the question of Rousseau's influence.

36. Moore, *Moral Purity*, p.77. On the third component, see n. 9.

37. See Arendt, *On Revolution*, pp. 76–90.

38. Blum, *Republic of Virtue*, pp. 159, 164.

39. Blum, *Republic of Virtue*, pp. 217, 223

40. Quoted in Blum, *Republic of Virtue*, p. 198. See also pp. 187, 196–98, 249.

41. Blum, *Republic of Virtue*, pp. 180, 255.

42. Moore, *Moral Purity*, chap. 3, traces the idea of purity as it functioned in the French Revolution. His discussion of the speeches of Hébert, Robespierre, and Saint Juste provides considerable supporting evidence for the claims made here. His analytic focus is the secularization of the politics of purity during the Revolution.

43. Moore, *Moral Purity*, p. 166 and chap. 9.

44. See Mona Ozouf, in *Critical Dictionary*, s.v. "Regeneration."

45. Furet, "Rousseau and the French Revolution," pp. 179–181. See also Carla Hesse, "Precedent and Invention: The Problem of the Past in Revolutionary Politics," unpublished paper delivered at the National Humanities Center, Research Triangle Park, NC, November 1, 2002. On the connection between the Terror and civic education, see Blum, *Republic of Virtue*, chap. 10.

46. See Andrew Delbanco, *The Death of Satan: How Americans Have Lost the Sense of Evil* (New York: Farrar, Strauss and Giroux, 1995), chap. 2. Delbanco describes the tensions in this period between emerging Enlightenment rationalism and traditional Christian teachings concerning sin.

47. It should be noted that "evil" could mean any kind of pain or suffering. The term was not restricted to cruelty, nor did it connote extreme immorality, as it often does today. I am indebted to David Wootton for this point and for other illuminating comments on this paper. See also Delbanco, *Death of Satan*, p. 76.

48. See, for example, the speeches of Melancton Smith in the New York ratifying convention. Herbert J. Storing, ed., *The Anti-Federalist* (Chicago: University of Chicago Press, 1981, 1985), 331ff.

49. This is not to say that there are not also natural sentiments that support sociability.

50. See Alexander Hamilton, James Madison, and John Jay, *The Federalist Papers* (New York: New American Library, 1961), *The Federalist*, no. 1; and John Locke, *Of the Conduct of the Understanding* in *Some Thoughts Concerning Education and Of the Conduct of the Understanding*, ed. Ruth W. Grant and Nathan Tarcov (Indianapolis: Hackett, 1996).

51. *Federalist*, no. 51

52. This is why the question of perpetuation of institutions and the longevity of the regime is so important.

53. In this particular respect, there is a similarity in the rhetoric justifying injustices towards women and blacks in America.

54. See George Orwell, "Reflections on Gandhi," in *A Collection of Essays* (Garden City, NY: Doubleday and Co., 1954); Max Weber, "Politics as a Vocation," in *From Max Weber: Essays in Sociology*, trans. and ed. by H. H. Gerth and C. Wright Mills (New York: Oxford University Press, 1958). See also David Wong, "Evil and the Morality of Conviction," in this volume.

55. Edmund Burke, *Reflections on the Revolution in France* (Indianapolis: Bobbs- Merrill, 1955), p. 162.

56. Burke, *Reflections*, p. 46.

57. See Philip G. Zimbardo, "A Situationist Perspective on the Psychology of Evil: Understanding How Good People Are Transformed into Perpetrators," in *The Social Psychology of Good and Evil: Understanding Our Capacity for Kindness and Cruelty,* ed. Arthur Miller (New York: Guilford, 2004).

Chapter 4

Nannerl O. Keohane

Inequality and the Problem of Evil

Many contemporary moral philosophers are reluctant to use the term "evil." They are made uncomfortable by its religious overtones, and this discomfort is heightened by the loose usage of the word in popular discourse. Yet as Andrew Delbanco notes, "despite the shriveling of old words and concepts, we cannot do without some conceptual means for thinking about the sorts of experiences that used to go under the term evil."[1] There are times, after all, when saying "That's very bad behavior" is as far off the mark as calling Yosemite Valley "a pretty landscape." We need words to name things that elicit awe or horror, not merely routine pleasure or distaste.

Inequality, unlike evil, is discussed frequently by philosophers these days. In this paper, I shall argue that inequality is closely connected with evil. I hope to suggest a pathway for considering the phenomenon of evil in human life that is especially appropriate for contemporary moral philosophy. To make this case, I will rely principally on a writer who was crucial in shaping a secular understanding of evil, Jean-Jacques Rousseau.[2]

In the context of radical evils such as the Holocaust and genocide, an emphasis on inequality may seem an odd choice. Is it not more plausible to say, as Claudia Card does in a recent study of atrocity: "inequalities are not themselves evils" but "tend to accompany the evils of exploitation and oppression"?[3] Rousseau presents the case for seeing inequality not just as an occasional accompaniment of evil but as the primary source and cause of the evils human beings experience in our lives.

Inequality both creates the contexts in which evildoing is likely to occur and can itself be the motivation for severe mistreatment. Inequality establishes conditions in which some people are heavily dependent on others. This prompts some human beings to take advantage of others, to pursue their self-interest at the expense of those who are less advantaged than they. Such impulses can lead to cruelty or to sustained oppression. It can prompt those who are dependent to strike back violently. Inequality also distances human beings from each other, making it easy to see another human being as on a different plane of being from oneself, radically "other," deficient in some way. In this way, inequality diminishes the natural pity that provides a check on impulses toward cruelty. Rousseau shows how each of these features of inequality can lead directly to behavior that deserves to be called "evil."

The more familiar assumption that inequality is only an adjunct of evil reflects a concept of equality dominant in moral philosophy today. Our current focus on distributive equity as the primary factor in assessing equality can be traced in large part to John Rawls's profoundly influential *Theory of Justice.* But distributive equity is not the only point at issue in understanding equality as a precept of moral philosophy. For centuries, the ideal of equality has also carried a more generous interpretation, referring to the basic normative status of all human beings as sentient individuals with distinctive hopes and fears, each worthy of respect.

In a recent essay, Jeremy Waldron distinguishes these two concepts of equality. The first, as "a political aim," brings to the fore "particular egalitarian principles like the principle of equality of opportunity" that are the substance of most contemporary discussions. The second, "the basic equality of all humans as an assumption of moral and political thought," implies that "we all have the same standing or significance for moral purposes."[4] This more generous concept of equality will provide the background for my argument.

Rawls himself was willing to speak of evil, although he rarely did so. In a brief but suggestive passage toward the end of *A Theory of Justice,* he offers an interpretation of evil that depends on equality denoting equal worth or moral status rather than on the political sense of distributive equity. Rawls notes that what he has called "the full theory of the good" allows us "to distinguish different sorts of moral worth, or the lack of it. Thus we can distinguish between the unjust, the bad, and the evil man." The unjust man wants too much of something which in itself is good, such as wealth or security. The bad man enjoys the sense of mastery and "seeks social acclaim." In both cases, the actors have "an inordinate desire for things which when duly circumscribed are good, namely, the esteem of others and the sense of self-command."

The "evil man," by contrast, wants specifically to "manifest his superiority and affront the self-respect of others." He aspires to violate "what independent persons would consent to in an original position of equality," and is moved by the "love of injustice." The evil man delights in "the impotence and humiliation of those subject to his power" and relishes "being recognized by them as the willful author of their degradation." In this way, malicious perversity distinguishes evil persons from those who act badly or commit injustice to secure something that they want.[5]

Those who wrestle with the problem of evil sometimes ask whether it makes most sense to think in terms of evil persons, evil acts, or both. Rawls's concept of the "evil man" appears to take a clear side in this dispute. Yet his definition also emphasizes the connections or relationships between persons that allow one to degrade or humiliate the other. I shall argue, following Rousseau, that social interaction is the crucial context for understanding evil. One could imagine a sad recluse who spends all his time conceiving terrible tortures to which he might subject other human beings; we might plausibly refer to such a person as an "evil man." But if only hermits could be evil, and evil acts could be done only in imagination, the world would be an immensely better place. What we care most about is evil in action, evildoers, people who carry their principles into practice and bring great harm to other human beings.[6]

Rousseau on "the State of Nature"

Rousseau's observations on inequality and evil are scattered throughout his political and autobiographical writings and are prominent in his novel, *Émile*. They are developed most fully in response to a question about the origins of inequality posed by the Academy of Dijon, in an essay entitled "On the Origin and Foundations of Inequality among Men." This essay, also known as the *Second Discourse*, was published in 1755. Rousseau is motivated throughout this discourse by the clear conviction that human inequality is at the root of all the ills that beset the world. I shall first note those aspects of this account that are most salient for our topic and then assess the value of Rousseau's perspective for our modern world.

In responding to the academy's question, Rousseau embarked on a thought experiment to determine the most plausible innate characteristics of a single human individual in the "state of nature," abstracted from all social ties. Rousseau believes that human beings are best understood as independent individuals, not members of societies or communities of any kind. He is convinced that we are happiest when we are self-sufficient and our social relations are kept in proportion and under our control. The image of the solitary savage is used as a baseline to throw into high relief the consequences of social interactions.

This is clearly an unusual approach. It has been well established by archaeology, anthropology, and history that human beings, like most primates and many other mammals, "naturally" live in groups. Rousseau may have accepted early explorers' accounts of humanlike primates, probably orangutans, who were reported to live solitary lives; he may have been reflecting his own penchant for solitude as a way of life. He may even have meant his statements about the purely hypothetical, ahistorical nature of his approach to be taken seriously.[7] In any case, it is easy for readers to dismiss his account because of his starting point and fail to credit the acuteness of his perception in describing the stages of human development.[8] One of the major points of this account of "the state of nature" is that individual disparities become significant only when human beings have repeated interactions.

Rousseau's savage individuals have no need of one another (except for occasional ephemeral couplings to satisfy sexual desire), and as a result, they have no claims on one other. Their desires do not exceed their physical needs; these are easily satisfied without competing with or encumbering anyone else in an environment where food and water are readily available. The single savage displaced from his rustic bed or bested in collecting acorns by a stronger or younger person can simply move on to the next tree. Rousseau emphasizes the personal wholeness of these isolated individuals; savage man "carries himself entire, as it were, about him." As society develops, this original wholeness is lost, dissolved in what a person owns or needs; thus, the rich "are vulnerable in every part of their goods."[9] But in the "state of nature," there are no grounds for claiming authority or obedience, nor any way to hold another in your power. For, says Rousseau, "what can be the chains of dependence among men who possess nothing?"[10] This connection between dependence and possession is one of the keys to Rousseau's concept of human moral development or, more accurately, corruption.

In some of his other works, including the *Discourse on the Arts and Sciences* and *Émile*, Rousseau famously claims that man is naturally good and that society has made him evil. In one of his notes to the *Second Discourse*, he makes the same claim. But in the text itself, his claim is more modest, and more subtle. It is not that we are naturally good, but that good and evil have no meaning for an individual in the state of nature, who has no "moral relationship" with anyone else nor any "known duties" to his fellows.[11]

Rousseau also posits several "moral and metaphysical qualities" that are distinctive to our species, including free will—the ability to choose our actions rather than simply follow instinct and what he rather ironically calls "perfectibility"—the capacity of our species, unlike other animals, to develop and adapt. These qualities also include the native capacity for pity or commiseration, putting oneself in the place of another suffering being. This tempers the fourth factor, care for one's own preservation, which Rousseau describes as "self-love," *amour de soi-même*.[12] He shows how these qualities interacted with physical alterations in climate and fertility to bring us from solitary savagery to the modern world, and eventually to evil.[13]

The Development of Inequality

Rousseau asserts that there are "two sorts of inequality in the human species: one, which I call natural or physical, because it is established by nature and consists in the difference of ages, health, bodily strength and qualities of mind or soul; the other, which may be called moral or political inequality, because it depends upon a sort of convention which is established, or at least authorized, by the consent of men."[14] It is important to note what does *not* appear in this list of natural inequalities. There is no reference to sex, race, or physical attractiveness—"natural" qualities that are often linked with inequality in modern life. Among moral or political inequalities, Rousseau names various "different privileges that some men enjoy to the prejudice of others," including being wealthier, more powerful, or more honored than other individuals. This second sort of inequality identifies advantages that only make sense, and can indeed only be enjoyed, in a social context. One of the major purposes of the *Second Discourse* is to explore both the differences and the connections between these two types of inequality and their relevance for human life.

In Rousseau's account, when human beings first began using tools and measuring themselves against other animals, they developed a concept of "relationships," drawn from the emerging aptitude for using other things or other people to advance one's own purposes. Encounters with other human beings began to cumulate; human beings first lived together in families, in huts that they constructed with primitive tools. They began to depend on the instruments they made and the things those allowed men to enjoy. The direct connection (or proportion, as Rousseau describes it) between men's desires or needs, as well as the ability to satisfy them easily and single-handedly, is broken.[15] As the crucial next step, Rousseau names the habit of comparing oneself to other human beings, wanting to demonstrate superior qualities in order to prove one's own worth and elicit the admiration or deference of others, which he calls *amour-propre*, a deformed version of self-love that arises only in society.[16]

Rousseau's argument in the *Second Discourse* is tightly constructed. In just a few pages from this point forward, he offers a powerful account of the close interaction among *amour-propre*, economic dependence, physical inequalities, and environmental circumstances. It is especially important to his project as he conceives it that he not repeat Hobbes's mistake in *Leviathan*, by reading back into the state of nature factors that could only have been developed when human beings became "civilized." Rousseau's intention is to show how all these things work together in society to produce misery and evil.[17] Yet at this crucial point, he accepts without explanation a major disproportionality in human life that he says explicitly is not naturally found among solitary individuals.

According to Rousseau's account, there are no significant natural differences between the sexes apart from a woman's ability to bear children, which does not, on his account, incapacitate her or render her in any way unequal. In his list of physical or natural inequalities, "sex" is notable for its absence. And in his narrative of human development, Rousseau says explicitly that "savage women" were quite capable of caring for their young alone and otherwise lived precisely as did their male counterparts, satisfying their needs as independent individuals. They also developed a kind of habitual affectionate attachment for their offspring, the first instance of sustained caring for another individual in human history, on Rousseau's account.[18] Thus it is clear that inequality between the sexes must be an instance of "moral or political inequality," the sort of inequality that depends on convention and is authorized by a kind of consent.

After the establishment of families and the building of huts, "women became more sedentary and grew accustomed to tend the hut and the children, while the man went to seek their common subsistence."[19] In this instance, Rousseau's speculative anthropology conforms reasonably well to the way we now believe our species developed, through a primitive division of labor linked to semipermanent living spaces. In this hut society, men for the first time experience sentiments of attachment to other persons, conjugal and paternal love, along with the early stages of what later would become the grounds for inequality and evil. But in a narrative that scrupulously accounts for every crucial step in our development as a species, Rousseau never explains why "savage woman" should have relinquished her capacity to take care of herself and her child in order to become dependent on a man. He never explores what female human beings lost (or gained) by this transaction. This is a glaring omission given his determination to understand human beings first of all as individuals and his heavy stress on dependence as the source of much that is evil in our lives.

Radical inequalities between the sexes are among the most obvious occasions for evildoing in many societies, as men abuse their power, wealth, and status to dominate and demean the women who are dependent on them. Rousseau himself offers reasons why traditional sexual inequalities might serve human beings well in other writings—notably the fifth book of *Émile*—and also deplores some of their costs. It is therefore sobering that he ignores this issue in the *Second Discourse* and incorporates deep disparities between men and women into the development of society without a shred of justification. It is bewildering to find him asserting, in his parenthetical discussion of "the sentiment of love," that women "ought to obey" men. Voltaire was among the first of many readers to note in the margin at this passage: "Pourquoi?"[20]

From this point forward, the story Rousseau tells is solely about savage men and their gains and losses from this new way of living. Thus sexual inequality stands virtually alone as a stale importation from conventional morality in a carefully developed account of human evolution in which conventional morality is specifically ruled out as evidence.

The Loss of Proportionality and the Origins of Evil

Despite the nascent ills he has identified, Rousseau regards the "hut society" as "the happiest and most durable epoch," the "veritable prime [jeunesse] of the world."[21] Evil and misery come only with economic dependence on other human beings and, closely connected with this, the institution of property.[22] Two arts, metallurgy and agriculture, first made possible, and then made necessary, the division of labor and the institution of property. Even at this late stage, says Rousseau, evils could have been avoided if things had been evenly balanced so that people needed one another equally and no one had significant grounds for dominance or superiority. But at this crucial point, "natural" inequality becomes important in ways that had never been relevant before, and in a very real sense, the rest is history.

When metallurgy and agriculture are invented, the "proportionality"—that is, the rough equality—between the farmer and the blacksmith is broken, as one individual proves shrewder, stronger, more fortunate, or less scrupulous than the other. For the first time, they depend on another's services and productivity. Farmers need tools; blacksmiths depend on the farmers' food. They are no longer able to satisfy their own needs individually, and those who are less productive are to some extent at the mercy of the others.

Since stronger people could work harder and cleverer people find better ways of doing things, what Rousseau calls the proportionality among human beings and their activities was destroyed in this fashion. Because all these workers depended on each other, the implications of their differential success in accomplishing their tasks begin to cumulate. More successful individuals accumulate wealth and thus improve their capacities to satisfy their wants and persuade or force others to help them do so. "Thus does natural inequality imperceptibly manifest itself along with contrived inequality [celle de combinaison]; and thus do the differences among men, developed by those of circumstances, become more perceptible, more permanent in their effects" and more consequential.[23]

Concern about loss of proportion is one of the keys to understanding Rousseau's argument throughout this essay. This theme encompasses not only the disproportion that develops through the division of labor and the radical inequalities that result from it, but also the developing disproportion between the desires and the capacities of human beings as we become civilized. The basic consonance between our simple needs and our ability to satisfy them dissolves. We want (or need) more than we can individually provide for ourselves, and we seek with increasing ingenuity and intensity to satisfy those wants. This brings not satisfaction and greater happiness but misery and disappointment. In these varied instances of disproportionality, we see the origins of dependence among human beings, and of evil.[24]

Rousseau identifies several stages in the development of inequality: First, the division of labor and the establishment of property, which created the status of rich and poor; then the institution of government, arising from a parody of the social contract devised by the rich to protect their property, which authorized the status of the powerful and the weak. At this point in his narrative, Rousseau describes an inexorable slide into misery. "Due to a multitude of new needs," men became radically dependent on one another.

> It is first of all a question of providing for the necessary, and then for the superfluous; next come delights, then immense wealth, and then subjects, and then slaves . . . so that after long prosperity, after having swallowed up many treasures and desolated many men, my hero will end up by ruining everything until he is the sole master of the universe. Such in brief [are] the secret pretensions of the heart of every civilized man.

"All these evils," claims Rousseau, "are the first effect of property and the inseparable consequences of nascent inequality."[25]

The rich are as dependent on others as the poor for the satisfaction of their more extensive needs, and the master as much a slave as those he dominates, since he is unable to do without them. Each must try to get others to behave in ways that will satisfy his needs, "to interest them in his fate, and to make them find their own profit, in fact or appearance, in working for his." Given the power of *amour-propre,* competitive ambition leads men to harm each other in order to advance themselves.[26] The final stage of degradation is despotism, "the last degree of inequality and the limit to which all the others finally lead."[27]

Cumulative Inequalities

To understand how all this occurs, it is important to note the several ways in which inequalities cumulate in human life. As we have seen, physical inequalities have little relevance in Rousseau's state of nature. But in society, these physical inequalities leverage and undergird moral and political inequality and thus take on a great deal of relevance. Rousseau points out that those who enjoy strength, health, or wit—natural inequalities—use these advantages to gain wealth, power and social recognition.

And the connections work in both directions.[28] Those who enjoy such "moral inequalities" can use them in turn to improve their physical capacities. Social advantages provide opportunities for education, nutrition, or the acquisition of habits that promote bodily health and strength. Finally, instituted inequalities can compensate for physical weakness, age, or lack of wit. This leads to a common situation Rousseau regards as especially perverse, "the sort of inequality that reigns among all civilized people; since it is manifestly against the law of nature, in whatever manner it is defined, that a child command an old man, an imbecile lead a wise man, and a handful of men be glutted with superfluities while the starving multitude lacks necessities."[29]

Another of Rousseau's major points is the compounding effect of moral and political inequalities, the ways in which they tend to pave the way for and then reinforce each other. Rousseau regards wealth as the most basic form of "moral inequality," in the sense of being "the most immediately useful to well-being and the easiest to communicate" and notes that it can therefore be "easily used to buy all the rest." He notes explicitly that having wealth leads to having power in a political structure, and having power allows the magistrate to enrich himself and increase the difference in wealth and status between himself and ordinary citizens.[30]

Given these multiplier effects, it is no wonder, says Rousseau, that human beings who are roughly similar in the state of nature differ so vastly in society. Advantages of wealth and power allow some to have greater access to all kinds of good things than others do, and thus maximize both moral and physical inequalities. In this insight about the mutually reinforcing effect of several types of inequalities, he was clearly prescient as far as our more advanced modern society is concerned.

Those who are successful in the economic and political developments Rousseau describes take advantage of others. In turn, those who are the losers have to depend on or steal from the rich: "[A]nd from that began to arise, according to the diverse characters of the rich and the poor, domination and servitude or violence and rapine. The rich, for their part, had scarcely known the pleasure of domination when they soon disdained all others, and . . . thought only of subjugating and enslaving their neighbors: like famished wolves which, having once tasted human flesh, refuse all other food and thenceforth want only to devour men."[31]

Although he does not use different words to describe these different kinds of behavior, Rousseau in this account describes a continuum among types of wrongdoing; and the different stages along this continuum closely parallel the categories used by Rawls.[32] Those who behave unjustly grasp for more and more of the world's good things, in a pattern very close to Aristotle's *pleonexia*.[33] As these same people gain power as well as wealth, they begin to treat other human beings badly. Eventually, they come to regard others as members of a lesser species and behave in ways that can only be described as "evil." In each case, increasing inequality is implicated in the complex situation that calls forth such behavior.

Power is crucial in this account as a distinctive, radical form of inequality. Situations involving serious power imbalances—or "disproportions," to use Rousseau's term—readily conduce to evil. If we reflect on paradigmatic situations of evil, such as the Holocaust, torture in prisons or genocide, the power held by the torturers or killers over their victims must be a prominent part of the explanation, along with the suppression of the impulse to pity that allows them to treat the victims as less than human.

The Role of Pity or Commiseration

For Rousseau, pity provides the most significant natural antidote to the evils he describes. He notes that this primordial instinct that we share with beasts is commonly accepted as a human virtue even by detractors of our species such as Mandeville; indeed Rousseau is willing to describe it as the source of all "the social virtues."[34] Generosity, clemency, humanity, even benevolence and friendship are, in his view, variants of the instinct to empathize with another sentient being or put ourselves in his or her place. Rousseau argues that the sentiment of commiseration is just as natural as our desire to improve our personal situation, or *amour de soi-même*. We note instinctively that others can suffer and recognize that a sensitive being has the "right not to be uselessly mistreated."[35]

We can pity people who are our equals in all respects except the misfortune that occasions our feeling of compassion; or we can pity people who are dramatically less fortunate in wealth or status. In either case, our impulse to relieve their suffering and improve their lot can be a genuine act of human sympathy, not a veiled attempt to improve our own situation or advance our reputation. Rousseau emphasizes that "it is in this natural sentiment, rather than in subtle arguments, that we must seek the cause of the repugnance every man would feel in doing evil, even independently of the maxims of education." He clearly believes that a significant part of what we might hope for in reducing evils and increasing the level of good comes from the exercise of this natural facility.[36] Pity for other human beings blocks the impulses to evil behavior more effectively than any other natural feature of our lives.

But the force of pity on this account is radically diminished in modern times.[37] Rousseau asserts that the identification of an observing animal with one who suffers "must have been infinitely closer in the state of nature than in the state of reasoning. Reason . . . turns man back upon himself, it separates him from all that bothers and afflicts him. Philosophy isolates him; because of it he says in secret, at the sight of a suffering man: Perish if you will, I am safe. No longer can anything except dangers to the entire society trouble the tranquil sleep of the philosopher and tear him from his bed. His fellow man can be murdered with impunity right under his window; he has only to put his hands over his ears and argue with him-self a bit to prevent nature, which revolts within him, from identifying him with the man who is being assassinated."

We are very familiar with the power of this contention in thinking about urban life and the deliberate repression of human sensitivity that contemporary societies routinely encourage or require. As Rousseau points out, it is easy to rationalize our disinclination to help a fellow human being in need, because there are so many of them. Thus our natural com-passion is blunted or dulled by our exposure to repetitive examples. As a result, willful disconnection is one of the distinguishing characteristics of our complex lives. It is hard to imagine a savage individual or the resident of a traditional small town passing a fellow resident in need or danger without immediate reactions of compassion, but this happens in modern life with depressing frequency. Even the Good Samaritans among us make rational calculations about the time and place for such reactions, just as Rousseau predicted.

It is true that countervailing forces in modern life make it possible for us to pity human beings many thousands of miles away. The media bring to our attention the victims of 9/11, of tsunamis, famines, floods, or geno-cides, and our "natural impulse" to pity leads many people to send aid or even to travel to the sites of devastation to help those who are suffering. Through globalization, our capacity for pity can thus operate on a larger scale, and some of the tendencies toward tribalism or suspicion of strangers that marked earlier societies can be overcome.[38]

On balance, however, Rousseau's conviction that modern life is marked by a decline in the natural pity that might otherwise block impulses toward evil actions is well founded. In many aspects of our com-plex modern lives, pity has clear limitations as a check on evil behavior; and one of the major reasons for this is a phenomenon I will call "dis-tancing."

Inequality and Distancing

Rousseau notes with dismay the sense of separation that sophisticated contemporary human beings experience—and foster—from other human beings, a distancing that allows us to ignore others who are in pain. This sense of separation can be either deliberate or unconscious. In either case, such distancing readily blocks our natural tendency to feel pity for those who are suffering or in danger. It can lead us either to cause such suffering or fail to intervene when others are causing it. To take an extreme example of this point, note how the characteristics of modern warfare often depend on a radical distancing of the warrior from the victim, in the firebombings of World War Two or the dropping of an atomic bomb.

Physical distancing, however, is not the essence of the problem. It is easier to ignore the plight of those who are not geographically close to us since we do not directly observe their suffering; but distancing in this sense is a matter not of physical space but of psychological impairment. We can be "distanced" from sufferers even when they are immediately before us, if we fail to regard them as deserving of our compassion or having any claim on our assistance. We see this in the demeaning or humiliation of prisoners, or sometimes even in the treatment of civilians in war zones. Closer to home, all of us experience this "distancing" when we pass beggars or homeless persons on the street and rationalize our behavior in not aiding them directly.

Inequality is closely linked with this phenomenon of "distancing," because it makes it easy to dismiss the suffering person as inferior to ourselves, not worthy of our compassion, even in some sense deserving of his fate. Inequalities that are not natural but peculiar to society in Rousseau's sense, including race, religion, and sex as well as social status, wealth, and power, all tend with particular force to this kind of distancing. By contrast, difficulties associated with obvious physical inequalities such as early childhood, old age, serious disease or loss of limbs are more likely to call forth the sentiment of pity in most of us, without the intervening sense of distancing.[39] Given the multiplier effects of inequality in complex societies described above, if I imagine myself radically unequal to another, that almost inevitably suppresses instincts toward pity and creates a great psychological distance between us.[40] And in the end, I can easily regard myself as a member of an entirely different, and superior, species.

Much modern psychological research focuses on contextual explanations for cruelty and severe mistreatment. In the Stanford prison experiments, Phillip Zimbardo and his colleagues distinguish between "dispositional" and "situational" roots of evil acts and emphasize the importance of the latter. They argue that when institutional structures and rules are so aligned, ordinary people will behave in evil ways. These experiments involve simulated prisons, where some volunteers are charged with acting as prison guards; they quickly begin treating the "prisoners" in demeaning and cruel ways. The artificial but very clear inequality among the guards and prisoners, volunteers who are all, in "real life," ordinary Stanford undergraduates with similar characteristics on all counts, elicits this treatment. The gap between guards and prisoners opens up with surprising rapidity and has very ugly consequences.[41]

Stanley Milgram's famous experiments make the same basic point. In these experiments, high percentages of "ordinary people" administer what they believe to be very painful shocks to another person posing as a "learner." Milgram refers to a "deeply ingrained disposition not to harm others" as characteristic of human beings, and tries to explain the factors— including especially obedience to authority—that led so many subjects to overcome that innate tendency to avoid harming others and behave as they did.[42] One of the factors correlated with the occasional refusal to administer such shocks is the physical proximity of the "learner" to the subject, making it harder to distance oneself from the pain being expressed by the learner. But a surprisingly large number of subjects are willing to submit other volunteers to what they believe to be very serious and painful shocks, even when they are sitting right next to them.

Both Zimbardo's study and Milgram's emphasize that one mechanism employed by the subjects to justify their activities is demeaning or deprecating their victims. The person who administers the shock readily tends to identify the "learner" as stupid if he cannot perform the assigned task, and this makes it easier to punish him. The "prison guard" sees the "prisoners" in their loose smocks, nylon stocking caps, identification numbers, and tiny cells as ridiculous and inferior. Thus, yet again, inequality turns out to be closely implicated in evil.

Those who administer severe shocks or harass prisoners in these experiments are responding to institutional situations in which inequality in the form of power differentials is a key factor. The experiments yield their results because of the suppression of pity and distancing from other human beings. Rousseau's argument, however, takes a crucial further step: that not just a few high-profile psychological experiments but the incentives and patterns of social interaction in modern society itself create multiple situations of significant inequality in which we are tempted to advance our own power, status, or esteem by harming others and will benefit from doing so.

As Judith Shklar noted, pity is both fleeting and uncertain and has limited usefulness in creating social bonds. When it operates effectively, pity "cures us of hatred, cruelty and envy, but it is no replacement for justice . . . In the long run, there must be less inequality" if our situation is to be fundamentally improved.[43] This is consonant with Rousseau's view: a society in which inequality—including, above all, economic inequality— is moderated, such as Geneva in his own times, is most likely to provide effective bulwarks against injustice and evildoing.

Rousseau and Modern Life

The *Discourse on the Origins of Inequality among Men,* like Rousseau's earlier *Discourse on the Sciences and the Arts,* stood very much athwart the assumptions and self-image of the age. During the flowering of what we now know as the Enlightenment, the benefits of society were broadly understood as tempering human depravity or savagery and making it possible for us to accomplish great things together as a species. Directly against this understanding, Rousseau contended that the apparatus of civilization itself is at fault in human evil.[44]

In much the same way, the *Second Discourse* stands athwart the assumptions of our own times. Like our Enlightenment precursors, we assume that education, society, and civilization knock off the ruder angles of human nature and make it possible for us to live together amicably and pursue collective goals. This is why we find it so difficult to understand how manifestly civilized people like the Germans during the Holocaust, or well-educated Muslims planning terrorist acts today, can behave in ways that seem to us transparently evil.

Assumptions about "original sin" no longer stand behind such views, for many moderns. It is not that we think human beings are naturally depraved or barbarous and that only adherence to divine or social mores and laws can make us tolerable to each other. Instead we believe, with Rousseau, that human individuals are "naturally" malleable and diverse, not inexorably prone to evildoing. But unlike Rousseau, and like his Enlightenment counterparts, we assume that such malleability is best shaped through the incentives, institutions, and opportunities that society routinely provides. These factors adapt the raw material of our "nature" to the needs of socially connected human beings, allow us to live our ordinary lives, and occasionally accomplish great things. There are always some who defy the institutions or break the laws, and it is those who are "evil," not those who play by the familiar rules.

Rousseau saw things differently. For him, the very incentives and structures we associate with society tempt us toward evil, provide the stimulus and context for wrongdoing. As he put it, "the vices that make social institutions necessary are the same ones that make their abuse inevitable."[45] It is true that our connections with other human beings make possible some of the things that are best about us—love of our families, desire to collaborate with others in our communities, awareness of arts, sciences, and technologies. But in the context of increasing dependence on other human beings, each of these otherwise good aspects of our human lives can become noxious. This fundamental tension between our basic human nature and the structures and pressures of society is the central element in Rousseau's account of the origins of evil.

Rousseau's conception of the economics of modern life is very much a zero-sum game.[46] This is one of the main points on which he was at odds with common wisdom, then and now. Most of his contemporaries were fascinated by the ways in which men pursuing their own selfish interest contribute to the common good through commerce and services. For Rousseau, the assumptions here are fundamentally flawed. One man's wealth is made at the expense of others, more land and property for me means less for you. This eventually leads some to have much more than they need and others to face want and privation. And his conception of human psychology means that once this process is underway, people are rarely content with what they have, and connections between wealth, power, and status rapidly come into play.

Rousseau's key contention here is that very little of what we regard as collaborative in our lives is truly so. Most of our interactions are based on comparisons or competitions that have inevitably invidious dimensions. We work for wealth within a market economy and, in the spirit of Adam Smith and other eighteenth-century thinkers, celebrate the ways in which this system leads us to serve others in order to advance our own self-interest. Rousseau emphasized instead that our desire to get ahead and improve our own situation is at the bottom of our interactions, not any desire to help or serve another human being. The motivation is deeply selfish, not altruistic; we are not brought out of ourselves in genuine concern for or connection to another human being. "If I am answered that society is so constituted that each man gains by serving others," he notes, "I shall reply that this would be very well, if he did not gain still more by harming them. There is no profit, however legitimate, that is not surpassed by one that can be made illegitimately, and wrong done to one's neighbor is always more lucrative than services."[47]

The same is true of rank or status, which by definition depends for its rewarding aspects on others being beneath you or being less highly esteemed. Rousseau is clear that the advantages of social inequalities for people in complex societies have a great deal to do with relative status and derive their attractiveness specifically from the fact that others are less privileged. So he notes that "if one sees a handful of powerful and rich men at the height of grandeur and fortune, while the crowd grovels in obscurity and misery, it is because the former prize the things they enjoy only insofar as the others are deprived of them; and because, without changing their status, they would cease to be happy if the people ceased to be miserable."[48] Thus the institutions and incentives that are supposed to civilize us become the terrains and provide the stimulus for besting others and advancing our own interest at their expense.

In passages such as these, Rousseau exaggerates the perverse aspects of human interdependence in a civilized society and understates the benefits. We do not usually attempt to rip off our neighbors, clients, or customers in the transactions of daily life, and Adam Smith was neither the first nor the last to note the impressive advantages of a market economy in making all participants better off, compared with any alternative. Because Rousseau emphasizes the ills of modern society and fails to note that most of us enjoy countless goods and services as well as health and opportunities that we could never obtain alone, it is easy to dismiss his observations as romantic, perverse, and/or irrelevant. But such a reaction would be shortsighted; these insights offer important lessons about our own lives.

The most useful aspect of Rousseau's account is to put us on notice, to make us more cautious about features of our modern lives that are easy to take for granted. Our dependence on all the good things we enjoy can lead us to overlook the problems with our economic and social structures. For instance, we may not acknowledge those who cannot obtain basic human goods, because the market has no need of the labor or the skills they offer or because any available work provides recompense that is insufficient to meet their most basic needs. When such people have no alternative ways to feed or clothe or house or heal their families, we have a serious problem in our society; but those of us who are comparatively well-off tend to ignore these people and their problems. It is especially easy for those who enjoy privileged positions in societies that are themselves advantaged to ignore the "negative externalities" our demands and enjoyments impose on others near to us and far away. We prefer to think of the ways such demands provide opportunities for employment and trade. Pondering Rousseau's account makes it harder to be unaware of the multiple implications of these connections in our lives and may even motivate us to attempt to modify such radical disproportionality.

Rousseau also helps us recognize that dependence on other human beings is the source both of some of our most admirable and despicable behavior. Acknowledging that power can indeed corrupt the power holder, that situations in which human beings have power over others are prime locations for cruelty and mistreatment and must therefore be watched and checked if we wish to minimize evil in the world, is another crucial step. Noting that wealth leads to the cumulation of inequalities and thus to especially damaging forms of dependence allows us to recognize the impulse toward greater economic equality in society as not just a vague prescript of disappointed socialists, but a recurrent historic insight that, if acted on, would lead to fewer opportunities for the degradation or mistreatment of other human beings.

So What Is to Be Done

Ruth Grant points out in this volume that a radical attempt to root out evil can easily produce more evil in its train.[49] Communist societies that attempted to introduce equality and justice through draconian measures are good examples of this difficulty. There is a difference, however, between radical measures and more cautious and prudent efforts to keep burgeoning inequalities in check within the economic and social structures that characterize the modern world. If we ponder the connections that Rousseau has drawn between inequality, power, dependence, human suffering, and evil, we should be wary of the untrammeled development of these aspects of the modern world and more conscious of the importance of providing effective limits to such dependencies and inequalities.

Rousseau's own writings offer three alternative solutions to the evils he describes, identified by numerous interpreters of his work.[50] First there is Émile, who is raised from birth not to be dependent on other human beings and prepared to find his natural instincts of compassion refined and deepened through love for another human being. Next, there is the citizen of the state described in the *Social Contract,* who achieves a new form of wholeness by giving himself totally to the political community. Finally, there is Jean-Jacques himself as a solitary walker pursuing his reveries later in life with only minimal ties to other human beings. None of these offers much consolation to those of us already living in modern society, having reached adulthood in flawed political communities without the benefit of Émile's highly specialized educational experience, with responsibilities to others that we cannot simply jettison to wander about in our private reveries.

However, Rousseau's diagnosis points us in the direction of quite a different solution, the liberal emphasis on institutional checks and balances for the control of power in order to deter evildoing. One of the most valuable lessons from Rousseau is a version of Judith Shklar's "liberalism of fear," the caution about allowing accumulations of power, wealth, and rank, because of what they make it possible for human beings to do to one another and the behaviors they provide temptations for. This claim may be surprising, since Rousseau is often regarded as one of the first of the "anti-liberals."[51] But the *Second Discourse* describes in vivid terms the human tendencies toward public and private cruelties that are the essence of what liberalism has to fear and identifies them, as Shklar does, as the first of the vices. On this reading, Rousseau would understand Madison's motivations in the tenth *Federalist Paper* in establishing institutions designed to control "factions" that attempt to bend the government to their more narrow private purposes, and Jefferson's concern about dramatic inequalities and the importance of protecting basic rights and civil liberty.

Yet Rousseau emphasizes not just threats from the excessive concentration of power in the hands of political leaders or governments but also the occasions for abuse and evil in "private" social interactions, including economic interchanges and status hierarchies. In this way, his diagnostic insights are more consonant with modern liberal perspectives than those of the Founders, despite the fact that his own proposed solutions have clear authoritarian or utopian dimensions. Rousseau's version of the "liberalism of fear" would call attention not only to the potential abuses of power by state institutions but also to abuses by others who hold power in society in contexts that are not formally political. Establishing laws and institutions that provide effective hedges against such behavior was not directly Rousseau's conclusion; but such teachings are consistent with the "Dedication to the Republic of Geneva" that precedes the essay and with the political observations in the final sections of *Émile*.[52]

Such insights are particularly pertinent in advanced democracies today, and relevant for those who would offer such systems as models for others. It is easy to assume that limits on the abuse of governmental power are all that is required to establish a democracy. Rousseau reminds us that we must also take deliberate steps to combat radical socioeconomic inequalities and their accompanying evils in order to create or sustain the kind of moral or political equality in society that makes democracy meaningful or even possible.

Conclusion

In light of Rousseau's emphasis on "proportionality," it is interesting to note that in the *Oxford English Dictionary* the etymology of "evil" refers to "exceeding due measure" or "overstepping proper limits" as the root meaning of this term in medieval English and other Germanic languages. Evil in this original sense supports Rousseau's interpretation. Evil flows from the socially generated phenomenon he calls *amour-propre:* from pride, ambition, vanity, and disregard for "proper limits." Self-love, perverted by society, takes the form of a deliberate desire for superiority over others, the desire to be *unequal,* which then leads to radical artificial differences among human beings that provide both the context for and the stimulus to evil.

In this way, evil is neither imposed on human beings by something outside ourselves such as a devil or a Satan, nor something innate to all human beings, nor one inscrutable component of a larger creative design. Instead, evil results from the dialectical interaction between the practices human beings develop in our attempts to improve our lot and the basic characteristics that naturally define us as human individuals.

In their attempts to understand evil, some of our forebears projected this sense of "overstepping proper limits" onto a proud ambitious angel as the embodiment of evil in the universe. In so doing, they followed a path parallel to Ludwig Feuerbach's claim that human beings have created God in their image by projecting onto the divine being all that is good about themselves.[53] Milton's Satan—the proud, rebellious archangel Lucifer—is the paradigmatic image of one who "exceeds due measure"; his *amour-propre* leads him to defy all order and constraints to pursue his overweening purposes. More pedestrian versions of Satan build on the same tendency: to project malicious cruelty, deceit, ambition, pride, and other vices onto a larger being, whom we then blame for the evil that we do and the misfortunes that we suffer.

Many theologians and religious people today are aware of the problems we store up by creating God in our own image. We should learn the same lesson about Satan. Evil is not something comfortably—or frighteningly—outside ourselves, embodied in some malevolent being. Nor should we identify evil simply as a psychological abnormality that marks a few perverse individuals like Hitler or Stalin and is limited to those "evil men." Most people most of the time do not commit evil acts. But in Rousseau's view, the potential is always there. Evil emerges from interactions among human beings that conflict with or erode our own good instincts. It depends on regarding others with whom we interact or over whom we have some power as in no way our equals in dignity or worth and thus as less human than ourselves. This is Rousseau's message, and it is one we need to hear today.

ACKNOWLEDGMENT

I am grateful to colleagues in the Moral Judgment Seminar at Duke University and at Stanford University and the Center for Advanced Study in the Behavioral Sciences, who commented on earlier drafts of this paper.

NOTES

1. Andrew Delbanco, *The Death of Satan: How Americans Have Lost the Sense of Evil* (New York: Farrar, Straus and Giroux, 1995), p. 9. One recent volume that explores secular meanings of "evil" is *Monist* 85, no. 2 (April 2002), general topic "Evil," Adam Morton, advisory editor; essays pertinent to this paper include those by Paul Thompson, Roy W. Perrett, and Eve Garrard.

2. Ernst Cassirer, *The Question of Jean-Jacques Rousseau*, trans. by Peter Gay (New York: Columbia University Press, 1954), p. 75, credits Rousseau with solving the problem of evil by "placing responsibility at a point where no one before him had looked for it," in human society rather than the individual. Among recent interpreters, see Susan Neiman, *Evil in Modern Thought: An Alternative History of Philosophy* (Princeton: Princeton University Press, 2002), pp. 3–57; John T. Scott, "The Theodicy of the *Second Discourse*: The 'Pure State of Nature' and Rousseau's Political Thought," *American Political Science Review* 86, no. 3 (September 1992): 696–711; and Arthur M. Melzer, *The Natural Goodness of Man: On the System of Rousseau's Thought* (Chicago: University of Chicago Press, 1990).

One difficulty in reading Rousseau on evil is that the French language, like other Romance languages, lacks a specific term for "evil" that immediately distinguishes it from "bad." In translating Rousseau into English, "evil" is conventionally used to translate "mal" or "méchant" in contexts where Rousseau speaks of degradation and perversity.

3. Claudia Card, *The Atrocity Paradigm: A Theory of Evil* (Oxford: Oxford University Press, 2002), p. 100.

4. Jeremy Waldron, "Does 'Equal Moral Status' Add Anything to Right Reason?" paper presented to the American Political Science Association, September 2004. Waldron's first footnote refers to other moral philosophers who have discussed the more basic concept of equality in recent years, including Ronald Dworkin, Gregory Vlastos, Bernard Williams, and more than half a dozen others.

5. John Rawls, *A Theory of Justice* (Cambridge, MA: Belknap Press of Harvard University, 1971), p. 439.

6. Daniel M. Haybron, "Moral Monsters and Saints," *Monist* 85, no. 2 (April 2002): 276–280, offers arguments against the position that "evil action" is what truly matters.

7. This is the interpretation of Cassirer, *Question of Jean-Jacques Rousseau*, p. 50. Rousseau says at the outset of his essay: "Let us therefore begin by putting the facts aside, for they do not affect the question." Jean-Jacques Rousseau, *The First and Second Discourses*, ed. Roger D. Masters, trans. by Roger D. and Judith R. Masters (Boston: St. Martin's, 1964), p. 103. Many other readers assume that this statement was intended to protect Rousseau against persecution by religious authorities, for whom the facts were securely recorded in the book of Genesis.

8. As Roger Masters, *The Political Philosophy of Rousseau* (Princeton: Princeton University Press, 1968), p. 107, notes, Rousseau's account of the earliest stages of human life in "the state of nature" parallels that of Lucretius, *De Rerum Natura*, book 5, sections 925–1136. But the points he makes in describing the development of society have more in common with the observations of modern anthropologists. Claude Lévi-Strauss called him the "founder of the sciences of man"; for Immanuel Kant, he was the "Newton of the moral order." John Hope Mason, ed., *The Indispensable Rousseau* (London: Quartet Books, 1979), p. 3.

9. *Discourses*, pp. 107, 162. In French this last phrase is even more striking: "les riches étant, pour ainsi dire, sensibles dans toutes les parties de leurs Biens." In Bernard Gagnebin and Marcel Raymond, ed., *Oeuvres complètes*, vol. 3 (Paris: Gallimard, 1964), p. 179.

10. *Discourses*, p. 139; these individuals have "no kind of commerce among themselves" and "consequently knew neither vanity, nor consideration, or esteem, nor contempt." He describes such beings (p. 133) as "more untamed than evil [*plutôt farouches que méchans*]."

11. *Discourses*, note 1 (p. 193) and pp. 128–130. Rousseau specifically rejects the doctrine of original sin. "Letter to Christophe de Beaumont," in Mason, *Indispensable Rousseau*, p. 232.

12. *Discourses*, p. 130. In the preface (p. 95), Rousseau describes "two principles anterior to reason . . . the first and simplest operations of the human soul," one of which "interests us ardently in our well-being and our self-preservation, and the other inspires in us a natural repugnance to see any sensitive being perish or suffer, principally our fellowmen."

13. *Discourses*, pp. 113–115. Sanford Lakoff points out a paradox here: nature gives us free will and perfectibility, and the physical events, differences of climate and environment, that call forth those capacities are natural as well. But if nature is responsible for all the factors that come together to produce human evil, then is not evil natural, after all? *Equality in Political Philosophy* (Cambridge, MA: Harvard University Press, 1964), pp. 107–108. Rousseau himself seems uneasily aware of this difficulty; he claims that "Nature" herself would have kept us from the course we have followed, had she been able. But in the end, Rousseau insists that even if the factors that combine to create evil are all "natural," individuals are not "naturally" evil: the ills we suffer and the wrongdoing of which we are guilty are all features of social interaction, not innate to any one of us. George Armstrong Kelly sums it up succinctly: "For Rousseau, nature is a wise guide, man is an open question, and history is a tale of horror." In "A General Overview," *The Cambridge Companion to Rousseau*, ed. Patrick Riley (Cambridge: Cambridge University Press, 2001), p. 8.

14. *Discourses*, p. 101.

15. *Discourses*, p. 147. Rousseau says that these "commodities" were "the first yoke" men imposed on themselves and the "first source of the evils they prepared for their descendants."

16. Rousseau ascribes the earliest significant instance of this sentiment to adolescent sexuality. As families gathered into troops with more fixed settlements, young people began to see each other more often and to "acquire ideas of merit and beauty, which produce sentiments of preference." *Discourses*, p. 149. See the parallel account in *The Essay on the Origin of Languages*, with its memorable story of young girls and boys meeting at water holes in dry climates: "Imperceptibly water came to be more needed, the cattle were thirsty more often; one arrived in haste, and left with reluctance." In Victor Gourevitch, ed., *The Discourses and Other Early Political Writings* (Cambridge: Cambridge University Press, 1997), p. 277.

17. The reference to Hobbes is *Discourses*, pp. 128–130.

18. *Discourses*, pp. 112, 121, 130, and note L, p. 219.

19. *Discourses*, p. 147; for a fuller discussion of this theme, see Susan Moller Okin, *Women in Western Political Thought* (Princeton: Princeton University Press, 1979), pp. 106–115; and N. Keohane, " 'But for her sex . . .': The Domestication of Sophie," in *Trent Rousseau Papers*, ed. Jim MacAdam et al. (Ottawa: University of Ottawa Press, 1980), pp. 135–157. In stark contrast with these views, Susan Meld Shell speculates that the "hut society" was a result of covert female initiative; "*Émile*: Nature and the Education of Sophie," in *The Cambridge Companion to Rousseau*, ed. Patrick Riley (Cambridge: Cambridge University Press, 2001), pp. 279–284.

20. *Discourses*, p. 135; Voltaire's comment is noted in *Oeuvres complètes*, vol. 3, note on p. 1335.

21. *Discourses*, p. 151. Jonathan Marks, "The Savage Pattern: The Unity of Rousseau's Thought Revisited," *Polity* 31, no. 1 (fall 1998), sees this as the model for all Rousseau's political solutions.

22. *Discourses*, p. 151. In the *Essay on the Origin of Languages*, p. 272, he makes clear that this analysis is grounded in economics, so that "everything is related in its principle to the means by which men provide for their subsistence."

23. *Discourses*, p. 155. The crucial factor here is the *interconnection* of "natural" and "contrived" inequality, not the creation of a whole new sort of inequality. It is in conjunction with the activities of labor and commerce that our natural gifts become politically and socially salient.

24. As he sums it up in one of his notes: "When, on the one hand, one considers the vast labors of men, so many sciences fathomed, so many arts invented, so many forces employed . . . ; and when, on the other hand, one searches with a little meditation for the true advantages that have resulted from all this for the happiness of the species, one cannot fail to be struck by the astounding *disproportion* prevailing between these things, and deplore man's blindness, which, to feed his foolish pride and an indefinable vain admiration for himself, makes him run avidly after all the miseries of which he is susceptible, and which beneficent nature had taken care to keep from him." *Discourses*, p. 193 (note 1), emphasis added; the word in French, here and at other points cited, is indeed "la disproportion."

25. *Discourses*, p. 156 and note 1, p. 195.

26. In the "Letter to Christophe de Beaumont," Rousseau describes how "self love is fermented into self interest." Mason's edition, p. 233. The French—*mis en fermentation*—calls up vivid images of natural decay; *Oeuvres complètes*, vol. 4, p. 937 and note a. Ruth Grant, *Hypocrisy and Integrity: Machiavelli, Rousseau and the Ethics of Politics* (Chicago: University of Chicago Press, 1997), argues that *amour-propre* is the most basic of three factors contributing to human corruption (pp. 143–153).

27. *Discourses*, pp. 157–160, 172, 177.

28. *Discourses*, p 138, where Rousseau notes "how much natural inequality must increase in the human species through instituted inequality."

29. *Discourses*, p. 181. In the sentence that comes just before this passage, Rousseau asserts surprisingly that "moral inequality, authorized by positive right alone, is contrary to natural right whenever it is not combined *in the same proportion* with physical inequality" (emphasis added). By implication, this seems to condone extreme social inequalities if they match up correctly with their physical counterparts. But once again, the crucial concept is "proportion." He frequently asserts that natural or physical inequalities are relatively minor, and thus there is no possible way in which the dramatic social inequalities we see in modern society could be proportional to anything characteristic of single individuals.

30. *Discourses*, p. 174. He notes a few paragraphs earlier (p. 173) that "political distinctions necessarily bring about civil distinctions. The growing inequality between the people and its chiefs soon makes itself felt among individuals, where it is modified in a thousand ways according to passions, talents, and events."

31. *Discourses*, p. 157.

32. Rawls, *Theory of Justice*, p. 439; see discussion in the introductory section of this essay.

33. *Nicomachean Ethics* V: 12–14, 1129a–b.

34. *Discourses*, pp. 130–133; in this essay Rousseau uses "la pitié" and "la commiseration" interchangeably; he rarely uses "la compassion," although sometimes it seems the most appropriate English word to use, carrying broader connotations than "pity." Pity and compassion become central in the argument of *Émile*, where the concepts are more fully developed. Carl G. Hedman provides a fine account of compassion in *Émile*, in "Rousseau on Self-Interest, Compassion and Moral Progress," *Trent Rousseau Papers*, pp. 181–198. David Konstan, *Pity Transformed* (London: Duckworth, 2001), provides in the introduction a valuable overview of pity as an emotion and its place in the history of ideas since classical times. On pity and sympathy in the development of moral philosophy in the eighteenth century, see Charles L. Griswold, Jr., *Adam Smith and the Virtues of the Enlightenment* (Cambridge: Cambridge University Press, 1999), chap. 2; and David Marshall, *The Surprising Effects of Sympathy: Marivaux, Diderot, Rousseau and Mary Shelley* (Chicago: University of Chicago Press, 1988).

35. *Discourses*, p. 96. Jonathan Haidt and Craig Joseph, "Intuitive Ethics," in *Daedalus* (fall 2004): 59, include "compassion" as one of three "winners," along with "fairness" and "respect," in their survey of works by "a variety of social scientists to locate a common core of moral values" across cultures. As they note: "It seems that in all human cultures,

individuals often react with flashes of feeling linked to moral intuitions . . . when they see others (particularly young others) suffering." They go on to emphasize "that a flash of intuition is not a virtue. But it is an essential tool in the construction of a virtue" (p. 63).

36. Marshall, *The Surprising Effects of Sympathy*, pp. 202–203, notes that in the *Essai sur l'origine des langues*, Rousseau identifies a problem with "natural pity" that he ignores in the *Second Discourse*: the tribal tendency for people in small groups—such as the "hut society"—to identify much more closely with those with whom they are familiar, and regard others suspiciously as strangers.

37. *Discourses*, p. 132.

38. Anthony Giddens, *The Consequences of Modernity* (Stanford: Stanford University Press 1990), part 1, provides an interesting perspective on this topic; he invokes (p. 14) a concept of "time-space distanciation" quite different from the kind of "distancing" I describe below.

39. This generalization holds as long as we do not feel threatened by this physical disability; if old age reminds us too much of our own mortality, or disease threatens us with contagion, self-love trumps the sentiment of commiseration just as Rousseau would have predicted, and the phenomenon of distancing can come just as surely into play.

40. As Richard Boyd notes in his thoughtful recent essay, "Pity's Pathologies Portrayed: Rousseau and the Limits of Democratic Compassion," *Political Theory* 32, no. 4 (August 2004): 534, "Only by a colossal leap of the imagination can the rich recognize anything of themselves in the poor, downtrodden, and oppressed."

41. Craig Haney, Curtis Banks, and Philip Zimbardo, "Interpersonal Dynamics in a Simulated Prison," *International Journal of Criminology and Penology* 1 (1973): 69–97. In a recent commentary, "Reflections on the Stanford Prison Experiment," Zimbardo, Haney, and Christina Maslach describe their experiments, and Stanley Milgram's, as providing evidence of "the power of social situations to overwhelm individual dispositions and even to degrade the quality of human nature." In their words: "The value of the Stanford Prison Experiment . . . resides in demonstrating the evil that good people can be readily induced into doing to other good people" within a social and institutional context that supports such behavior. *Obedience to Authority: Current Perspectives on the Milgram Paradigm* (Mahwah, NJ: Lawrence Erlbaum Associates, 2000), pp. 193–194.

42. Stanley Milgram, *Obedience to Authority: An Experimental View* (New York: Harper & Row, 1974), p. 42.

43. Shklar makes these points in her essay, "Jean-Jacques Rousseau and Equality," reprinted in *Rousseau's Political Writings*, ed. Alex Ritter and Julia Conaway Bondanella (New York: Norton and Co., 1988), p. 273.

44. On this theme, see N. Keohane, "'The Masterpiece of Policy in Our Century': Rousseau on the Morality of the Enlightenment," *Political Theory* 6, no. 4 (November 1978): 457–484; Christopher Brooke, "Rousseau's Political Philosophy" in *The Cambridge Companion to Rousseau*, ed. Patrick Riley (Cambridge: Cambridge University Press, 2001), pp. 112–118; and Joseph Reisert, *Jean-Jacques Rousseau: A Friend of Virtue* (Ithaca: Cornell University Press, 2003), pp. 69–71.

45. *Discourses*, pp. 172–173.

46. In the second of his *Lettres morales* (*Oeuvres complètes*, vol. 4, p. 1089), Rousseau says: "Luxury in cities brings to the countryside misery, hunger, despair; . . . In multiplying the commodities of life for a few rich people, one has only forced the majority to consider themselves miserable." This point is made especially strongly in the preface to Rousseau's play *Narcisse*, included in Gourevitch, *Discourses and Other Early Political Writings*, p. 100: "What a wonderful thing, then, to have put men in a position where they can only live together by obstructing, supplanting, deceiving, betraying, destroying one another!" See also Arthur M. Melzer, "Rousseau and the Modern Cult of Sincerity," in *The Legacy of Rousseau*, ed. Clifford Orwin and Nathan Tarcov (Chicago: University of Chicago Press, 1997), p. 281.

47. *Discourses*, pp. 194–195 (note 1); on pp. 193–194, he says: "Let human society be as highly admired as one wants; it is nonetheless true that it necessarily brings men to hate each other in proportion to the conflict of their interests, to render each other apparent services and in fact do every imaginable harm to one another." He catalogs situations in which someone gains from another's misfortune and concludes: "Thus do we find our advantage in the detriment of our fellow-men, and someone's loss almost always creates another's prosperity."

48. *Discourses*, p. 175.

49. "The Rousseauan Revolution and the Problem of Evil."

50. See most recently Laurence D. Cooper, *Rousseau, Nature and the Problem of the Good Life* (University Park: Pennsylvania State University Press 1999), introduction.

51. "The liberalism of fear" is described in *Ordinary Vices* (Cambridge, MA: Harvard University Press, 1984), chap. 6. On Rousseau as an antiliberal, see Stephen Holmes, "The Permanent Structure of Antiliberal Thought," in *Liberalism and the Moral Life*, ed. Nancy L. Rosenblum (Cambridge, MA: Harvard University Press, 1989), p. 227. This same volume (pp. 21–38) includes an essay by Judith Shklar, "The Liberalism of Fear," which builds on the analysis of *Ordinary Vices*.

52. See also *Rousseau, Judge of Jean-Jacques* (the *Dialogues*), where he asserts that "he always insisted on the preservation of existing institutions, holding that their destruction would only remove the palliatives while leaving the vices and substituting brigandage for corruption." In the *Collected Writings of Rousseau*, trans. Judith R. Bush, Christopher Kelly, and Roger D. Masters (Hanover, NH: University Press of New England, 1990), p. 213.

53. Feuerbach, *The Essence of Christianity* [1841], trans. George Eliot (New York: Harper & Row 1957), chap. 1, esp. pp. 11–14.

PART 2

Making Judgments, Passing Judgment,
Taking a Stand, Biting Your Tongue

Chapter 5

The Butler Did It

I

Evil is not an ordinary word even if ordinary people can be evil or do evil deeds. The word and idea are the heavy artillery of moral condemnation, kept in reserve to name and do battle against ethical and political atrocities whose depravity, cruelty, and viciousness seem inexplicable and inhuman, if not mad. Whatever else they are, evil men and women appear so much larger than life, so much outsized figures doing outsized deeds, that there seems little left to say about them other than insist that they are evil and leave it at that, except perhaps to detail and so bear witness to the horrors they commit. This mood or conclusion seems mandated by the Holocaust which, for all the writing on it, leaves one speechless.

I suggest that there are at least four other considerations that enter into the way we speak or do not speak about evil. One is the temptation of Manicheanism whenever the language of evil is deployed. We want—and need—the word "evil" as something that names events or people in the world. But evil can too easily function as a shut up word, preventing moral argument and political analysis. We are unlikely to understand the grievances that fuel Muslim resentment, violence, and sense of humiliation if we simply condemn them, accepting a binary between the "West" and "Islam" as if they represented uniform, identifiable entities within well-divided boundaries, thereby ignores the fissures within each category, the mutual indebtedness between them, and their cross-pollination that exists in the present. In both instances, Manicheanism becomes a self-fulfilling prophecy that brooks no challenge, complication, or contradiction.[1]

A second, related factor is that the concept of evil has become divorced from the theological scaffolding that provided a language and ontology for naming and understanding it. Perhaps it is less important to grasp the most profound reasons why a human being can take a knife to another person's throat and take his head off than to recognize that it has always happened and is happening now.[2] Yet I think something is lost when the theological sources for understanding the all-too-human fact of evil are neglected.

Yet, thirdly, it is also true that not every society has a notion of evil equivalent to our own. There are good reasons to believe that the ancient Greeks, for example, had no such word because polytheism did not pit a good god against an evil one, but powerful gods who would do what they wished to humans and were beyond good and evil. There certainly were words such as *kakos aischros* and *poneros* denoting shameful, ugly, disgusting actions, individuals, or statuses. But these were, at least in the late fifth or early fourth century B.C., closer to Aristotle's notion of akrasia (weakness of will) than to evil.[3]

Finally, there is the secret, revealed by Dante and Milton among others, that evil possesses a fascination that goodness lacks, except, perhaps, for the ominous innocence of a Billy Budd. In part, it is this mesmerizing aspect of evil that led Hannah Arendt to talk about evil's banality and Adolf Eichmann's "normalcy."[4] In one aspect, the banality of evil presents the frightening prospect that evil is, potentially at least, all around us in the apparent readiness of ordinary people to become complicit in extraordinary evil. But if evil is ordinary, rather than a monstrous intrusion in human life, then evil is not a power "beyond our capacity" to resist and overcome. Such "democratization" of evil suggests that "we" are to blame if evil drives goodness from the world.[5]

It is Arendt's idea of the banality of evil that provides me with a template for thinking about the relationship between "ordinary" evil, morality, responsibility and evasion, and political life. While it makes moral sense to regard the Holocaust as the quintessential embodiment of evil, there are problematic aspects in doing so. Samantha Power, for instance, worries that the Holocaust sets too high a bar for labeling mass murder genocide,[6] and even permits morally evasive responses to more recent killings which "only" reached eight hundred thousand. Then there is the question of what focusing on such flagrant examples of evil does to moral reflection as a whole.[7] Should we, for example, regard ordinary evil as an ethical oxymoron, or does Arendt's Eichmann prove otherwise? Does the

Holocaust and genocide "generally" (an idea appalling in itself) color the way we think about "lesser evils," as the issue of race in America does in debates over equality? Might it be that the example of genocide so dwarfs everyday evil (or wrongs) that we give ourselves something like an ethical free pass in regard to them, as when people elide the undemocratic aspects of America by contrasting it to authoritarian regimes? And most important, what is the relationship between political institutions, cultural forms, and historical circumstances on the one side, and moral wrongs, including genocide, on the other?[8]

I want to reflect on these questions by considering the butler, Stevens, in Kazuo Ishiguro's *The Remains of the Day*[9] and comparing him to Hannah Arendt's Adolf Eichmann. The novel tells the story of a butler who chooses his future employer for his goodness, integrity, and concern for justice but who, with this act cedes his own moral agency and judgment to his new "master" even as the latter is drawn into the quagmire of pro-Nazi sympathies. Arendt's book—she calls it a "report"—is a provocative reflection on the trial and character of Adolf Eichmann and on his role in carrying out Hitler's Final Solution. It is in this work that she coins the remarkably influential phrase, the "banality of evil."

The comparison of the two books may seem forced, yet I think the novel invites it, as well as the question of whether, if Stevens had lived under the Nazi regime, he would have been susceptible to the same temptations Eichmann was. For all Stevens's idiosyncrasies, what Arendt says about Eichmann might be said about him. "The trouble with Eichmann," she writes in the epilogue to *Eichmann in Jerusalem*, "is precisely that so many were like him, and that the many were neither perverted nor sadistic, that they were, and still are, terribly and terrifyingly normal."[10] Of course, Stevens and Eichmann lived in very different worlds, such that the ordinariness of their moral failings had incommensurable moral consequences. But why? Can we say something about the kind of politics that inhibits such ordinary moral failings from becoming evil?

Like Eichmann, Stevens's ordinariness dramatizes issues of moral responsibility and evasion as they are implicated in ideas and practices of patriotism, loyalty, citizenship, and democracy, are part of a class structure, and embedded in an ethos of professionalism. What becomes clear in the novel is that the separation of public from private life is problematic at best. Moral acts or inaction have political consequences; political commitments, or lack of them, have moral ones; and "individual" decisions have both. Thus, it is neither an accident nor a surprise that Stevens's epiphany about his wasted life involves both lost love and lost dignity.

II

"Eichmann was not Iago," Arendt writes, "and nothing would have been further from his mind than to determine with Richard III 'to prove a villain.'" Except for his extraordinary diligence in looking after his own personal advancement, "he had no motives at all." What Eichmann lacked, Arendt goes on, was the moral imagination to see the world from another's point of view and so the ability to think about what he was doing. It was this "thoughtlessness" rather than anti-Semitism, Nazi ideology, or evil motives that "predisposed him to become one of the greatest criminals of the Nazi era."[11] Later, reflecting on these reflections, she wonders, as Socrates did, whether the "problem of good and evil, the faculty for telling right from wrong [might be] connected with our faculty of thought?" Not that thinking could somehow "produce" good people or deeds, but that "the activity of thinking as such, the habit of examining whatever happens to come to pass or to attract attention regardless of results or specific content" may "be among the conditions that make men abstain from evil doing or even . . . condition them against it."[12] As an argument, this is far too vague, but as a question it directs us to a crucial dimension of the relationship between thought and moral action in *The Remains of the Day*. In the novel, Lord Darlington's godson is incredulous that Stevens has no curiosity about the politics and morality of what his employer is doing by bringing English aristocrats and Nazi officials together. "Are you not," the godson asks Stevens, "at least *curious* about what I am saying?" Stevens is not. Instead of being inquisitive or eager to understand what is happening, Stevens is stubbornly, even perversely, indifferent to it.

What are we to make of this? Surely, Stevens is responsible for his credulity. Perhaps his credulity is like that of a spouse who knows, but does not know because he or she does not want to know, that their partner is cheating. But this will not do, given the moral and political stakes here. So the question *again* is what can be done about such credulity? What sort of institutional or cultural forms *and* forms of disturbance are most likely to encourage the moral imagination Arendt celebrates and the impartiality she regards as its issue? How do we "make" people curious about their world and so less willing to take refuge in indifference and diffidence? Might such curiosity direct us to the play of power in its invisibility and ordinariness, in the way it sometimes seems to speak our mind and at other times seems an alien force?

But I also want to insist that Stevens is not very different from the rest of us. Remember that he is neither an Eichmann nor a Iago. He is complicit in no murders and would no more join the marching columns of the Third Reich as fly to Mars. Nor is he thoughtless in the way Arendt says Eichmann was. He reflects on the meaning of dignity, responsibility, goodness, and justice, and if these reflections are sometimes self-serving and naïve, how unique to him is this? And if he chooses to look away rather than face hard choices and wrenching moral dilemmas, how often have we tolerated injustices for the sake of a little peace and quiet? Recall Rousseau's man who argues a little with himself before putting his hands over his ears, blocking the cries of the innocent being murdered beneath his window.[13]

It is true that Stevens has difficulty acknowledging that in the story of his life there is an authority exercised by what he has done and not merely by what he has done intentionally.[14] But once again, he is surely not alone in that. And if he is, as critics are quick to claim, an unreliable narrator, which one of us, trying to tell the story of our lives, is not? We, too, are unable to order our memories or keep our stories "straight." Memories are like ghosts. They appear unbidden, refashioning the ensemble of cultural imaginings, affective experience, animated objects, marginal voices, narrative densities, and eccentric traces of power that appear to have been left behind but remain as what Avery Gordon calls a "seething presence."[15] That Stevens's memories and construction of the past should be selective, confused, and contradictory is less a pathology than a condition of us all.

But it is a common condition that the uncritiquable position of critique nullifies. "In various ways," Geoffrey Harpham writes, "contemporary thinkers try to preserve their self-righteousness intact by remaining on the margins . . . avoiding the disorder and equivocality that attend worldly agency."[16] This desire for purity can too easily translate into passivity of the kind critics attribute to Stevens. Surely one thing our responsibility requires is imagining ourselves in the position, both powerful and vulnerable, of the actor—which is why I am Stevens's companion as much as his analyst.

To his credit, Stevens is aware of his own lapses in memory and what they signify. As he reads and rereads Miss Kenton's letter, he realizes that and what he is reading into it. The words, differently inflected with each reading, become the occasions for various patternings of his life as well as his realization that there are not many years remaining in his day. That is why the letter becomes a template upon which is written the longings he has so doggedly denied. When he says that "at this very moment no doubt she [Miss Kenton] is pondering with regret decisions made in the far off past that have now left her deep in middle age, so alone and desolate" (48), it is as much a description of his life as of hers. Indeed more so, since she eventually goes back to a husband who loves her and is soon to be a grandmother, while Stevens is left alone with work that lacks purpose and meaning.

None of this is meant to excuse Stevens for what he has done and not done. Because something is common or ordinary does not excuse it. But it does or should make us cautious in excoriating others for what we also do. But we must confront the question Arendt asked regarding Eichmann: what exactly did Stevens do and what standards of responsibility can we hold him to without self-righteousness? Should he have actively protested Darlington's political aims or have resigned (as Miss Kenton, the chief housekeeper, threatened to do) when Darlington insisted that two Jewish maids be dismissed instead of simply following his order? And what are we to make of his reference to this dismissal as "insignificant," his all-too-familiar assertion (after Darlington admitted his demand was "wrong") that he was internally opposed to the dismissal or the fact that he calls "the incident" a "misunderstanding" even after Darlington accepts moral responsibility for it? Is this an example of bad judgment or evil, an ordinary vice or something more sinister? And are Stevens's actions mitigated by the possibility that he is a man whose good will, energy, trust, and dedication has been abused? Once more, is he responsible for his credulity? How much so, given the class structure of England? Does historical accident mitigate otherwise immoral behavior? Arendt admits that there is a sense in which Eichmann was a victim too. If he had lived in another place at another time he would almost certainly not be complicit in genocide. "In fact," Thomas Laqueur writes, "had circumstances not intervened, party priorities not changed, and new opportunities for advancement not presented themselves," Eichmann would have gone down in history as the Nazi expert on Freemasons.[17]

But Eichmann lived when he did, where he did, and did what he did. Whatever the circumstances, he did make choices and mistakes, however much those have to be placed within a larger historical and political narrative that explains without justifying.

III

The Remains of the Day opens a decade after the end of World War Two with Stevens's new American employer suggesting that he take his car and time off to see the English countryside. That someone like Stevens, for whom order and routine are paramount values and traits, undertaking such a trip is out of character. He tells us, as he so often will, that the reason he undertook the trip is professional, since a letter from Miss Kenton, who left Darlington Hall twenty years ago to get married, indicates a certain nostalgia for Darlington Hall and a disappointment with her current life, talking with her about a possible return would solve what he calls his "staff" problem.

But there are more compelling reasons for the trip he does not, and perhaps cannot, yet acknowledge: boredom, isolation, and loneliness now that the community of butlers no longer exists; the disappearance of "great" houses where history was made and whose significance reflected on him; his repressed love for Miss Kenton, which the letter rekindles; and the fact that approaching old age *he* has become the staffing problem his father was twenty years before. The words he uses to characterize his lapses in the present—"a series of small errors . . . quite trivial in themselves"—are exactly the words Lord Darlington used about his father whom Stevens had hired, but whose old age prevented him from performing all but the most menial tasks.

So this is no ordinary journey. The risks are substantial, the stakes even more so. An elderly man, Stevens is finally leaving the social, moral, and political cocoon of Darlington Hall. Even if this "great house" had provided him with a sense of place and significance, his life then was like being in a minimum security prison. Emotionally cauterized by the rigid hierarchies of class and status as well as by self-denying professionalism that was both his fate and his choice, Stevens takes a trip that opens his life to a world outside and a world within that he has persistently, even desperately, held at bay.

Whatever sense of place and purpose Darlington Hall had provided, the era it represents has become a historical curiosity, leaving Stevens adrift in a social world whose cues are alien to him. (He is at a loss about how to respond to his new employer's playfulness.) Given such circumstances, he has little choice but to reconsider the narrative of his life and the ends that have defined it.

As that narrative opens space for thought and memory, the immediate trials of this otherwise unremarkable man become something far more substantial: meditations on mortality and loss, the possibility for love and companionship, and a search for moral redemption. Haltingly, imperfectly, even reluctantly, Stevens confronts evidence that his life has been wasted, or worse: that he has been complicit in shameful political and moral actions and that what he regarded as his best traits, what gave him pride and dignity, were partly responsible for this. He travels forward in space and back in time until the two meet in a present full of loss and regret. That present is captured by two moments. Learning that Miss Kenton is, unexpectedly, going back to her husband after hearing her admit that she often thought of their possible life together, Stevens says (to himself), "Indeed—why should I not admit it—at that moment my heart was breaking" (239). Finally recognizing what his uncritical loyalty to Darlington has meant and cost him, Stevens says:

> Lord Darlington wasn't a bad man. . . . And at least he had the privilege of being able to say at the end of his life that he made his own mistakes. . . . He chose a certain path in life, it proved to be a misguided one, but he chose it, he can say that at least. As for myself I cannot ever claim that. You see I TRUSTED. I trusted in his lordship's wisdom. All those years I served him, I trusted I was doing something worthwhile. I can't even say I made my own mistakes. Really—one has to ask oneself—what dignity is there in that? (243)

And this from a man for whom dignity has been a goal and subject of reflection his whole professional life.

If he did not make his own mistakes, who did? Stevens doesn't say he was not *allowed* to make his own mistakes, only that he *did* not. This sounds less like a denial of responsibility than an admission or lament. But by putting it this way, is he suggesting that the abuse of his trust by others is a mitigating circumstance that absolves him from complicity in the moral and political naiveté of his employer. And what about his "personal mistakes"? Certainly his uncritical trust in Lord Darlington did not require his obliviousness to Miss Kenton's feelings for him or to his sometimes supercilious petty criticisms of her.[18] His conclusion, made halfway through this journey of discovery and self-discovery, that there "was surely nothing to indicate at the time that such evidently small incidents [his criticism and coldness toward her] would render whole dreams forever irredeemable" (179) is moving but not wholly persuasive. As I suggested, these mistakes seem to be his and his alone.

But what about his relationship with Lord Darlington? We know that Stevens was confronted by criticism of Darlington's politics and attitudes (unlike Eichmann, who was morally convinced by the unanimity of "respectable" people's endorsement of the final solution). To begin with, we are told by Stevens that he had ongoing conversations with his fellow butlers not only about what constituted a "great" butler but about the events of the day and what they read in the newspapers, which suggests that he probably encountered views that contradicted Darlington's. Then there is Miss Kenton's outrage at the firing of the Jewish housekeepers, the sardonic toast by an American representative to one of Darlington's international conferences in which "His Lordship" is dismissed as an "amateur" who does not know what he is doing, and Lord Darlington's godson who attempts to enlist Stevens in saving Darlington from the stupidity of his good intentions. Miss Kenton could be dismissed as just a servant. Lewis (the American) is portrayed by Stevens as a boor. But the godson is another matter. As we saw, his response to the godson's criticism of Darlington is a combination of stunning indifference and stubborn diffidence. He has placed his trust in Lord Darlington's doing what is "highest and noblest," and that trust is unequivocal. More damning still is the fact that he *chose* Lord Darlington as an employer out of moral concern and personal ambition. For his "idealistic" generation of butlers, "what mattered was the moral status of the employer," a status that was based on the degree to which he was "furthering the progress of humanity" (114). Only by serving such a personage could Stevens realize his professional ambitions. To serve "great men" of "great houses" in whose hands "the fate of civilization" rested was a necessary condition for being a "great" butler. "A great butler can only be one who can point to his years of service and say that he has applied his talents to serving great gentlemen and thus serving humanity," from which it follows that, if the "great" man has done a disservice to humanity, the butler cannot regard himself as great. It also follows that choosing Lord Darlington was a mistake and that Stevens made it.

But this is too pat. How could he know that it was a mistake at the time? And, given his chosen profession, how could he expect employment if he wrangled with his employers who were, in any case, far better educated and situated? Perhaps Stevens is right; to be a great butler there are things one must do and a kind of person one must be. Foremost is the duty to provide good service and this is impossible if butlers are critical of their employers and seek to meddle in the "great" affairs of the nation. To render independent judgments ruined the careers of many promising butlers. One must exercise such judgment in choosing an employer who is "noble and admirable" and exercise the virtue of loyalty afterwards.

Of course, Stevens could have chosen another profession. But then, almost every profession has its code of conduct, standards of efficiency, premium on calculation and predictability, ideals of depersonalization (in the sense of excluding love, hatred, and personal feelings that intrude in the execution of official tasks), praise of loyalty and dependability, and a reliance on the rationality constituted by official discourse. And this profession was particularly compelling, given the physically and psychologically intimidating figure of his butler father whose perfect balance of "dignity and readiness to oblige" (38–39). Stevens so much admires. Admittedly, that admiration has a paradoxical, if not perverse, aspect. Stevens claims that he became a great butler (like his father) by ignoring him in order to manage an important international conference. His success, his "greatness," his "coming of age" as a butler was premised on paying more attention to the French delegate's swollen feet than to his father's death. Stevens honored, even became, his father by keeping his emotions in check and remaining calm under the most intense pressure, just as his father did when he attended a general whose stupidity had caused the death of Stevens's brother. No doubt there is something admirable in such stoicism. But given the personal and moral sacrifice demanded by such self-restraint in the case of Stevens junior, the father's Herculean self-control must have come at a considerable cost. We do not know what it took out of him, but we can guess, as we can at the emotional and moral scar the father's professionalism left on the son.[19]

From this point of view, Stevens's journey is an effort to escape the "dark severe presence" of his father, his father's fate (living in a tiny room described as a prison cell), talking less and less, and dying alone.

As Stevens distances himself from the confines of Darlington Hall, the ambivalent relationship he has with his father is replayed in his relationship with Lord Darlington. Initially, Stevens holds onto his sanitized memory of Darlington for dear life. He defends his employer's character and intentions, insists that he was a "good man at heart" and claims to be "proud and grateful for the privilege of serving him for 35 years" (61). Of course, this defense is also a self-defense. If Stevens's sacrifices were for naught, if his trust were abused, if his dedications to his profession proved to be a form of moral evasion and personal evisceration, then the world and his place in it unravel. Stevens had insisted that any butler who takes pride in his vocation, who "aspires to a dignity in keeping with his position," must "be seen to *inhabit* his role utterly and fully," except when he is entirely alone (169). But we (but not yet he) recognize that there is no such thing as his being alone, that his virtue as a butler consumed his virtue as a man. Caught reading a sentimental novel in the colorless butler's pantry he calls his headquarters (it is where he makes his "staff plan"), he justifies his reading it in professional terms (it improves his vocabulary)[20] as he does his quest to capture a lost unspoken love. Even the English countryside's virtues—understatement, lack of drama, dignified calm and order—sound suspiciously like the virtues of a butler.

Eventually, Stevens does separate himself from Lord Darlington and the life he led in thrall to him. But the process is not easy or wholly successful. The first step in that process finds Stevens impersonating Lord Darlington. Of course, there had always been parallels between them. Both were naive and "idealistic"; both had no experience with women, romance, or sex[21] (which made Darlington's request that Stevens tell his godson about the facts of life comical, poignant, and ironic); and both regarded getting one's house in order (whether it was Darlington House, or Italy, and Germany) as paramount. So these affinities suggest that there were reasons why Stevens chose Lord Darlington as an employer beyond his desire to serve a noble gentleman committed to justice and engaged in historically significant affairs.

But his impersonation is something else entirely. Finding himself in a small town mistaken for a gentleman, he talks about *his* good fortune to have had "the ear of Churchill, Eden, and Hallifax on many great issues of the day," and his "gratitude" at "having a part to play on the world's stage" (188). In fact, his part was to provide clean silver that put Lord Hallifax in a "good mood."

It is true that Stevens is relieved to have his charade discovered, admitting to the doctor who recognizes him as a gentleman's gentleman that things got out of hand. But the impersonation and the relief are more complicated than they seem. To begin with, "things got out of hand" sounds like an excuse. Then there is Miss Kenton's complaint that Stevens is always pretending; that he is nothing but pretense. In addition, he is, for the moment, reliving his life, imagining what it would have been like if he really had the power and influence he momentarily pretends to have had, even if that eventually meant making his own mistakes. Finally, his replacing Lord Darlington is a kind of ritual sacrifice, and a quid pro quo. With this he is able, finally, to acknowledge what Darlington's actions and his uncritical support of them has meant for his life.

It is only then that he can and does admit to being ashamed of having served Lord Darlington. He goes so far as to deny ever having known him. He may say that "it is illogical for me to feel responsibility" if Darlington's views "were shown to be misguided, even foolish." But he is, and is probably right to be so, even if the unpredictability of events lends a certain plausibility to his denial. Indeed, his shame is an acknowledgement of how much he has fallen short of what he had hoped for himself and that his failures have shamed and wronged others. Moreover, his sense of shame not only enables him to separate himself from Lord Darlington, it allows him to see the foolishness of sacrificing oneself for anyone and of identifying one's virtue as a human being with the virtue required by one's profession. There is, he realizes, no dignity in this.

But it would be wrong to see this process of separation as a narrative of liberation, both because it is not *a* narrative and because the outcome, that is, what there is at the end of the novel and the end of his life, "remains" uncertain.

Stevens's story is hardly linear. Most obviously, each chapter begins from a different place geographically, psychologically, and biographically. More significantly, his ruminations on the past criss-cross as memories press on the moment, then disappear only to reappear in an altered guise that escapes the form and place he had initially given them. Stevens is right in saying that, when one looks back on one's life, there are so many turning points that seemed so innocent and unfraught but which at a certain time in a certain light and in a certain place become the fulcrum of a life. He is aware that some accidental thought or event can transform patterns of experience and identity. He is not only aware of it, he exemplifies it.

The novel ends with Stevens sitting on a bench watching the lights go on in an amusement park at the close of the day. Perhaps the end of the day is, as an unnamed companion said a few minutes before, the most enjoyable part of the day. Perhaps he should concentrate on that, be more positive about the future instead of looking back so much on a past so full of loss and regret. "After all," he reflects, "what can we ever gain in forever looking back and blaming ourselves if our lives had not turned out quite as we might have wished?" The hard reality, he goes on, is

> surely that for the likes of you and I, there is little choice other than to leave our fate, ultimately in the hands of those great gentlemen at the hub of this world who employ our services. What is the point in worrying oneself too much about what one could or could not have done to control the course one's life took? Surely it is enough that the likes of you and I at least *try* to make our small contribution count for something true and worthy. (201)

Perhaps *this* is a stoicism that deserves our acceptance if not respect, especially when it is balanced by a newfound pleasure in laughter. Here surely is a less ponderous and joyless man, one whom we imagine bantering with his new American employer. But there are too many discomforting echoes in his words, too many ways this modest realism could invite moral evasion and passivity. We have seen what putting one's faith in great gentlemen has come to, how ignorant, naïve, and dangerous their views were and undeserved their confident superiority had been.

The uncertainty of the ending, with its presentation of a far more attractive and human Stevens who repeats unchastened earlier beliefs, does have one clear result: the novel abjures providing the sort of authority it reveals to be pernicious.

IV

Responding to Miss Kenton's outrage at having to fire two otherwise exemplary maids because they are Jewish, Stevens rebukes her with, "You are not well placed to judge." Later on, responding now to an argument that equal dignity was what England fought for against Germany, he thinks how absurd it is to suppose that "ordinary people" could be "expected to have strong opinions in all manner of things" (194).

These are familiar refrains, familiar not only in aristocratic England[22] between the wars or in Nazi Germany but in liberal democracies as well. Of course, few now would explicitly defend hierarchy on grounds of nature, breeding or race. Yet the questions—who am I to judge those in the know and in power, who am I to contest the decision of the experts and professionals, leaders and scientists—have shown a tenacity across time and space.

It was in the name of science that Stanley Milgram performed his famous experiments that "showed" how easily subjects adopted the perspective of those in authority and came to judge themselves by how competently they performed their task. Obeying authority became a moral imperative that overrode any identification with the victim. Here we had "normal" individuals accepting an "agentic state" in which they were the "instrument of another's will" such that they no longer felt personally responsible for the content of their actions. Caught in the culture of the experiment, disobedience, refusal to cooperate, and counter-initiatives seemed inappropriate if not immoral to them.[23] Yet not all the subjects agreed to go along or continue to inflict pain. A few (like Miss Kenton in *Remains*) did not parenthesize judgment or distance themselves from the victims. The lesson of Anton Schmidt, a Sergeant who aided Jews, Hannah Arendt argues, is that "under conditions of terror most people will comply but some people will not. . . . Humanly speaking no more is required and no more can reasonably be asked, for this planet to remain a fit place for human habitation."[24]

Politically speaking, authorities may no more lay claim to superior rights on the ground of superior merit than ordinary citizens can absolve themselves from partial responsibility for public policies on the ground that their "task is done when they have elected those who take active charge of the affairs of the polity." This is what Stevens does when, with impeccable Hobbesian logic, he selects Darlington as an authority and then obeys without qualms or questions. (Stevens claims that he internally dissented to the firing of the Jewish maids, but given the echo of Germans who claimed the same, that is not an excuse but a self-accusation.) It may be comforting to suppose that someone else is "competently in charge of the large and dangerous affairs of politics and that the rest of us can go about our business without guilt, responsibility or sharing the burden of citizenship."[25] But the combination of moral arrogance on the part of elites such as Darlington and his friends, and the taking of ethical holidays by people such as Stevens, is a lethal mixture that sanctions moral evasion as well as political irresponsibility.

The arrogance is obvious in one of the most painful moments in the novel. Lord Darlington and his friends humiliate Stevens by asking him difficult questions about political and economic policy that he cannot answer. His inability to respond—he keeps saying, "I cannot help you"—is a cause of contemptuous laughter and is taken as conclusive proof that, as Darlington puts it, "Democracy is something for a bygone era." The world is "far too complicated a place now" (198), and so the idea that the will of the people should count in politics is an absurdity. Of course they themselves display appalling ignorance, are credulous, and are easily manipulated. But what makes the incident particularly painful is that Stevens knows what's going on from the beginning: that he *is* perceptive and does indeed think for himself. "I saw the situation for what it was; I was supposed to be baffled by the questions" (195). Evidently the dignity of his profession requires him to be complicit in his own humiliation. Thus, the argument that he or Miss Kenton are not "well placed" to judge is belied by the ignorance of those who do and his own capacity to do so, which he chooses to discount.

But what about the argument against democracy, the assertion that "ordinary people" are too simple and ignorant to make thoughtful judgments about political issues? A disillusioned socialist tells Stevens that people just want to be left alone and uninvolved.

Not all people. Those at the top of the social hierarchy for whom status and power are expected rewards are very much involved. (Why they do not want or expect to be left alone is an interesting question but beyond the scope of this essay.) Of course, there are reasons to be unhappy about their involvement. Indeed, the novel suggests that amateurism will not do, if by amateurism we mean amateurs like Lord Darlington who are moralistic and naive about the place and play of power, unable to see the consequences on others and themselves of class privilege, and contemptuous of the demos.

But the person who criticizes these amateurs as gullible and unrealistic is himself a compromised character. He is portrayed (remember, it is by Stevens) as a boorish lout whose realism is based on accepting the lowest common denominator of human behavior as the basis of an amoral politics. More telling, because we do not have to rely on Stevens, is what professionalism has done to *him*. The lesson seems clear enough. Morality and politics must not be left to experts, whether ethicists, consultants, managerialists or thinktank habitués. And that means that judgments cannot be confined to a professional ethos without the virtue of a person becoming absorbed by the virtue of their work.

As this suggests, people must judge not only what they know well (or think they know well), but what they know less well. True, judgments of the latter sort are riskier. But not making them is riskier still. Furthermore, such judgments must be offered in public. Stevens claims that he internally dissented to Darlington's anti-Semitism. But in politics, silence and obedience are the same. In fact, all action is a risk. Being an agent and taking action means not only taking counsel with oneself in order to do the best one can to foresee the order of means and ends, but betting on the unknown and incomprehensible.[26] This means taking a risk on a historical terrain that remains partly impenetrable. That is why moral luck does not excuse Stevens any more than it does Eichmann, though what they are responsible for and why are different.

The ideas of moral luck and historical context challenge the idea that no one can be moral or free to choose if any ethically significant aspect of his person belongs to him simply as a result of a process by which he was contingently formed. It is no more possible for us than for the character Stevens to make our outlook available to critique so that every value we hold can become a consideration for us.[27] Insofar as Socrates demanded that we take ourselves as a whole into account when deciding how to act justly, he was setting a standard neither Stevens nor anyone else can meet. How could we see our life as a whole while we are still in the midst of living it? And if called upon for an account of that life, we are likely to trail off into inconsistencies and a vagueness dialectic cannot contain.[28]

As this implies, a division of labor between elites comfortable with their place as moral exemplars and wielders of power and "ordinary" people comfortable with letting them have it is an ethically and politically corrosive mixture. "Superpowers," Sheldon Wolin has recently argued, require "imperial citizens" by which he means men and women who accept the "remote relationship between the concerns of the citizen and those of the power holders, who welcome being relieved of participating obligations and who are fervently patriotic,"[29] which is, in its way, a fine description of Stevens. That is why democracy may require an element of distrust as a ground for politics. As we see with Stevens (and in Lord Darlington's trust of his Nazi visitors), trust can be too easily abused. In this context, skepticism towards those sure of their power and moral standing is a sign of political health, not a pathology.

Equally corrosive is a focus on order as the supreme political virtue. In the context of the novel, "getting your house in order" has ominous reverberations, both in Darlington Hall and the larger political world. Such a focus also inhibits the kind of thinking Arendt commends, though her story of Anton Schmidt may indicate that such moral reflection is not a prerequisite for living a moral life.

In the end, I do not think Stevens did anything "evil," which may have less to do with his character than with opportunity or lack of it. He probably would not have joined what Christopher Browning calls "those ordinary men who shot, day after day, at close range, men, women, and children by the hundreds of thousands."[30] But we will never know. What we do know is that Adorno's assumption that a "deviant personality" is necessary for someone to do great harm to his fellow creatures is, unfortunately, outdated, as the recurrence of genocides attests.

V

I do not have any solution to these problems except to ask, yet again, about the kinds of politics and culture that might make recourse to willful ignorance, studied incredulity, and ethical holidays less likely and attractive. But I do have a few summary thoughts.

Machiavelli's *Prince* is regarded as a handbook on how to gain and maintain power, and within limits, this is true enough. Yet at the heart of this work, so boastful about its mastery of politics, is the figure of *fortuna*. *Fortuna* has its attractive side—it embodies the idea of opportunity— but it is also a constant threat to the very possibility of human action. What we can do to minimize the threat of *fortuna*, which Machiavelli likens to a river, is to build dikes to contain the unforeseen and uncontrollable forces that *fortuna* represents. The question for us is what kind of dikes might best contain evil or, even better, encourage a concern for justice and goodness so that they do not become, in the face of evil's dominance, residual or derivative categories.

But if building dikes is too defensive and reactive, we are brought back to the issue about the kind of polity that could inhibit ordinary people from being susceptible to "ordinary" wrongs, which under certain historical circumstances can evolve into extraordinary ones. What sorts of counsel could we offer Stevens or take from our journey with him?

We might begin by acknowledging that the densities of human life make the proper assumption of responsibility difficult and that this difficulty is not an excuse. It is true that the demands and possibilities of life are multiple and unyielding in their opacity—which is why action entails risks, and forgiveness must be part of taking and assessing responsibility. But inaction seems no less a risk and its outcome no less opaque.

Second, we might want to explore curiosity as a political and ethical virtue or consider the ways in which it is a precondition or part of Arendt's notion of thoughtfulness. Freud talks about a child's curiosity as its destiny, as an urgency to know, an unsatisfied addiction for knowledge (in this case, knowledge of sexuality).[31] Third, we might want to reconsider the emphasis on trust as a political virtue and order as the end of politics, and strengthen our skepticism towards the claims of professional experts when these translate into sustained hierarchies of value and power.

But surely these considerations are more questions than answers, which, given *The Remains of the Day,* is as it should be.

NOTES

1. See Roxanne Euben, *Journeys to the Other Shore: Muslim and Western Travelers in Search of Knowledge* (Princeton: Princeton University Press, 2006).

2. Michael Ignatieff, "The Terrorist as Auteur," *New York Times Magazine*, November 14, 2004, p. 51.

3. This conclusion comes from conversations with my colleague Diskin Clay.

4. Hannah Arendt, *Eichmann in Jerusalem: A Report on the Banality of Evil* (New York: Viking, 1962). The Anti-Defamation League called Arendt's book "evil."

5. John McGowan, in his response to this paper at the conference "See No Evil," held at Duke University, January 27–29, 2005. The argument at Nuremberg was that the evils of National Socialism were due to the machinations of a small number of monsters. This argument, like Manicheanism, can stop political and ethical analysis in its tracks.

6. Samantha Power, *A Problem from Hell: America and the Age of Genocide* (New York: Basic Books, 2002).

7. See Stanley Hauerwas, "Seeing Darkness, Hearing Silence: Augustine's Account of Evil," in this volume.

8. Thomas Laqueur argues that the question is not how genocide is possible but how it is that certain societies in certain periods of history have been spared its ravages in "Four pfennige per track km," *London Review of Books*, 4 November 2004, p. 7.

9. Kazuo Ishiguro, *The Remains of the Day* (New York: Vantage, 1988). Page references will appear in the text.

10. Arendt, *Eichmann in Jerusalem*, p. 276.

11. Arendt, *Eichmann in Jerusalem*, p. p. 287. See her discussion of Kant in "The Crisis in Culture," in *Between Past and Future* (New York: Penguin, 1993).

12. Hannah Arendt, "Thinking," *Life of the Mind*, vol. 1 (London: Sacker and Warburg, 1971), p. 5.

13. See Judith Shklar, *Faces of Injustice* (Cambridge, MA: Yale University Press, 1990), p. 45.

14. See Bernard Williams, *Shame and Necessity* (Berkeley: University of California Press, 1994), pp. 164–68.

15. Avery Gordon, *Ghostly Matters: Haunting and the Sociological Imagination* (Minneapolis: University of Minnesota Press, 1996).

16. Geoffrey Galt Harpham, *Shadows of Ethics: Criticism and the Just Society* (Durham, NC: Duke University Press, 2002), pp. xiii and 3.

17. Laqueur, "Four pfennige per track km."

18. Professionalism often combines advertised adherence to a detailed code of conduct with pettiness and pique in something like Freud's return of the repressed.

19. Stevens's exchanges with his father are often chilling. His father has just had a stroke:

> Then he said slowly, "I hope I've been a good father to you."
> I laughed a little and said, "I am so glad father is feeling better now."
> "I'm proud of you. A good son. I hope I've been a good father to you. I suppose I haven't."
> "I'm afraid we are extremely busy now. . . ." (97)

20. The scene is full of sexual tension which petrifies Stevens. Later on, he admits that he took pleasure in reading these sentimental novels.

21. *Remains* is a masculinist novel in the sense that few women are present or mentioned. There is Miss Kenton, of course, and a woman friend (there is a hint of something more) of Lord Darlington's who is responsible for his increasing anti-Semitism. But there is not a word about Stevens's mother, or Darlington's for that matter.

22. On the ways in which Darlington embodies a political and social type, see Ian Kershaw, *Making Friends with Hitler: Londonderry, the Nazis and the Road to World War II* (New York: Penguin, 2004).

23. See Stanley Milgrim, *Obedience to Authority: An Experimental View* (New York: Perennial, 1974), pp. 14–26; and Craig Haney, Curtis Banks, and Phillip Zimbardo, "Interpersonal Dynamics in a Simulated Prison," *International Journal of Criminology and Penology* 1 (1973): 69–97; and Christopher R. Browning, *Ordinary Men* (New York: HarperCollins, 1992).

24. *Eichmann in Jerusalem*, p. 233.

25. Both this and the preceding quotation are from John H. Schaar, "Equality of Opportunity and Beyond," in *Legitimacy and the Modern State* (New Brunswick, NJ: Transaction Books, 1980), pp. 206–208.

26. Jean-Pierre Vernant and Pierre Vidal-Naquet, *Tragedy and Myth in Ancient Greece*, quoted in Williams, *Shame and Necessity*, p. 19.

27. Williams, *Shame and Necessity*, p. 158.

28. Jonathan Lear, *Happiness, Death and the Remainder of Life* (Cambridge, MA: Harvard University Press, 2000), pp. 3–14.

29. Sheldon Wolin, *Politics and Vision*, rev. ed. (Princeton: Princeton University Press, 2004), p. 565.

30. Browning, *Ordinary Men*, p. 159.

31. See Adam Phillips, *The Beast in the Nursery* (New York: Pantheon, 1998).

Evil and the Morality of Conviction

Mankind today is on the brink of a precipice . . . because humanity is devoid of those vital values which are necessary not only for its healthy development but also for its real progress. Even the Western world realizes that Western civilization is unable to present any healthy values for the guidance of mankind. It knows that it does not possess anything which will satisfy its own conscience and justify its existence.

Sayyid Qutb[1]

On a tape claiming responsibility for the atrocities in Madrid, a man is heard to say, "We choose death, while you choose life." . . . It is a mind set that rejoices in suicide, incites murder, and celebrates every death we mourn. And we who stand on the other side of the line must be equally clear and certain of our convictions. We do love life, the life given to us and to all. We believe in the values that uphold the dignity of life, tolerance, and freedom, and the right of conscience. And we know that this way of life is worth defending. There is no neutral ground—no neutral ground—in the fight between civilization and terror, because there is no neutral ground between good and evil, freedom and slavery, and life and death.

George W. Bush[2]

Introduction

Evil can arise malignantly from those who intend to produce it as evil, or it can arise from those who are convinced of their own righteousness and who believe themselves to be opposing malignant perpetrators of evil. In the second case, the righteous may come to see themselves as the sole, embattled agents of a morally urgent end, very often the preservation of civilization itself. The righteous may believe in the possibility of a final and complete victory over their evil opponents. These perceptions of the righteous self and malignant other can have disastrous consequences.

They weaken the power of constraints used to wage war on the enemy.[3] The results not only include terrorist attacks on civilians in self-declared wars on evil, but a greater willingness to set aside constraints against humiliation, torture, and presumption of innocence in the response to those attacks. In the case of the radical Islamist war on the United States and the corresponding "war on terrorism" waged by the United States, many on *both* sides see themselves as the righteous battling the malignantly evil. In such worst-case scenarios, each side feels increased permission to set aside constraints on war against the other, with the result that its actions confirm for the other side that it is truly a malignantly evil opponent that must be fought with few or no constraints, and so the spiral turns downward.

Moreover, those persuaded of their own righteousness tend to divide the world into those who are for "us" and those who are against "us." Because the world is divided so cleanly into good and evil, those who refuse to ally themselves with us are moral weaklings, passively complicit with the enemy, or actively cooperating with the enemy. Violent Islamic fundamentalists, on their side, tend to characterize the West as a monolithic entity, its culture godless and materialistic, and its aims imperialistic. On the American side of the second Iraq war, the labels of moral weakness and passive or active complicity often got pasted onto Americans who opposed the war, the French and the many other Western democracies who opposed it, and Saddam Hussein with his alleged connections to al Qaeda. This kind of polarization silences the voices of moderation and only serves those who wish to eliminate all the options except violent conflict.

This essay is about the moral psychology of those who do evil as they wage war upon evil. My focus is the "morality of conviction" that simplifies and polarizes for the sake of meaning, certitude, and decisiveness. My primary example will be the downward spiral dance between those Islamists who invoke fundamentalist views to motivate and justify terrorist attacks on the United States and its allies (many who hold radical fundamentalist views, of course, deny that attacks on civilians are justified), and those in the United States who oppose them but are fundamentally alike in misperceiving the motivations of the other side. By saying they are fundamentally alike in this respect, I am not saying that what is done on both sides is morally equivalent, all things considered, nor do I want to say that the fact of one's actions being somewhat, or even a lot, less bad than those on the other side constitutes a good excuse for those actions. A final qualification to make clear at the outset is that the perception of the other side as malignantly evil is but one motivating factor for the terrorist attacks and the U.S. response, and there is no claim here for the primacy of this perception as a motivating factor. The assumption of this paper, however, is that it was and continues to be a significant factor in the readiness to use violence without the usual acknowledged constraints.

Misperception of the Other Side as Malignantly Evil

Radical Islamist fundamentalism, if not Islam as a whole, is seen by Americans as a monolithic entity and often equated with aggression, fanaticism, irrationality, and antipathy toward women and human rights. The favored rhetoric of George W. Bush is that the terrorists are "enemies of freedom." He groups violent radical Islamists with the other evil movements of the last century: "by abandoning every value except the will to power—they follow in the path of fascism, and Nazism, and totalitarianism."[4] In the two years following the 9/11 attacks, substantial percentages (42–69) of the American public have expressed the opinion that Saddam Hussein was personally involved in the attacks,[5] and this thinking might simply continue Bush's assimilation of al Qaeda with any and all evil movements. Hussein is evil in the same undifferentiated way, and therefore he must be allied with al Qaeda.

What do we find when we actually try to understand the motivations of those who attacked the United States? Consider that Sayyid Qutb, perhaps the most influential Islamist fundamentalist of the twentieth century and a staple of the Islamic education of generations of jihadists, both moderate and extreme, peaceful and violent,[6] was preparing to take his place among the liberal, Western-oriented Egyptian elite when he visited the United States for two-and-one-half years. He was repulsed by its racism toward Arabs, its preoccupation with pleasure and material interest, and the cultural encouragement it gave to women to leave their proper roles of bringing up children "merely to be attractive, sexy and flirtatious," to use "their ability for material productivity rather than the training of human beings, because material production is considered to be more important, more valuable and more honourable than the development of human character."[7]

Compare these remarks with Christian evangelist Jerry Falwell's statement that the 9/11 attacks were God's judgment on America: "I really believe that the pagans and the abortionists and the feminists and the gays and the lesbians who are actively trying to make that an alternative lifestyle, the ACLU, People for the American Way, all of them who try to secularize America . . . I point the thing in their face and say you helped this happen."[8] Even though Falwell later stated that the terrorists were alone responsible for the attacks, his initial remarks accurately indicate that radical Islamists are far from alone in their condemnation of materialistic trends in American society and in their rejection of the cultural changes associated with the movement for gender equality. Falwell's remarks suggest that the attacks are not a clear case of "us" versus "them" but rather that there is some of "them" in "us."

Much, if not all, of what Qutb wrote has force for people of a wide variety of political, religious, and moral beliefs both inside and outside the United States. Many, for example, lament the American preoccupation with pleasure and material interest. The fundamental principle of Islamic economic theory, Qutb states, is that property belongs to the community in general, whereas individual possession is a stewardship that carries with it conditions and limitations. A proportion of all wealth belongs by right to the needy members of the community.[9] Indeed, one of his principles of economic justice is "to each according to his need."[10] Qutb's underlying analysis of what has gone wrong in the West centers on the secularization of its societies, on the segregation of Christianity to the otherworldly dimensions of life. Qutb takes the American philosophy of pragmatism as emblematic of the West's rejection of spirituality: only the useful is that which can be said to exist; even God is allowed to exist only if He proves to be useful.[11] Ideas of right and justice have no permanent place in American life or American international policy because such ideas must always be subordinated to material interest. By contrast, Qutb takes Islam to provide a comprehensive moral vision of life that cannot be separated from political philosophy and economics.

Many of us who would find ourselves surprised by agreeing with Falwell on anything also lament the American preoccupation with pleasure and material interest and its influence on American foreign policy. It is too close for any moral comfort that the United States has allied itself with two authoritarian states, Saudi Arabia and Egypt, from which nearly all the hijackers of 9/11 came, and that the United States has been exceedingly mild in its criticisms of these governments for the way they have treated their citizens. It is difficult to brush aside the perception of many Muslims, many of them not at all militant jihadists, who see in the words of John Esposito "a world dominated by corrupted authoritarian governments and a wealthy elite, a minority concerned solely with its own economic prosperity, rather than national development, a world awash in Western culture and values in dress, music, television, and movies," and "Western governments . . . as propping up oppressive regimes and exploiting the region's human and natural resources."[12] A common perception in the Middle East is that the United States sees it as nothing more than a gas station, and that American policy underneath all the rhetoric is geared to keep the pumps flowing. Even when George W. Bush articulated the need for democracy in the Middle East, he presented it in conjunction with the aim of neutralizing terrorist threats from that region.[13] Bush might be right or wrong about the connection between more democracy and less terrorism (and right or wrong about the possibility of a democracy emerging in Iraq under the conditions created by the war), but his justification simply confirms the common perception in the Middle East that the United States does what is right only by coincidence with its perceived self-interest.

Qutb shares a fundamental theme with other, very different groups in American society. As has been observed by Ahmad S. Moussalli, Qutb and other radical Islamist fundamentalists declare that human reason is simply too weak to understand God, prove the necessity of his existence, or comprehend his true nature. Hence they reject all claims for genuine knowledge based on rational proof or empirical observation.[14] Knowledge comes only through revelation, and different individuals will have different interpretations of what has been revealed to them that cannot be definitively adjudicated by reason or the traditional Islamic methods of jurisprudence, theology, and linguistics.[15]

Moussailli draws this portrait of fundamentalism with the aim of likening it to postmodernism, but many other than postmodern thinkers have accepted that our reasons for believing as we do often run out before the other side is convinced, even when the other side is considering our arguments in good faith. Serious disagreement creates a context of debate that removes the usual, agreed-upon stopping points, the places where everyone says, "Yes, I see now."[16] Running out of reasons can be especially threatening the more the opposing view represents a grave threat to oneself or to others one is defending. The sense of threat can motivate violence of the kind that shuts off consideration of other voices and views. It may take the form of a religious insistence on one's personal revelation as the only authentic revelation, or a simple secularized refusal to consider these other voices and views anymore, or a stonewalling declaration that the others are stubbornly denying the plain truth. It is pervasive in moral discourse. It may be asserted by those who shut off all arguments against the view that the fetus is a person who is murdered in an abortion (a position associated with religiously based views on the morality of abortion) and those who shut off all arguments against the right to abortion on demand (a position associated with a secularist view of abortion). Indeed, arguments do not work very well when we get to disagreements over fundamental values, for example, the liberal belief in the moral equality of all human beings versus the priority an Aristotelian might give to the realization of human excellence.

To shut off other voices when one's own reasons run out is not obviously an irrational thing to do, even though this move is often associated with profoundly antirationalist views. Indeed, one might form a perfectly coherent worldview by shutting out dissonant voices. On this basis, there is not much hope for Western societies to redeem themselves in the eyes of radical Islamists. A Western society that lives up to its ideals of right and justice far more closely than any of the major Western powers do now or for the foreseeable future would nevertheless violate the comprehensive ideal of a society united in worship of God. On the other side, it might seem unimaginably horrifying to subject an entire society to a detailed and uncompromising vision of a properly spiritual life on the basis of personal revelation.

On the other hand, not all of the conflict is accurately described as a brute conflict between ultimate visions of a proper human life. There are failures of perception on both sides that have nothing to do with inconsistencies of thought. As demonstrated by their use of the word 'Satan' to describe the United States or Israel, radical Islamists are guilty of the same kind of misperceptions as those who characterize them as irrational savages. Though there might be more than a little truth in the idea of the United States as a carrier of spiritual devastation, it is a moral failure to neglect the more complex truth of what it inflicts and what it has to offer. The Boroumands lament the Muslim world's failure to see that

> the West is a diverse, plural, and complex entity. Its political culture has
> produced horrors but also institutions that protect human dignity. One of
> these horrors was the imperialism imposed on Muslim and other lands, but
> even that did as much harm to the Europeans themselves as it did to us, as

anyone familiar with the casualty figures from the First World War will know.[17]

It is difficult to say how much of the conflict between radical Islamists and the United States is a brute confrontation between ultimate visions of human life and how much is based in failures of perception. Belief systems are dynamic in ways that undermine attempts to identify which parts are foundational and which derivative. However, the perception of the West as possessing merely sham values and, in practice, driven by pleasure and material interest is *no incidental part* of the radical Islamist vision. It is a crucial part of the Islamist web of belief that supports intolerance of not just non-Islamist beliefs but also traditional Islamic beliefs, practices, and institutions that are incompatible with Islamicism. Perhaps most importantly, this simplistic perception of the West feeds the willingness to set aside virtually all constraints on attacks against civilians, just as the American belief about the brute savagery of radical Islamists feeds the willingness to set aside constraints on treatment of U.S.-labeled enemy combatants. The simplistic perception on both sides tends to eliminate all courses of action except for a strategy of total defeat of the other.

It might be thought that, even if the perception of the other side as savagely malignant evildoers is correct, there still is no justification for the deliberate targeting of civilian noncombatants or for the torture of those suspected of being engaged in such targeting. However, the case for the absoluteness of such constraints is controversial and unpersuasive in the face of certain examples. There is a reason why a comparison to Hitler is also used as a conversation stopper in moral debates. The intentional terrorizing and killing of noncombatants might be justified if the stakes are high enough, for example, if civilization itself really is at stake. For Michael Walzer, the stakes must be that high for the deliberate killing of noncombatants to be morally necessary, and even then, for Walzer, it would also be a "determinate crime."[18] An extremist response to those perceived to be savagely malignant evildoers cannot be condemned on the basis of absolute side constraints, but must be judged according to the accuracy of its perceptions of the other side and the necessity of the actions it takes for achieving victory over the other side. Whether bombing of civilians is truly necessary for victory, of course, can itself be a controversial matter. The firebombing of German cities and the atom-bombing of Hiroshima and Nagasaki during World War Two, both with the intention of terrorizing and demoralizing the civilian population, may have come at a time when the ultimate outcome of the war was not in doubt (though the bombing of the Japanese cities had the purpose of shortening the war). In any case, both sides in the current conflict do allege that something like civilization is at stake, and we are back to the issues of how each side perceives the other.

It may be objected that relying on Qutb to understand the motivations of violent radical Islamists is to overintellectualize their motivations. Of course, all movements inspired by an ideology comprehend a diversity of motivations among their leaders and followers. But it is important to recognize how different kinds of motivations work together and mutually reinforce one another. Relatively sophisticated intellectual and moral justifications can support and be supported by the need for power, status, recognition, material gain, and an insecure and unstable sense of personal identity and self-worth, sometimes arising from severe economic problems, unemployment, and inability to provide for oneself and one's family. As Ervin Staub observes, intense political conflict, disorganization, and rapid social change add to social chaos and disorganization. People become disconnected from each other. Participating in a radical fundamentalist movement can provide them an identity and help them feel effective and in control; and the goals of the movement become the motivating force for members.[19] The ideologies need not be merely convenient excuses for satisfying these other needs. In fact, the ideologies better reinforce the needs if they hold some appeal in their own right.

Richard Mitchell, one of the first Western scholars to write about Qutb's Society of the Muslim Brothers, observed that the stereotype of the marginal, antimodern other was seriously misleading and could not explain how the Brotherhood could have attained the position of influence it attained in Egypt. It is important to recognize, Mitchell observed, that the society resonated with a Muslim search for authenticity as a necessary aspect of contending with the Muslim situation in the contemporary world.[20] Richard Antoun, in writing of Islamic, Jewish, and Christian forms of scripturalism, observes that they meet the need for certainty in a rapidly changing and disrupted society, giving people "confidence to continue their pursuits, often in situations where the odds are heavily against them," allowing them "to proceed in the face of adversity and often jeopardy when others without their faith do not."[21] He cites as an example the Ayatollah Khomeini's defiant reply in 1979 to U.S. threats to crush Iran with its economic and military might if American hostages were not returned: "as Sh'ites we welcome any opportunity for sacrificing our blood."[22]

There are more speculative psychoanalytic explanations that are difficult to endorse but also difficult to dismiss. One idea is that the zealous pursuit of goodness leads to evil because it requires repression of one's own darker side. This splitting might further lead to projection of one's unacceptable tendencies and traits onto others who are then despised. It is not very hard to see what the applications of this explanation might look like in our case at hand, again, on both sides. The problem lies in establishing the causal links suggested by the explanation.

In considering possible explanations for the failure to perceive the complexity and truth in the other side's views, furthermore, we must not neglect the pragmatic dimension. Sometimes we first decide to act against an enemy and then tailor our characterization of its motivations so as to strengthen resolve and gain adherents to our side. It is even possible to see that its motivations are more complex than one's characterization of them but to ignore that complexity for the sake of strengthening resolve behind the action one has already decided to take. Arguably, something like this might be true of both sides of the conflict in question.

The fact that motivations are typically mixed among those who participate in radical movements is not in itself an indictment of the movement. If it were, no movement could be free of criticism. It is not clear that violent radical Islamists are any guiltier of bad faith than others are in movements that might deserve our approval, all things considered. The range of motivations underlying the faulty perception of the righteous self and malignant other, however, helps us to better explain how such perception comes about.

Needs Met by Failures of Perception

On both sides of the conflict, then, there is a kind of brute assertion of a vision of human life against the other and also a failure to perceive the complexity and truth in the other side's views. Whatever the actual explanations for the failure, it seems likely that it is not an accidental overlooking. Failure to perceive complexity may answer a number of different psychological and political needs and can be deliberate. The crucial question to ask now is whether this failure is always a vice.

This question is not a simple matter of noting that failures of perception leave us farther from the truth. As we have seen, some part of the conflict is a radical disagreement over visions of a proper human life. And even when failures of perception are the issue, the vice is not simply a matter of getting things wrong any more than the virtue is simply a matter of getting it right. This is because the process of arriving at judgment is itself an activity that, to a significant degree, is under one's control. One incurs risks not only by failing to take enough time and care to assess the situation at hand, but also by taking too much time.

In an essay on the difficulty of being a pluralist and remaining committed to a single way of life, Joseph Raz gives an example that is perfect for the issue I want to pose here:

> I value long contemplation and patient examination: these are the qualities
> I require in my chosen course. Their life, by contrast, requires impetuosity,
> swift responses, and decisive action, and they despise the slow contempla-
> tive types as indecisive. They almost have to. To succeed in their chosen way,
> they have to be committed to it and to believe that the virtues it requires
> should be cultivated. They therefore cannot regard those others as virtues
> for them. By the same token it is only natural that they will value in others
> what they choose to emulate themselves. . . . Of course, pluralists can step
> back from their personal commitments and appreciate in the abstract the
> value of other ways of life. But this acknowledgment coexists with, and
> cannot replace, the feelings of rejection and dismissiveness. Tension is an
> inevitable concomitant of value pluralism. And it is a tension without stabil-
> ity, without the prospect of reconciliation of the two perspectives, the one
> recognizing the validity of competing values and the one hostile to them.
> One is forever moving from one to the other.[23]

Raz is right in seeing an incompatibility between the virtues associated with slow, patient examination on the one hand and swift decisiveness on the other. He is wrong in holding that it is impossible to appreciate both sets of virtues at the same time. It is of course difficult, if not impossible, to *possess* these virtues at the same time, but that is a different question. One can recognize both sets of virtues because there is a trade-off between the ways of life constituted by them.

The trade-off is illustrated by a famous chapter of the *Analects* (11.22). Here Confucius gives different advice in response to the same question posed by two different students. Zilu asked, "Should one immediately practice what one has heard?" Confucius said, "There are father and elder brother [to be consulted]." Ranyou asked the same question, but to him, Confucius said, "One should immediately practice what one has heard." When he was asked why he gave conflicting advice to the same question, Confucius replied that Ranyou was retiring and needed urging forward, but Zilu had more than one man's energy and needed to be kept back.

Analects 11.22 not only illustrates the trade-off between slow, patient examination and swift decisiveness but also suggests that there might be a mean between the traits Raz describes, at least if these traits are conceived as excesses or deficiencies. Zilu was rash in acting too soon before thinking while Ranyou deliberated too long, perhaps letting the occasion for acting pass. Perhaps, then, there are not two sets of virtues after all, but simply the virtue of giving a matter sufficient deliberation and then acting in a timely manner. The problem lies in the notion of a single ideal point of balance, especially in those circumstances in which the stakes are of the highest import, the consequences of various courses of action highly ramified and difficult to predict, and in which one's judgments are at least partly based on views for which our reasons have run out before we have eliminated their competitors. The very existence of a single ideal point becomes dubious in such circumstances, because one's conception of an ideal balance between deliberation and swift action will depend on one's relative tolerance for the risk of letting the time for acting pass versus the risk of acting too soon. And this tolerance itself is a matter of evaluative stance. Zilu might act too swiftly even in relation to an ideal of swift decisiveness, and Ranyou might have one or more thoughts too many even in relation to an ideal of slow, patient examination, but there is no guarantee of convergence even if the courageous soldier is taught patience and the cautious bureaucrat acquires some gumption.

In addition to the problem of varying ideals corresponding to differing stances on the relative disvalues of letting the time for acting pass versus acting too soon, there is also the question of how much of a duty one has to consider the other side's point of view when ultimate visions of human life conflict. It cannot always be wrong to insist on personal revelation, to refuse to consider any further other voices and views, or to simply declare that one's own views are those best supported by reason even when one's reasons have given out. It cannot always be wrong to stop talking, even to stop listening, and act. At times we must do so if our values are to mean anything to us. We have even more reason to do so when we see those values to be threatened, when *we* are threatened. Decisive action on behalf of those values can, and no doubt at times should, take precedence over the virtue of acknowledging and listening to other voices and views. And the question of when one has taken enough time and considered enough views may itself be an essentially contestable question. This is not to say that there aren't clear cases of wrongfully impetuous action, but we do not often have such clear cases. Or there will be disagreement on what constitutes a clear case.

The Will to Truth versus the Need for Action

One might fear that opposing a morality of conviction that demonizes and polarizes is to expose oneself to the moral danger of lack of conviction. Decisive action—particularly if it takes the form of an attack on others—can indeed be undermined by the will to carefully examine all sides of a conflict, to see one's own history of evil and some legitimacy in the grievances of one's enemies. Yet it is a mistake to think that those who oppose the demonizers have no ethical place to stand. That place is a strong commitment to moral truth, to all of it, even to that possessed by one's enemies. The will to moral truth is a will to see clearly whatever is there: clear, bright lines between good and evil where they do exist, and ambiguity and fuzziness where these exist. The will to moral truth refuses to give in to wishful thinking that there should be clear bright lines every time one needs to take action, however much one might need to take action out of fear and anger and grief and sorrow, as was the state of many Americans after 9/11. To will the moral truth is to recognize that the reasons for one's own moral views give out, as well as the reasons for views one rejects. Unlike the moral demonizers it opposes, this will to truth admits the contingency of its priority over other moral imperatives. To will the moral truth is to recognize that the need to act under severe circumstances might have to prevail over the will to search out complexity and ambiguity, and that this possibility is itself part of the moral truth.

In some circumstances, the will to moral truth *does* support decisiveness. It can help one stand firm against the demonizers when their haste promises disaster. The attacks of 9/11 created a sense of looming threat and urgency that was exacerbated by ignorance of what the United States was up against. It made decisiveness and aggressive response the preferred virtues for many Americans over reflective, tempered and nuanced response, over taking the time to learn more, say, about the possible connections between Iraq and al Qaeda, or the actual threat posed by Iraq in terms of nuclear and biological weapons, or the time to actually discuss and assess and actually plan for the ambitious vision of making Iraq a beacon of democracy that would transform the Middle East. The mainstream news media in the U.S was intimidated by the sense of siege and failed to vigorously interrogate the various and variable official rationales for the Iraq war. This failure to interrogate sprang from moral weakness and panic, not strength. It takes courage and resolution to stand firm in the face of panic. Moreover, when the right course of action is compromise, negotiation, and efforts to achieve rapprochement, it can be served by the recognition of ambiguity.[24]

With that said, it must be granted that the will to truth can run against the grain of human nature in ways that other of our moral ideals do. When people have an emotional investment in moral norms and when these norms are violated, they tend not to consider the motivations and viewpoints of the violators but to judge simply on the basis of outcome.[25] That is why people tend to react with outrage when civilians in their country are killed as a result of "collateral damage," even if it is clear from a more detached perspective that the deaths were unintended and that measures were taken to avoid them. That is why people tend not to take seriously the motivations for terrorist attacks on their societies, even if from a more detached perspective these motivations are based on some truth. The problem posed by this tendency is not special to terrorism and perceptions of Western exploitation of the Middle East, however. That is why judges explicitly instruct juries that they must take into account the intentions of those being tried for serious crimes,[26] and jury members do take heed at least some of the time.

The demonization of others is very much connected with the human tendency to distinguish between in-groups and out-groups. Experiments have divided subjects into groups on the basis of criteria they know to be arbitrary and/or trivial, but they still tend to associate more desirable attributes to their own groups, to behave in more prosocial and cooperative ways toward members of their own groups, and to overestimate the similarities with members of their own groups and their dissimilarities with members of other groups. When prejudicial attitudes toward real, socially defined groups (e.g., racial and ethnic groups) are investigated, people demonstrate a tendency to recognize more diversity of attributes possessed by members of their own groups and to see members of other groups as similar and interchangeable (Osama bin Laden equals Saddam Hussein). People tend to explain negative behaviors of out-group members by reference to enduring personality traits of these members and to ignore situational explanations. They give the reverse explanation for positive behaviors of out-group members. One theory purporting to explain such biases is that favoritism toward one's own group is an outgrowth of the urge to bolster self-esteem. Another factor might be the epistemic need to rely on simplifying social categories to manage the intake of potentially overwhelming information about one's social environment. Thus motivations and needs that are unobjectionable and even inevitable help to create perceptions and attitudes that cause and exacerbate conflict.[27]

Such tendencies present problems for any ethic that requires fair and respectful treatment of those outside one's social groups—problems, therefore, for any ethic that holds any promise to help us navigate in an increasingly globalized and interdependent world. Some hope lies in the recognition that bolstering self-esteem need not always result in denigration of out-groups. Though we do tend to judge how well we are doing by comparison with others around us, feeling better about ourselves does not *necessarily* require viewing others in an unfavorable light. Studies of groups formed for the purpose of experimentation reveals that when combined in a "super" group united by pursuit of a common goal, subjects tend to judge former out-group members as favorably as their former in-group members.[28] Studies of socially established groups also point to intergroup cooperation toward common ends as sometimes promoting reductions in prejudice, but only when the pursuit of common ends meet with success.[29] Another relevant theme from social psychology is that minority groups over time can have an impact on the views of majority groups, at least if the former have channels of communication to the latter and are consistent in the dissenting messages they send.[30] We must pursue such hopes for greater understanding of others and ourselves, tempered, as these hopes must be, with sobering qualification.

Conclusions

It is not difficult to see much of ourselves in the other we condemn as savagely malignant. We see in them our tendency to demonize others who pose a severe threat to us; we see in ourselves their tendency to shut off other views and voices from those they already view as threats. These perceptions can be vices, but not always. We must exercise our best judgment as to when we are justified in our perceptions and when ambiguity persists in the matter of how much truth is on our side and on theirs. It will sometimes be right to stay our hand. At other times we might reach the point of having to act against the other side with violence and with the consequences of foreseeable death to innocents.

The one unambiguous virtue we might exhibit in such circumstances is being honest about shutting off the other voices when we do so, for the sake of decisiveness, for the sake of a conviction that cannot be fully explained or justified to skeptical others. And to be honest to others, we must be honest with ourselves, and that is difficult because it may undermine our ability to act on our perceptions. It is much easier to act against others when we have managed to persuade ourselves that we have listened to them as much as they merit, and that they are as savagely malignant as we need to believe they are. Decisive action, especially when it takes the form of violence against others, can be easier to undertake when we are willing to exercise selective attention to support the rightness of what we are doing and at the same time deny that we are exercising selective attention. It is easier to approve of sending young people off to their deaths in combat if one lets oneself believe they will be fighting malignant evildoers rather than to acknowledge that the evildoers might have some truth on their side and yet decide that they must be fought anyway. It is also dangerous to be blinded to whatever truth the other side's views embody, because it prevents one from addressing issues on which the other side gains adherents. It may or may not be true that the U.S. invasion of Iraq ultimately wins more adherents to al Qaeda's cause than it kills or scares off, but we had better not let it distract us from features of U.S. policy that alienate those who would not otherwise be sympathetic to al Qaeda. In this respect the demonization of al Qaeda and its agglomeration with Saddam Hussein can amount to a self-inflicted wound.

Isaiah Berlin, at the end of his famous essay, "Two Concepts of Liberty," quotes Joseph Schumpeter: "To realise the relative validity of one's convictions and yet to stand unflinchingly for them is what distinguishes a civilised [person] from a barbarian."[31] This remark has the air of paradox. How could one stand unflinchingly for one's convictions and at the same time be aware of their "relative validity?" And why is this civilized? The conclusion of this essay suggests that the mark of a civilized person is willingness to confront whatever truth is held by one's enemies; it is willingness to listen to and pursue their truth at risk to oneself and one's own; but one must judge when the risk is too high and act to oppose them. One stands unflinchingly because one must decide when one can no longer listen; and one must then take responsibility for the consequences of that decision, especially when one's actions have regrettable results or are based on mistaken assumptions. It may strike many that the line from W.B. Yeats's "The Second Coming," applies to our time: "The best lack all conviction, and the worst are full of passionate intensity." The argument of this paper is for a conclusion less striking, and fortunately, less pessimistic: the best are able to act in the face of moral ambiguity when they ought, with full awareness of the ways in which they may have contributed to that ambiguity through their own hypocrisy and injustice. And the worst are simply full of blind self-righteousness.

ACKNOWLEDGMENT

Thanks to the participants in the "Speak No Evil" conference for their helpful comments and especially to my respondent, Philip Costanzo, who provided an illuminating psychologist's perspective on my essay. I offer my keenest appreciation to Ruth Grant for her detailed and thoughtful editor's comments and more generally for serving as the intellectual and spiritual force behind not only the conference but also the faculty seminar that gave birth to our essays.

NOTES

1. Sayyid Qutb, *Milestones* (Chicago: Kazi Publications, 1993), p. 7.

2. Remarks by President Bush on Operation Iraqi Freedom and Operation Enduring Freedom, March 19, 2004, text at http://www.whitehouse.gov/news/releases/2004/03/20040319-3.html (accessed July 7, 2004).

3. There might be good reasons to weaken such constraints, e.g., if the enemy truly presents a realistic threat to civilization itself, but such a reason does not apply to al Qaeda. The fact that it seemed willing to stop at nothing to accomplish its ends is not a sufficient moral reason to loosen constraints on combating it. It requires a realistic threat of tremendous magnitude.

4. Address to a Joint Session of Congress and the American People, September 20, 2001, transcript at http://www.whitehouse.gov/news/releases/2001/09/20010920-8.html (accessed July 20, 2004).

5. A CBS/New York Times poll taken on March 7–9, 2003 revealed that 45 percent of the American public thought that Saddam was personally involved. See http://www.cbsnews.com/htdocs/CBSNews_polls/iraq_back310.pdf. A Washington Post poll taken from August 7–11, 2003, revealed that 69 percent of the American public believed that it is very likely (32 percent) or somewhat likely (37 percent) that Saddam Hussein was personally involved in the 9/11 attacks. See *Washington Post*, Saturday 6, 2003. Results available at http://www.washingtonpost.com/wp-srv/politics/polls/vault/stories/data082303.htm (accessed July 25, 2004).

6. John L. Esposito, *Unholy War: Terror in the Name of Islam* (Oxford: Oxford University Press, 2002), p. 8. Esposito also points out that one of Qutb's brothers, Dr. Muhammed Qutb, was one of Osama bin Laden's teachers.

7. Qutb, *Milestones*, pp. 97–98.

8. The "700 Club" telecast on Sept 13, 2001. A transcript of the relevant remarks are available on http://www.truthorfiction.com/rumors/f/falwell-robertson-wtc.htm (accessed July 18, 2004).

9. Sayyid Qutb, *Social Justice in Islam*, trans. John B. Hardie (Oneonta, New York: Islamic Publications International, 1953), p. 135.

10. Qutb, *Social Justice in Islam*, p. 257.

11. Qutb, *Social Justice in Islam*, pp. 292, 315.

12. John L. Esposito, *Terror in the Name of Islam*, p. 27.

13. In his State of the Union address on February 2, 2005, for example. See http://www.whitehouse.gov/stateoftheunion/2005/ (accessed May 11, 2005).

14. Ahmad S. Moussalli, *Moderate and Radical Islamic Fundamentalism: The Quest for Modernity, Legitimacy, and the Islamic State* (Gainesville: University Press of Florida, 1999), p. 48.

15. Moussalli, *Moderate and Radical Islamic Fundamentalism*, p. 184.

16. Robert Fogelin argues persuasively that this removal of the usual parameters is ultimately behind forms of skepticism about knowledge. Skeptical doubts create contexts of justification that outstrip any arsenal of reasons in our possession. See *Walking the Tightrope of Reason: The Precarious Life of a Rational Animal* (New York: Oxford University Press, 2003).

17. Ladan and Roya Bouroumand, "Terror, Islam, and Democracy," *Journal of Democracy* 13 (2002): 17–18.

18. Michael Walzer, "World War II: Why Was This War Different?" *Philosophy and Public Affairs* 1 (1971): 18–19.

19. Ervin Staub in *The Psychology of Good and Evil: Why Children, Adults, and Groups Help and Harm Others* (Cambridge: Cambridge University Press, 2003), pp. 353–354.

20. Richard P. Mitchell, "The Islamic Movement: Its Current Condition and Future Prospects," in *The Islamic Impulse*, ed. Barbara Freyer Stowasser (London: Croom Helm, 1987), pp. 84–85. A good discussion of Mitchell's views can be found in John O. Voll's foreword to *The Society of the Muslim Brothers* by Richard P. Mitchell (New York: Oxford University Press, 1993).

21. Richard T. Antoun, *Understanding Fundamentalism: Christian, Islamic, and Jewish Movements* (Walnut Creek, CA: Altamira Press, 2001), p. 42.

22. Cited in Antoun, *Understanding Fundamentalism*, pp. 42–43, from the *New York Times*, November 1, 1979.

23. Joseph Raz, "Multiculturalism: A Liberal Perspective," *Dissent* 41 (1994): 73.

24. There is considerable irony in the fact that fulminations against "moral relativism" have degenerated into unreflective bashing of those pointing out moral ambiguity and that reasons run out on both sides in serious and fundamental moral conflict. Such crusaders for "moral truth" seldom offer careful defense of their truth against rival conceptions. Unreflective moral absolutists show a curious subjectivism about what the moral truth is at the same time they are claiming objectivity for their conceptions of the moral truth.

25. See Philip Costanzo, "Morals, Mothers, and Memories: The Social Context of Developing Social Cognition," in *Context and Development*, ed. R. Cohen and A.W. Siegal (Hillsdale, NJ: Erlbaum, 1991), pp. 91–132. I have extracted (hopefully in an accurate fashion) but one implication of a very rich study of the ways that people's commitments to values and norms can affect the way they judge the actions of others in ways that do not conform to impersonal norms for reasoning.

26. A point made by Costanzo in "Morals, Mothers, and Memories," p. 109.

27. Thanks to Philip Costanzo for pointing me in the direction of the relevant psychological studies of the psychological tendencies underlying demonization. The results of studies mentioned here are described in Patricia G. Devine, "Prejudice and Out-Group Perception," in *Advanced Social Psychology*, ed. Abraham Tesser (New York: McGraw-Hill, 1995), pp. 467–478.

28. Devine, "Prejudice and Out-Group Perception," pp. 479–480.

29. Devine, "Prejudice and Out-Group Perception," p. 500. The theme of intergroup cooperation towards common ends brings to mind the initial lack of response from the White House to the 2004 natural disasters of the earthquake and tsunami that struck countries bordering the Indian Ocean, including Indonesia, the most populous Muslim-majority nation in the world. In particular, the lack of comment from President Bush for three days, and the relatively small amount of aid initially pledged by the United States, constituted a missed opportunity for the United States to mitigate the hostility between Muslim peoples and the U.S. The fact that the White House seemed to recognize this mistake and took some steps to undo it is again some cause for sobered hope.

30. Serge Moscovici has been especially influential in articulating this theme. See his *Social Influence and Social Change* (London: Academic Press, 1976).

31. Joseph Schumpeter, *Capitalism, Socialism, and Democracy* (London: Harper and Brothers, 1943), p. 243; as quoted by Isaiah Berlin in "Two Concepts of Liberty," in *Liberty: Incorporating Four Essays on Liberty* (Oxford: Oxford University Press, 2002), p. 217.

Combining Clarity and Complexity
A Layered Approach to Cross-Cultural Ethics

Can moral judgment combine the virtues of clarity and complexity? Too often, the answer seems to be *no*. We find ourselves lurching between two visions of ethics, the first a confident absolutism of black-and-white judgments, the second an ethic of contingency that paints moral life in a shimmer of grays.

Geoffrey Harpham regards this tension between bright lines and "proliferating distinctions [and] refinements" as "central to the ethical enterprise itself."[1] It is, in any case, a core moral dilemma of our era. Its difficulty stems from the way each ethic attracts as well as repels. A morality of bright lines stands for something: it is an ethic of strong convictions and principled action. But it can also lack moral imagination, lapsing into self-righteousness, dogmatism, even fanaticism. By contrast, a morality of nuanced judgment exhibits a rich moral imagination, an intelligent and self-critical encounter with a complex world. But its logic of "on the one hand, on the other hand" qualifications all too often results in moral paralysis and an evasion of moral responsibility.

The danger, hauntingly captured by William Butler Yeats in "The Second Coming," is that the shadow sides of clarity and complexity will come to dominate our moral life and discourse, pitting fanaticism against moral equivocation. In such a world, Yeats warned,

> the best lack all conviction, while the worst
> are filled with passionate intensity.[2]

Cross-cultural moral disagreements are especially prone to these twin dangers of dogmatism and moral paralysis. Confronted by a practice that has substantial support within another culture or group but is widely condemned within our own (or vice versa), we may be tempted to issue a summary judgment, to stand firm while making little or no effort to understand the other's perspective or to reflect critically on our own. Or we may strenuously seek to engage with other perspectives and, in the process, lose all sense of where we stand, ultimately throwing up our hands and exclaiming, "Who am I to judge?"

Five Layers of Moral Judgment

The challenge is to construct approaches to moral judgment that combine the virtues of clarity and complexity while avoiding their vices. In this chapter, I attempt to do this by distinguishing among five layers of moral judgment—judgments about the rightness or wrongness of

1. an action or practice;
2. the motivations, interests, and goals of individuals who engage in or defend it;
3. the social contexts that shape, sustain, and give meaning to it;
4. our own standing, motivations, and responsibilities in relation to it; and
5. our possible responses to it.

While each of these is familiar to moral theorists, conceiving them as *layers* highlights their role as elements of an overarching moral assessment. Each layer raises distinct and important moral questions and choices, which are to some degree independent of one another, so that black-and-white judgments in one layer are compatible with more complex judgments in other layers. At the same time, judgments within one layer help clarify the moral stakes in other layers. Ignoring any of the layers diminishes our capacity to understand, evaluate, and respond to a situation. Indeed, the moral weaknesses of both dogmatism and moral equivocation can be traced to a refusal or inability to confront one or more of the layers.

I develop this model of moral judgment through a discussion of two contemporary practices that inspire deep cross-cultural moral disagreement. The first is terrorism, and particularly the tactic of suicide bombings—or what its proponents term "martyrdom operations."[3] The second is female genital mutilation, also called female genital cutting, circumcision, or surgery, as well as by a variety of traditional terms such as "purification."

While they are obviously very different, these practices share features that make them appropriate for this analysis. Both involve the infliction of irreparable physical injury. Both are defended, even venerated, as moral acts that help to ensure a community's survival and dignity. And both have been condemned as cruel or evil practices that must be stopped in the interest of humanity and civilization.

There is also an instructive contrast between them. In the wake of the 9/11 attacks, terrorism has attained, for many Westerners and especially Americans, the status of a prime evil. We have seen the emergence of a Manichean public rhetoric about the war on terror that bears all the hallmarks of an ethic of clarity in its most extreme form. By contrast, Western responses to female genital mutilation have been far less confident and indeed more prone to the opposite reaction of a suspension of moral judgment in the face of paralyzing complexity.[4]

The "War on Terror" and the Appeal of Manicheanism

The al Qaeda attacks in the United States on September 11, 2001, as well as in Kenya, Tanzania, Bali, and Egypt, the U.S. declaration of a war on terror, the invasions of Afghanistan and Iraq, the Oklahoma City bombing, the second Palestinian intifada and the Israeli occupation, the Russian-Chechen conflict, and hostage takings in Russia, Iraq, and Afghanistan, have made terrorism and the responses to it one of the central moral and political challenges of our age. The choice of terrorism itself reveals deep moral polarization—people adopt terrorist tactics out of rage and resentment against a despised enemy. But judgments *about* terrorism also tend to take a stark and polarized form.

Indeed, one of the striking features of moral judgment in the aftermath of 9/11, particularly in the United States, has been the emergence of a Manichean rhetoric about a global war on terror that labels terrorism and all terrorists as utterly evil and, at the same time, brands any attempt to articulate a more complex moral judgment, whether about terrorists, the causes they advocate, appropriate ways of responding to terrorism, or the conditions that promote or obstruct terrorism, as a lapse in moral judgment. This morality of bright lines confidently proclaims that we, who represent civilization, freedom, and goodness, face a battle with a demonic global force, the "enemies of freedom." "We" are decent, courageous, and heroic, whereas "they" are cowards who envy and hate us. Those who take issue with any part of this vision are immediately under suspicion of being "soft on terror," or insensitive to the victims of terror, or even treacherously disloyal to our side.[5]

To be sure, we occasionally encounter a different Manichean rhetoric that is almost a mirror image of the first. In this, the critique of terrorism is regarded as a distraction from the true source of evil, which is American imperialism or Israeli or Russian state terror, and the resort to terrorist tactics by the victims of these forces is portrayed as an inevitable and reasonable response. This morality of bright lines confidently proclaims that the true enemies of freedom and justice are not those who are labeled terrorists but those who do the labeling. Anyone who tries to articulate a more complex moral position by, for instance, condemning those who choose, condone, or glorify terrorism in the service of any cause, however just, is immediately under suspicion for failing to grasp the heart of the matter.

Both of these Manichean responses to terrorism focus on a single, powerful villain. Both are deeply suspicious of moral complexity, of any suggestions that there are fateful moral and political choices, legitimate interests, and potential villainies on all sides. Such moral simplification is, of course, typical in wartime. It is also logically flawed and morally dangerous.

The logical flaw of this response is to suppose that any second moral judgment weakens or vitiates the first, particularly if the second judgment is an acknowledgment of wrongdoing on "our side" or of legitimate grievances on "their side." So, for instance, we cannot condemn the Beslan school hostage atrocity while also condemning the Russian army's gross human rights violations in Chechnya, because the second judgment undermines the first. Yet this is not the case. We can simultaneously criticize the Russian army's campaign of murder, rape, looting, and destruction (and note that it is helping to create the conditions for Shamil Basayev's Chechen-Muslim extremist movement to arise and grow), while condemning Basayev's tactics of killing and terrorizing Russian civilians as morally inexcusable.[6] In fact, both of these judgments are rooted in the same commitments to human dignity and rights and the same prohibitions against targeting noncombatants.

Or, to take another example, we can condemn terrorism while drawing moral distinctions among individual terrorists—between, for instance, the culpability of men like Basayev, who took credit for the Beslan school hostage taking, or the leaders of the al Aqsa Martyrs' Brigades who recruit and train teenagers for suicide missions, and that of Hussam Abdo, the fifteen-year-old would-be suicide bomber who, after he was disarmed by Israeli soldiers, admitted that his main reasons for volunteering to perform his mission were to avenge the death of a school friend, to avoid having to go back to school, and because all the kids at his school thought martyrdom was "better than being a singer or a footballer."[7]

Thus drawing one moral line (killing and terrorizing schoolchildren or commuters is horribly wrong) does not prevent us from drawing another one (between adults who dream up schemes to kill and terrorize commuters and schoolchildren, and recruit others—including children—to carry them out, and a child who thoughtlessly succumbs to their influence).

The moral danger of adopting two-dimensional Manichean rhetoric about terrorism is that it makes us lose sight of these and many other morally relevant features of the situation, and especially that it blinds us to the moral dangers and stakes involved in our own responses to it. If we see ourselves as engaged in a cosmic battle of good against evil, we are likely to be blind to our own capacities for evil and more willing to set aside moral constraints, such as those against torture or indiscriminate targeting, in waging war.

But can we resist these dangerous moral simplifications and develop a more complex set of judgments about terrorism without lapsing into the opposite vices of murkiness and equivocation? That is, is it possible to engage the layered complexities of terrorism while still coming to a clear moral judgment about terrorism as a tactic? I want to demonstrate that it is possible by taking each of the five layers of moral judgment in turn.

(1) Judging the practice of terrorism

How should we judge terrorism? Is it unequivocally wrong? Or, as the adage goes, is "one man's terrorist another man's freedom fighter"? One curious feature of discussions of terrorism is the degree of disagreement that persists over the word's definition. The United Nations, for example, has no official definition of terrorism but a hodgepodge of twelve conventions outlawing specific terrorist acts, from hijacking to hostage taking.[8] Commentators differ on whether terrorism can be committed by states or only by nonstate actors, on whether its targets must be civilians, on whether victims must be selected at random (so that assassination, for instance, would not count as terrorism), on whether terrorism can only occur in peacetime (so that the same actions in wartime would count as war crimes, not terrorism) and on whether terrorist acts must aim to cause widespread terror in order to influence the behavior of a "target" group or government in a particular way.

I will employ what I believe is the clearest and most coherent definition of terrorism: *the deliberate use of violence against civilians or noncombatants in pursuit of a cause.* Terrorism is a tactic that intentionally targets ordinary civilians. It is distinct from guerilla warfare, which typically targets combatants, as well as from precisely targeted assassinations. It is the nature of the target that defines terrorism. Thus terrorism can be employed by states as well as by nonstate actors, in peacetime as well as in the conduct of an officially declared war.[9]

Is there a bright moral line that terrorism crosses, a line that must not be crossed? I believe there is. Terrorism is evil because it uses force against defenseless individuals who should not be targeted.[10] The immunity of noncombatants derives from a belief in the value of individual human life, as well as from fundamental notions of fair play in the employment of violence.[11] It also rests on a recognition that violence is humanity's most terrible and dangerous capacity, which must be controlled and constrained by ethics and law. Among our impulses to violence, targeting the defenseless—who since time immemorial have been "soft targets"—is both the easiest and the most brutal and horrifying. Protecting noncombatants is therefore central to the preservation of our humanity and, for those of us who are not pacifists, to any coherent conception of justified violence.

The principle of noncombatant immunity has an ancient pedigree. It is at the heart of the medieval Christian just war tradition[12] and has been most elaborately developed in this context. But it also appears in many other religious and ethical traditions. For instance, the Hindu *Laws of Manu* provide a detailed list of targets a warrior may not strike, including "anyone asleep, without armor, naked, without a weapon, not fighting, looking on, or engaged with someone else."[13] And both the Koran and Islamic prophetic traditions contain injunctions to show restraint and not to strike, maim, or kill women, children, and those who are not fighting.[14]

The term "terrorism" itself is of course already morally laden. Those who defend the targeting of noncombatants generally describe their tactics in different terms. They speak of wars of political and psychological liberation, as Jean-Paul Sartre did in defending Algerian terrorism.[15] Or they refer to "martyrdom operations" as Palestinian organizations engaged in suicide bombings do.[16] Or they call the bombing of civilians by euphemisms such as "area bombing" or "efforts to weaken enemy morale," as defenders of Allied obliteration bombing did during World War Two.[17]

Defenders of terrorist tactics generally appeal to one, or a combination, of three types of justification. The first is a claim of "supreme emergency"—the assertion that our community or cause is faced with an overwhelming existential threat and must resort to killing civilians in order to avoid annihilation. This argument is often invoked to justify Palestinian suicide bombings,[18] with many proponents drawing a parallel to Muhammad's decision to launch a jihad against the Meccans when the threat to the Islamic community in Medina had become unbearable.[19] Similar appeals to supreme emergency were invoked to justify the use of carpet bombing against German cities during World War Two.[20] A weaker form of this claim appeals to "military necessity," suggesting that, whether or not a community's survival is on the line, war cannot be waged successfully without resort to terrorist tactics.

The second justification for terrorism appeals to the principle of *lex talionis,* "an eye for an eye," and asserts that the targeting of civilians is justified retribution for violence suffered by civilians on our side. Osama bin Laden has invoked the idea that Allah permits "the wronged one to retaliate against the oppressor in kind," arguing that the World Trade Center bombing was justified retribution for the 1982 bombardment of Lebanon, which destroyed twin high rises and killed civilians.[21] Palestinian defenders of suicide bombings, including the bombers themselves in their last wills and testaments, make similar claims.[22] John Ford cataloged numerous public appeals to *lex talionis* in defense of the large-scale bombing of German civilians. "We will mete out to the Germans the measure and more than the measure that they have meted out to us," Churchill declared in one speech, adding in another: "there is something after all in the old and still valid Golden Rule." "Once the enemy starts it," asserted a 1944 American editorial defending obliteration bombing, poison gas, and other tactics, "it becomes no longer a moral but a military question." And another asked, "Why be nice about the undefended towns and cities? . . . The time-honored system of tit for tat is the only one which Hitler and his Germans can understand." [23]

Finally, the third justification for terrorism is the claim that it is impossible or inappropriate to distinguish between soldiers and civilians, combatants and noncombatants. This argument has been made about modern warfare in general, citing the wartime mobilization of populations, on the one hand, and the frequent conscription of soldiers, on the other.[24] It has also been claimed about particular states or peoples. For instance, Barry Buzan recently questioned what he called the "Western fetish" of noncombatant immunity, arguing that the legitimacy of targeting civilians depends on whether the people support and "deserve" their government and suggesting that in some instances, including Israel, Palestine, and Serbia, war against civilians may be morally permissible.[25] In a similar vein, Sheikh Ahmed Yassin, founder of Hamas, wrote, "Are there any civilians in Israel? They are all soldiers, men and women, except those religious persons who do not serve in the army. The rest are all soldiers. The only difference is that they wear civilians clothes when they are in Israel, and military clothes when they come to us."[26]

It is interesting to note that each of these justifications assumes that the targeting of civilians requires special moral justification. None simply asserts the permissibility of killing civilians. In this sense terrorism is different from genocide, which conceives a people's annihilation as a good to be achieved, as well as from the kind of warfare depicted in the Iliad or in the Athenian attack on Melos—aggression against whole communities for the sake of power, plunder, and glory, what William James termed "piratical war."[27]

The moral logic I want to defend rejects these justifications for terrorism and draws a bright line in the same way that the ban on torture does. It states that it is never morally permissible to resort to the tactic of deliberately targeting civilians, no matter how just your cause. Nor is it permissible to employ torture or terrorist violence because your opponent does.

It is possible to condemn terrorist tactics and to think there is little more to say about terrorism except that it must be defeated at all costs. This is the Manichean position I sketched earlier, which moves from a confident judgment about the practice to confident judgments about the need and the means to destroy it. The clear ban on terrorism I want to defend, however, is not only compatible with, but in some respects dependent on, an acknowledgment of complexity. That is, it draws part of its insistence on a bright line from a recognition of the power and danger of the arguments justifying terrorism.

The weakest of these arguments is the claim that it is impossible to distinguish between soldiers and civilians, combatants and noncombatants. To assert that there is no morally relevant distinction between civilians in a sidewalk café or on a commercial flight and armed soldiers in a fortified position is absurd. To be sure, there are gray areas (for instance, civilians who work in munitions or in telecommunications facilities vital to the war effort) and situations in which drawing the combatant/noncombatant distinction is genuinely difficult, as when indigenous peoples face territorial invasion by armed settlers. Nevertheless, the presence of hard cases does not render the distinction itself meaningless, particularly since the overwhelming majority of terrorist attacks victimize people who are unambiguously noncombatants. As John Ford noted, "it is a fairly common fallacy in legal and moral argumentation to conclude that all is lost because there is a field of uncertainty to which our carefully formulated moral principles cannot be applied with precision."[28]

A far stronger challenge is posed to the principle of noncombatant immunity by *lex talionis,* an eye for an eye, since this represents a rival clear and coherent moral logic for judging terrorism. The idea of *lex talionis,* of justice requiring proportional retribution, has deep roots in many cultures and religions (including, notably, the culture of Hollywood), and is one of the strongest candidates for being a universal cross-cultural moral value.[29] Moreover, in some cultures *lex talionis* has been linked to a conception of collective guilt that permitted retribution not only against the individual perpetrator but also against members of a perpetrator's family, tribe, or community, thus justifying attacks against random civilians in reprisal for civilian deaths on one's own side. To reject *lex talionis* in favor of an alternative moral vision of noncombatant immunity requires an act of judgment that noncombatant immunity affirms a higher conception of human dignity and has a better chance of making our world less ferocious and more humane. In making this judgment, however, it is important to recognize the enduring appeal of ideas of collective retribution—in order both to understand our enemies and to recognize our own side's temptation to seek indiscriminate retribution in fighting them.

The most difficult challenge to a bright line ban on terrorism comes from appeals to "supreme emergency." Just as with torture, so with terrorism, there is debate over whether there are extreme circumstances in which a purportedly absolute ban can and must be overridden. In a "ticking bomb" scenario, is it permissible to torture a suspect in custody if there is no other alternative for gathering information that could save many lives? And when the very survival of a community is at stake, when "a weaker party is threatened with annihilation or enslavement by a stronger one," is it permissible to resort to terrorism? These are agonizingly difficult moral questions.[30] Many Westerners defend Winston Churchill's decision to employ carpet bombing against German cities, killing hundreds of thousands of civilians, on the grounds that the horrifying prospect of an imminent Nazi victory compelled the Allies to override the rules of war.[31]

The problem with the argument from supreme emergency is threefold. First, our judgments about existential threats are notoriously biased and manipulable. The rhetoric of supreme emergency is pervasive in statements by terrorist organizations, and in many cases based on genuine fear. Yet is it truly the case that Palestinians or Serbians face imminent annihilation and have no other option but to target civilians? There is little evidence that any actually existing terrorist movement has arisen out of a situation of "supreme emergency" or in a context where no other alternative was available. Second, we have seen, time and again, the horrifying ways that torture and terrorism, once employed, get normalized as legitimate forms of violence. The dramatic rise of suicide bombings in the past two decades as an element of the "accepted repertoire" of violence is one example.[32] Closer to home, the danger was demonstrated, in the case of torture, by the U.S. Justice Department's August 2002 memorandum defending the use of torture in times of national emergency and subsequent revelations of torture being practiced at U.S. detention centers in Iraq, Afghanistan, and Cuba.[33] Those who defend Allied carpet bombings in the period immediately after the fall of France have to acknowledge that the deliberate mass killing of German civilians continued well past any reasonable claim of military necessity, culminating in the devastating firebombing of Dresden in the spring of 1945 when the war was almost over. Indeed, even Churchill began to wonder whether the time had come "when the question of bombing German cities simply for the sake of increasing the terror . . . should be reviewed."[34] Finally, while the issue requires far more analysis than I can provide here, the military and prudential arguments for resorting to terrorism are themselves highly problematic. Did the Allied bombings weaken or stiffen German resistance? Did the second Palestinian intifada make the survival of a Palestinian political community more or less likely?

It is all too human to invoke "extraordinary circumstances" in an expansive way and to allow atrocities to become routinized. So while the argument from "supreme emergency" is quite compelling, its slippery power should prompt us to adopt an absolute prohibition on terrorist tactics. As Thomas Nagel noted, it is "important not to lose confidence in our absolutist intuitions, for they are often the only barrier before the abyss of utilitarian apologetics for large-scale murder."[35]

I have tried to show that a bright line ban on terrorist tactics is compatible with an acknowledgment of moral complexity in judging the practice of terrorism. Consideration of the other layers of moral judgment shows that the condemnation of the practice is only the beginning of a chain of fateful moral choices.

(2) Judging the motivations, interests, and goals of those who engage in or defend terrorism

While a Manichean approach to terrorism paints a sweeping and monochromatic portrait of terrorists as evil enemies of freedom, a layered model of moral judgment compels us to engage in a more fine-grained analysis of the motivations, interests, and goals of those who engage in or defend terrorism. It brings into sharper focus the human realities of those who lead or get swept up in terrorist movements. The dour fanatic Mohammad Atta and the barely reformed playboy Ziad Jarrah, two of the 9/11 pilots, are very different individuals, as are the arrogant warlord Shamil Basayev and the naïve teenage suicide bomber Hussam Abdo. Bringing them into focus does not obscure the horror of their deeds, but it prompts us to think more deeply and intelligently about how they came to engage in them—to examine, for instance, how a cult of martyrdom gets established and what it will take to dismantle it. It allows us, too, to judge individual terrorists more fairly, not as interchangeable perpetrators but as individual human beings who, in different ways, came to participate in a cruel and evil practice.

The growing phenomenon of suicide bombings poses a special challenge in evaluating the motives of terrorists, for it associates the widely admired figure of the martyr with the tactic of terrorism. We consider people who are willing to give their lives for a cause brave and unselfish. To what extent should a suicide bomber's willingness to die affect our judgment of him or her?[36]

Mohammed Hafez's study of Palestinian suicide bombings provides a nuanced analysis of the reasons why individuals and organizations engage in suicide terrorist attacks. Drawing on the last wills and testaments of suicide bombers as well as on interviews with family members and with bombers whose missions were foiled, Hafez presents a portrait of young men and women "dying for God and country," who see their action as a righteous form of religious and patriotic self-sacrifice grounded in a vision of "redemption, empowerment, and defiance against unjust authorities."[37] For some, the decision to volunteer is grounded in a specific desire to seek revenge for the death of a loved one or of victims with whom they identify. For others, it is an effort to prove themselves before their families and comrades.

Hafez argues that while the individual motivations of suicide bombers tend to have a high-minded character, the rhetoric of the organizations that employ the tactic is dramatically different. Among both religious and secular groups, it focuses on instrumental calculations in the context of asymmetric warfare (suicide bombing is a low-risk, low-tech way to achieve a higher ratio of Israelis to Palestinians killed), as well as on factional competition among insurgent groups, who successively adopted suicide bombing once they realized its tactical and publicity value.[38]

Judging the motives behind terrorism is thus more complicated than it may first appear to be. In the Palestinian case, individual suicide bombers profess reasons reminiscent of young volunteer soldiers else-where, whereas organizational leaders reveal a cold-blooded military cal-culus that "counts" civilian deaths as valuable prizes and supports a cult of martyrdom to assist in recruiting more "human bombs." Rather than conceiving terrorists as a monolithic class of perpetrators, it is appropri-ate to draw moral distinctions between terrorist leaders who recruit sui-cide bombers, especially young or gullible ones, and the suicide bombers themselves. But this does not change our assessment of their deeds. The willingness to die does not justify taking civilian victims with you. Nor should it make us forget the indifference to the fear and suffering of victims, the willed hardheartedness, that is a central feature of the moral psychology of terrorism.

A more fine-grained analysis also allows us to draw important dis-tinctions among the ideological visions and political goals of those who employ terrorism. Sweeping generalizations about a single global net-work of terrorists bent on destroying freedom blinds us to the particu-larities of, for instance, al Qaeda's vision of theocracy, making us ill-equipped to make common cause with those best positioned to argue against it. It also blinds us to the just causes and legitimate grievances that have become entangled in terrorist movements, such as the Chechen and Palestinian peoples' desire for recognition and political autonomy or self-determination, or their opposition to the indignities and deprivations of occupation.

We can condemn an action while rendering a distinct judgment about whether it was performed in a just or unjust cause—as, for instance, the South African Truth and Reconciliation Commission did when it con-demned torture unequivocally, whether it was committed by policemen defending the apartheid regime or by antiapartheid activists, even while making it clear that apartheid was an unjust system and opposition to it, a just cause.

A willingness to engage this second layer of judgment is important for both moral and prudential reasons. It enables us to understand the phe-nomenon of terrorism more fully and fairly and is more likely, in the long run, to lead to stable solutions. But confronting the complexity of this second layer can also be difficult, because it requires us to abandon the psychological distancing that fuels the simple us-versus-them duali-ties of Manicheanism and to recognize the humanity of our enemies.

A focus on motivation also raises a different, fateful moral difficulty. On my definition, terrorism is limited to *intentional* targeting of civilians. This approach draws a sharp moral distinction between intentionally inflicted civilian deaths and civilian deaths inflicted as a byproduct of

military action, deaths that are frequently labeled with the awful euphe-
mism, "collateral damage." David Rodin has recently proposed expand-
ing the definition of terrorism to encompass what he calls "reckless or
negligent infliction of civilian casualties" in addition to intentional
ones.[39] I am sympathetic to his reasons for proposing this, since from the
point of view of civilians and their loved ones, the death and suffering
inflicted "unintentionally" is indistinguishable from that inflicted deliberately. Yet there remains, I believe, a moral need to capture the particular horror of policies that *deliberately* target civilians, and I would want to
reserve the term "terrorism" for such policies, while also condemning
military strategies that negligently or recklessly inflict civilian death and
suffering. This is analogous to the distinction between *murder* and
manslaughter in our legal system. Indeed, it would be useful to coin a term,
similar to manslaughter, for military strategies that negligently or recklessly inflict civilian death and suffering.

The moral distinction between intentionally and unintentionally
caused civilian deaths is explained in the just war tradition through the
much-debated doctrine of double effect, which distinguishes between the
culpability of those who intentionally inflict death and suffering on noncombatants and those who foreseeably but unintentionally do so. While
this doctrine can all too easily be misused to rationalize negligently or
recklessly inflicted civilian deaths, in its more rigorous formulations,
and as part of a broader theory of a just war, it offers a coherent and
defensible framework of responsibility and culpability in wartime. Still,
it is crucial to remember that, from the perspective of many of those who
embrace the moral logic of *lex talionis,* deliberately and negligently
inflicted civilian deaths are morally indistinguishable. This makes it especially sobering that according to some sources more noncombatants
were killed in the American invasion of Afghanistan than died in the
attacks of 9/11.[40] The second layer of moral judgment, by focusing on
issues of motive and interest, compels us to be vigilant about our own
motives and to reject efforts to exonerate ourselves through misuses of
the doctrine of double effect.

(3) Judging the social and political contexts that shape, sustain, and give
meaning to terrorism

One of the leitmotifs of the Manichean rhetoric about terrorism is that
all attempts to identify "root causes" are, in effect, attempts to "blame the
victim." A layered model of moral judgment shows, however, that a crucial aspect of judging terrorism is understanding and evaluating the

social contexts that sustain it. Far from "blaming the victims" (who, as civilian noncombatants, are tragically blameless), this analysis will point, in part, to a broader network of people and institutions who promote terrorism through what they teach in schools, preach in houses of worship, and advocate in the media. For example, the cult of martyrdom among Palestinian youth was fueled by one-sided media coverage that portrayed nearly every Israeli military action as a "massacre" and employed melodramatic music and haunting, evocative chants of "shaheed" (martyr) to heighten the emotional impact of images of Palestinian youths killed by Israeli soldiers.[41] Religious authorities also contributed through selective citation of Islamic texts, repeating passages about punishment and retribution while omitting subsequent phrases such as "but do not transgress limits, for God does not love transgressors" or "But if one is patient in adversity and forgives, this is indeed the best resolution of affairs."[42]

Attention to this layer also allows us to see how other institutions and groups help create the conditions in which terrorists can recruit followers, from the brutality of the Russian destruction of the Chechen capital of Grozny to the daily indignities of Israeli occupation. The extraordinary rise in Palestinian public support for suicide bombings—which went from 26.1 percent in March 1999 to 73.7 percent in April 2001[43]—reflected a vicious polarizing spiral between overly aggressive Israeli military action (as well as provocative political events such as the election of Ariel Sharon) and responses on the Palestinian side.

It is important to see how this layer illuminates others, particularly the assessment of terrorist motives. Understanding what people on all sides of a conflict have done and are doing to make terrorist action more likely is essential to reversing these trends and waging an intelligent "war on terrorism." It does not, however, negate the question of the rightness or wrongness of terrorism itself. A layered approach helps us to avoid the dangers of both Manicheanism and moral equivocation. For while the former rejects this layer and thereby deprives itself of crucial moral and practical insight into terrorism, the latter allows it to become an excuse that denies those subjected to oppression or propaganda the dignity of moral choice.

(4) Judging our own moral standing and motivations in relation to terrorism

While condemning terrorism in all circumstances, a layered moral analysis does not assume that terrorists are the only actual or potential wrongdoers in the situation. This crucial layer of moral assessment asks us to understand and acknowledge our own moral standing and motivations in relation to, and in our responses to, a terrorist movement or incident. If, as is so often the case, there are victims and perpetrators on all sides of a conflict, denying this and portraying our own side as a blameless victim or a pure paragon of virtue is morally dangerous because it fuels the same indifference to others' suffering that we condemn in terrorist moral psychology. If we see ourselves as warriors in a cosmic battle between good and evil we will consider it a waste of time to try to respond to, much less to anticipate and prevent, wrongdoing by our side. A failure to acknowledge the moral weaknesses and failures of our own side also cuts off the possibility of the kinds of mutually beneficial negotiated solutions that deprive terrorist organizations of the widespread resentment and indignity that fuels their work. The Russian-Chechen conflict, for example, will never truly be resolved unless there is acknowledgment on both sides of the horror suffered by civilian victims, both in Beslan and Moscow and throughout Chechnya. The same is true of Israel and Palestine.

Assessing our own moral standing requires a capacity to see ourselves as others see us, an imaginative attempt to adopt their perspective as our own. It requires a willingness to balance our tendency to see ourselves in an overly positive light with an acknowledgment that others may see us primarily through the prism of our worst misdeeds. Onuma Yasuaki offers a clear-eyed appraisal of the liabilities Japan must overcome, given its brutal imperialist past, in any effort to champion human rights.[44] As Americans we must be willing to do something analogous and acknowledge that the least attractive aspects of our civilization—from our worst materialist excesses[45] to the legacies of Hiroshima, slavery, the Trail of Tears, and Vietnam—are an important part of how others see us.

Manicheans aggressively resist this layer of judgment, regarding it as a sign of weakness or moral confusion. Yet the inability or unwillingness to see ourselves as others see us is not only a moral liability but also a prudential one. Mohammad Hafez cautions Western governments to avoid pronouncements about Islamic doctrine or calls to reform religious education, since such statements will almost certainly backfire.[46] And a failure to anticipate the resentment Iraqis would feel toward an occupying army, particularly one whose ethnic and religious background and cultural mores are so alien, has had deadly consequences for all sides in the Iraq war.

(5) Judging appropriate and effective responses to terrorism

The fifth layer of moral judgment builds on and synthesizes all the rest. If terrorism is evil, we must seek to build a world in which terrorist movements languish rather than grow and in which there is a growing global consensus that terrorism is not an acceptable use of force. Given the complexities of our layers of moral judgment, we need to develop intelligent strategies that are likely to build such a consensus.

Developing appropriate and effective responses to any particular terrorist incident or movement will depend on specific moral, political, and strategic judgments; there is no "one size fits all" strategy and no easy solutions. Responding to al Qaeda, Hamas, Basayev's Chechen separatists, or the Basque separatist group, ETA, will, in each case, require distinct analysis. A layered model of moral judgment is, however, much better suited to the task than a Manichean vision of a simple battle between good and evil. Without a clear and honest assessment of the motives and contexts fueling terrorism and of our own standing in relation to them, we run a far greater risk of adopting strategies that sow the seeds of future atrocities in our present efforts to fight the "war on terror." Responses to terrorism that are informed by a layered approach will:

- unequivocally condemn terrorist tactics, whether used by enemies or friends;
- seek to build a broad moral consensus against terrorism, particularly among those who share a culture or religion with the terrorist movement in question, in order to weaken support for the movement rather than strengthen it;
- seek to depolarize conflicts and to address the fears and legitimate interests that fuel (but do not justify) both terrorism and excessive responses to it;
- take into account our own moral liabilities and craft strategies and policies that seek to remedy them;
- and take vigorous steps to avoid civilian casualties, since this feeds the moral logic of *lex talionis* and, in many people's eyes, serves to legitimate terrorist action.

This last point deserves further emphasis. If we appeal to the principle of noncombatant immunity as the basis of our moral condemnation of terrorism, we are under a very strong obligation, on both principled and pragmatic grounds, to prevent and avoid civilian casualties in the war on terror. This is one of the most important practical consequences of adopting a bright line ban on terrorism while taking seriously the other layers of moral judgment. It raises grave concerns about a variety of tactics used by the United States and its allies in response to terrorism and insurgencies, from "shoot to kill" policies in the occupied territories to the use of cluster bombs and cheaper but less accurate GPS-directed weapons, instead of laser-guided ones, in Afghanistan and Iraq.[47] It also suggests that the U.S. military's current policy of refusing to estimate civilian casualties is indefensible: if our reasons for condemning terrorism are that every civilian counts, then we must try to count civilian casualties inflicted by our side. Not doing so is a striking example of bad faith and double standards. Some small steps have been taken in the right direction, including efforts to distribute "condolence and collateral damage" payments to Iraqi civilians.[48] But human rights workers and Iraqis seeking information about, or compensation for, civilian deaths and injuries have faced humiliating and Kafkaesque treatment and, all too often, blanket assertions of impunity on the grounds that the deaths in question occurred in "combat situations" very expansively defined.[49]

Imaginative identification with the victims of terror propels us to take a stand and work for a world free of terrorism. But it will take more than sheer resolve and military might to achieve this goal. A layered model of moral judgment allows us to combine a clear and principled stand *against* terrorism and *for* human rights and noncombatant immunity with an appreciation of the complexities of judging and responding to terrorism. Manichean moral responses, while tempting in their simplicity, blind us to the moral stakes involved in judging terrorism and responding to it. Combating terrorism well requires us to cultivate our capacities for a more nuanced and critical moral judgment.

Female Genital Mutilation: The Challenge of Harmful Traditions[50]

While recent responses to terrorism have been characterized by a Manichean clarity that ignores or denies important moral nuances, Western assessments of female genital mutilation have often shown the opposite vice of moral equivocation in the name of nuance and sensitivity. Confronted by a widespread practice embedded in a complex network of religious and cultural meanings, a practice apparently not motivated by any intent to cause harm, many people throw up their hands and exclaim, "Who am I to judge?" So Isabelle Gunning asks, "By what right [do] I, as a Western Feminist, criticize as right or wrong the practices of an entirely different culture?"[51] Rhoda Howard, in other respects a stalwart proponent of human rights as a vehicle for cultural change, suggests that, since female genital mutilation is "truly a cultural practice that no political authority and no socially dominant group initiates or defends," and since it is supported by "strong popular sentiment," it falls into the category of "occasional and strictly limited local variations and exceptions to human rights" permitted by what Jack Donnelly has termed "weak cultural relativism."[52] And Alison Dundes Renteln cautions against the tendency to speak of female genital mutilation (FGM) as "morally abhorrent" or even "hazardous to the health of young girls," since such statements will be viewed as culturally insensitive and "cannot alter the reality that the practice is accepted as moral by members of the culture."[53]

Yet the cluster of practices termed FGM cause irreparable harm to millions of women and children. According to the World Health Organization, there are four major types of FGM:

Type I (clitoridectomy): removal of the prepuce or clitoral hood and sometimes part or all of the clitoris.

Type II (excision): removal of the labia minora (usually done in conjunction with clitoridectomy).

Type III (infibulation): clitoridectomy, excision, and cutting of the labia majora, then stitching together of the vagina, leaving only a small hole for urination and menstruation.

Type IV: miscellaneous practices including pricking, stretching, cauterizing, scraping, and corroding of the clitoris and/or labia.[54]

FGM is found in twenty-eight African countries, with estimated prevalence rates ranging from 5 percent in Uganda to near or over 90 percent in Djibouti, Egypt, Eritrea, Mali, Sierra Leone, Somalia, and Sudan.[55] The U.S. Department of State estimates that 130 million women worldwide have undergone FGM, with an additional two million girls at risk every year. FGM is practiced among people of all education levels and social classes in both urban and rural settings, and among a variety of ethnic groups and religious communities, including Muslims, Christians, and Jews. It is most commonly performed on girls between the ages of four and twelve, and there is evidence that the average age at which girls undergo FGM is decreasing. An increase in the number of African immigrants in the United States, Canada, and Europe has brought FGM to these countries and posed complex legal and medical dilemmas.

FGM is commonly performed by traditional practitioners, almost always women, using razors, scissors, knives, or even sharp stones, and without anesthetic or sterilization. Among more affluent groups, FGM may be performed in a health care setting with anesthetic.

The origins of FGM are a mystery, although recent scholarship suggests the practice began approximately two thousand years ago in southern Egypt or northern Sudan, perhaps as a way of controlling the sexuality of female slaves.[56] It became more widespread in the nineteenth and twentieth centuries[57] and today is generally regarded as a prerequisite to marriage and a way of ensuring the chastity, fidelity, and honor of young women. The most common justification offered for FGM is an appeal to "custom" or "tradition." Many defenders of the practice consider it a religious requirement, particularly one associated with Islam, although there is no mention of FGM in the Koran and the practice is unknown in most of the Muslim world. As with many cultural practices, there are a variety of sometimes conflicting explanations and justifications offered for it. Some argue that FGM is required to curb women's excessive sexual appetite and to prevent the clitoris from growing so large that it interferes with sexual intercourse or childbirth. Others claim that it enhances men's—or even women's—sexual pleasure. Many of its defenders invoke the idea that FGM makes women clean and beautiful, since the external female genitalia are viewed as unsanitary and unattractive; or assert that FGM guarantees paternity or is an essential component of cultural identity.[58] It is described as a rite of passage into womanhood—but often practiced on young girls. As with footbinding in China, some advocates assert that the pain associated with FGM and its aftereffects is a form of noble moral discipline for girls and women, while others deny that FGM is painful. In Somali filmmaker Soraya Mire's fascinating 1994 documentary *Fire Eyes,* an affluent-looking Somali man explains that he supports infibulation because he wants to keep his wife "locked," just as he locks the door of his house to protect his television and stereo from theft, an argument that evokes howls of protest from a group of Somali women when Mire shows them the footage and films their response.

In areas of Africa where FGM is widely practiced, girls who have not been cut are ostracized and are not considered suitable marriage partners. Since women gain social status and economic livelihood through marriage, there is strong social pressure to perpetuate the practice, and many parents regard it as the only responsible and loving course of action to take with their daughters.[59]

(1) Judging—and naming—the practice of FGM

How should we judge FGM? On the one hand, it is embraced by many people in Africa and regarded as an integral part of their culture and religion. Surveys and polls reveal that, in many areas, a large majority of both women and men support the practice.[60] Proponents are often vocal about their willingness to defy efforts to ban it. Former Kenyan president Jomo Kenyatta made support for FGM a central feature of his anticolonial vision.[61] More recently, Osman Antar, the mayor of Sabee, 400 kilometers south of Cairo, was quoted in Egyptian newspapers calling the Egyptian High Court's ruling upholding a Health Ministry ban on FGM in hospitals and clinics "absurd." He added, "The government can do what it wants and we, too, will do what we want. We will all circumcise our daughters, no matter what the punishments."[62]

On the other hand, a growing chorus of African and Western states and international organizations condemns FGM. The 1981 African Charter on Human and Peoples' Rights speaks in general terms about eliminating discrimination against women and protecting the rights of women and children. The Protocol on the Rights of African Women, or the Kigali Protocol, which was finalized in 2000 and adopted by the African Union in 2003, goes further, explicitly prohibiting female genital mutilation as a practice that is "physically and/or morally harmful to women and girls."[63] Many African countries, including Kenya, have outlawed FGM.[64] The United Nations has declared its support for efforts to eradicate the practice.[65] The United States has declared FGM a "harmful traditional practice" that "threatens the health and violates the human rights of women" and "hinders economic and social development."[66] The performance of FGM on persons under the age of eighteen was made a crime in the United States in 1996 (18 U.S.C.A. 116), and FGM is also outlawed by sixteen states.

As with the debate over terrorism, one feature of the debate over FGM is disagreement over what to call it. Should it be termed "female genital mutilation," a clearly condemnatory phrase, or something less judgmental such as "female circumcision," "female genital surgeries," or "female genital cutting"? Some prefer "circumcision" because it signals the ritual aspects of the practice.[67] Many reject "genital surgeries" because it misleadingly associates the practice with medical therapy. Recently "female genital cutting" has gained currency as a more neutral label less likely to evoke charges of cultural imperialism, although FGM still remains, since around 1990, the dominant term within the international community and among activists.[68] Different terms may in fact be appropriate to different contexts—public health workers in Kenyan villages, for instance, are well advised not to use the term "female genital mutilation" when conducting health seminars. And terms may shift over time, in surprising ways: "female circumcision" was the most widely used term in the 1980s, but was abandoned out of a sense that it implied too close an analogy to male circumcision, a far milder and arguably harmless practice. Now, a small but growing movement is opposing *male* circumcision and claiming that it has far graver effects on men's health, well-being, and sexuality than has been acknowledged.[69] My own view is that "female genital mutilation," while it may not be the right term to use in all contexts and for all time, is a morally appropriate term that captures the physical effects of the practice but does not, in and of itself, vitiate the complexity of other judgments we can and should make about it.

Why should we judge FGM to be a harmful and, indeed, an evil practice? I want to focus on three reasons. First, FGM harms women's physical and sexual health and well-being. Second, it inflicts these lifelong and irreversible effects on girls and women who, in the overwhelming majority of cases, have little or no choice in the matter. Third, it plays a key role in reinforcing women's unequal social status and opportunities.

FGM poses serious health threats and can result in premature death or lifelong pain and suffering. It is condemned as a medically unnecessary and dangerous practice by, among others, the World Health Organization, the World Medical Association, the American Medical Association, and the International Federation of Gynecology and Obstetrics.[70] While its negative health effects vary widely depending on the severity of the procedure, the sanitary conditions in which it is performed, the competence of the practitioner, and the strength of the girl's resistance, all but the mildest forms of type IV FGM cause "irreparable physical injury"[71] and threaten serious health consequences.

According to the U.S. Department of State, short-term health consequences of FGM include

- bleeding (often hemorrhaging from rupture of the blood vessels of the clitoris), including risk of severe bleeding and death;
- postoperative shock;
- damage to other organs resulting from lack of surgical expertise of the person performing the procedure and the violence of the resistance of the patient when anesthesia is not used;
- infections, including tetanus and septicemia, because of the use of unsterilized or poorly disinfected equipment;
- urine retention caused by swelling and inflammation.

Long-term consequences include

- chronic infections of the bladder and vagina. In type III FGM, the urine and menstrual blood can only leave the body drop by drop; the buildup inside the abdomen and the fluid retention often cause infections and inflammation that can lead to infertility;
- dysmenorrhoea, or extremely painful menstruation;
- excessive scar tissue at the site of the operation;

- formation of cysts on the stitch line;
- childbirth obstruction, which can result in the development of fistulas, tearing in the vaginal and/or bladder wall; and chronic incontinence;
- increased risk of HIV infection.

Because it leaves only a small genital opening, type III FGM (infibulation) also poses a danger of brain damage during childbirth[72] and of a heightened risk of infant mortality.[73]

It is worth noting that some of the negative effects of FGM may go unremarked by victims because they lack a basis for comparison, especially when they undergo the procedure as young children. For instance, interviewers have found that women who reported "normal" urination subsequently explained it took them fifteen minutes to urinate; they believed this was the norm for women.[74] While few scientific studies have been done on the psychological effects of the practice, nightmares, depression, shock, passivity, and feelings of betrayal have been observed among girls subjected to FGM,[75] and it is reasonable to assume that such psychological trauma will be exacerbated in cases where children are forced to undergo FGM against their will. Given taboos about women's sexuality, there has also been little rigorous research done on the effects of FGM on sexual function, although it is clear that the more severe forms of FGM have a profound effect on women's capacity for sexual pleasure as well as on reproductive health and childbirth—indeed, for many infibulated women, sex is excruciatingly painful. In sum, then, FGM causes profound physical harm, suffering, and dysfunction.

The second reason to condemn FGM is that the girls who undergo it have little or no choice in the matter. Many are literally physically overpowered. Others are willing participants in an important cultural rite, but have no sense of its long-term effects on their bodies and lives. Some may be persuaded by false myths, such as the belief that an uncut clitoris will grow so large that it interferes with sexual intercourse and childbirth. Those who oppose the practice or try to protect their female children are frequently denounced by family, friends, and community and may face social ostracization and even threats or acts of physical violence.[76] Parents opposed to the practice may find it impossible to protect their daughters, as anecdotal accounts abound of relatives intervening by force and having the procedure performed without parental consent.[77] Dissenters like Fauziya Kasinga, the young woman from Togo at the center of the first successful U.S. political asylum case centered on FGM as a form of persecution,[78] are told that if they do not have FGM performed they will be unmarriageable, and if they do not marry, they will have no social status or economic sustenance.

Third, as Kasinga's case makes clear, FGM contributes to the oppression of women. It is part of a mutually reinforcing and systematically related framework of barriers—one wire of a birdcage, to use Marilyn Frye's evocative metaphor[79]—that also includes lack of educational and economic opportunities, discriminatory property rights regimes, and family customs, and that reinforce women's status as unequal and subordinate.

As with terrorism, the condemnation of FGM rests on certain moral beliefs and commitments. Some of these are widely shared: that it is right to promote health and well-being and to protect people from unnecessary physical injury and suffering, as well as to strive to base our actions and practices in truth rather than falsehood. Others are more controversial, including a commitment to women's autonomy, sexual agency, and equal moral and civic status. FGM threatens all of these values and is therefore unequivocally wrong.

One could adopt a Manichean stance against FGM similar to that found in our dominant discourse about terrorism and say that FGM and all who support or condone it are evil—or perhaps brutal, primitive, and irrational. Such a sweeping and simple-minded condemnation would avoid facing the complexities that make FGM such a poignant, and characteristically human, phenomenon. The evil of FGM is not the evil of cruel and murderous intent directed at defenseless people. But it is evil nevertheless, and of a particularly common and wrenching kind: the infliction of profound harm on other human beings out of a sincere belief that it is in their best social, moral, and physical interest.[80]

To fully understand and evaluate FGM requires a full engagement with the other layers of moral judgment. The problem is that too many commentators become absorbed in these other layers and lose sight of the first. In the process they evade the core moral question, as Geoffrey Harpham put it, of "Whose side are you on? . . . Which principles and whose rights should prevail?"[81]

For example, moral nuance lapses into moral equivocation in the influential work of Isabelle Gunning. Gunning persuasively argues for the importance of a layered approach to FGM focused on a respectful dialogue with African women, a dialogue shaped by an effort to "see the 'other' in her own context," as well as to see "oneself in historical context and as the 'other' sees you." Yet while she is obviously in favor of ending what she called "female genital surgeries," she never states a clear moral judgment against it. Instead, she worries about whether it is "appropriate to use the human rights system to outlaw or even criticize a specific culture's norm" and advocates an "open-ended" dialogue that "does not inevitably lead to the eradication of the surgery."[82] Ironically, Gunning reserves her strongest critique for what she calls the "arrogant perceiver approach" taken by Fran Hosken, an American scholar who was one of the pioneers bringing the issue of FGM to international attention in the early 1980s. A similar moral reticence and maddening "on the one hand, on the other hand" ambiguity is evident in the work of several other commentators on FGM.[83]

Gunning and others are right to argue for a culturally and contextually sensitive approach. But I take issue with their reluctance to offer a negative judgment about FGM as a practice. It is possible both to condemn FGM for the harm it wreaks on millions of women and to recognize the complexities of FGM within its social and cultural context, of our own standing in relation to it, and of the search for effective strategies to end the practice.

(2) Judging the motivations, interests, and goals of those who engage in or defend FGM

Perhaps the most challenging element of moral judgment about FGM is the recognition that the mothers and fathers who choose to have it performed on their daughters are very often motivated by the best interests of their child and that, given the range of options available to women and the importance of marriage to their social status and well-being, this judgment is well founded. Moreover, while some defenders of FGM are explicitly motivated by a vision of women as inferior to men and indeed as men's property, there is no *necessary* logical link between support for FGM and sexism, even though FGM serves to reinforce gender hierarchies in practice. Thus FGM is a practice that, by virtue of the gravity of the harms it causes, can appropriately be called evil, yet it is not done out of evil intent.

As we have seen, some of those who support FGM do so, at least in part, out of factual ignorance—they believe, for instance, that everyone in the world, or for instance all Muslims, practice FGM, or that without FGM a woman's clitoris will grow so long that it will be a health hazard to her husband during intercourse.

Others may support FGM on aesthetic grounds—claiming that a woman's natural genitals are ugly and unclean. While such an aesthetic judgment is deeply problematic in its implicit rejection of women's bodies (making FGM similar in this respect to footbinding in China and to the many bizarre aesthetic judgments and practices focused on women's bodies in the West, including breast augmentation and starvation diets), and while the other harms caused by FGM far outweigh this aesthetic argument, as an aesthetic argument it is simply an example of human cultural variety.

In many parts of Africa, FGM is performed by traditional practitioners who are "wise women" in their communities, and resistance to change on the part of these practitioners is also understandable, given the threat to their livelihood and social status.

Thus any approach to FGM that condemns those who engage in it as if they were intentionally harming girls and women is unfair and unjustified, particularly in those contexts where people are least likely to be aware of arguments against FGM. Even in situations where parents are likely to be aware of alternatives to FGM, as in the case of African immigrant communities in Western societies, their overriding motive for perpetuating the custom will often be a morally unobjectionable and understandable one ("I want to preserve my culture."). This makes some of the Western legal responses to FGM—such as the effort to criminalize it as a form of child abuse—deeply problematic.[84] Yet while it is important to grasp the complexities driving individual decisions to participate in FGM, this does not vitiate the harmfulness of the practice.

The voices of African women themselves are only beginning to emerge in the research on FGM. Interviews and surveys suggest a wide range of judgments on the part of women, from unambiguous affirmation or opposition to deep feelings of ambivalence or traumatized silence. Many of the Somali women interviewed by Soraya Mire[85] offer a strikingly layered assessment, expressing the hope that their daughters will not have to undergo the same suffering that they did while affirming their pride in Somali culture and their resistance to criticisms of FGM that condemn or belittle that culture as a whole.

(3) Judging the social contexts that shape, sustain, and give meaning to FGM

As the previous section suggests, moral judgments about FGM will be radically inadequate without a deeper understanding of the broader social contexts that shape, sustain, and give meaning to it. These include traditional gender roles and constraints on women's social and economic opportunities, the linkage that has emerged in many places between FGM and anticolonialism, and assumptions about the relationship between FGM and Islam. They also include a desire on the part of many parents to preserve traditions, including ritual acknowledgements of rites of passage, and the centrality of FGM within such traditions.

Over the past century, FGM has been outlawed (to little effect) by colonial and postcolonial authorities, proudly embraced by nationalist leaders as a symbol of African culture, declared a moral and political battleground between Western and African feminists, and treated with breathtaking callousness by American judges.[86] Only in the past twenty years has it attained legitimacy as an international health and human rights issue, as a basis for political asylum, and as the impetus for major grassroots organizing effort by African women.[87]

The ways in which FGM has come within some communities to stand for cultural or religious pride and defiance in the face of Western imperialism, are especially important to a layered assessment of FGM. This is true not only for strategic reasons but also for moral ones. Strategically, it is crucial that efforts to stop FGM not be seen as a movement to impose Western values on Africans or Muslims. Morally, it is important to acknowledge how the desire to preserve FGM is entangled, for many people, with the desire to uphold cultural values and to keep their children from succumbing to the materialism and hypersexualization they (rightly) associate with Western culture. Stopping FGM will require disentangling some of these issues, so that people feel they are not betraying their culture or religion by protecting their daughters from mutilation.

At the same time, however, it is important not to romanticize the traditional values that uphold FGM. For example, as the documentary *Fire Eyes* demonstrates, some of FGM's defenders openly regard women as men's property. Because of its link to ideals of female chastity, honor, and subservience, FGM plays an important role, along with lack of educational and economic opportunities, in maintaining the subordinate status of women in many African communities, a subordinate status that, in turn, inhibits public discussion of or opposition to the practice.[88]

(4) Judging our own moral standing and motivations in relation to FGM

In evaluating FGM, it is important for us to think deeply and critically about how others see us and about how our own ignorance, privilege, and cultural distance, as well as the persistent power of racism and of "primitive" stereotypes of Africa, can shape and distort our attitudes and actions. Gunning's concern about "arrogant perception" is in some ways well taken. It is easy for discussions of FGM to take on a whiff of smug superiority grounded more in pity than in empathy or solidarity. Our at times lurid fascination with FGM can blind us to the concern raised by some African feminists that, in the context of illiteracy, lack of access to drinking water, lack of property rights, civil war, genocide, and the AIDS epidemic, FGM is not at the top of their list of issues to address. As one of my students aptly pointed out, some of our repugnance at the practice may also reflect our own expectations as these are shaped by lives of relative privilege. We are appalled that FGM is inflicted on young girls in unhygienic conditions but forget that they lack access to good hygiene in all aspects of their lives.[89] If we focus our moral concern too exclusively on FGM we risk losing sight of a larger reality of suffering, inequality, and wasted human potential.

The temptation to unconsciously adopt a stance of cultural superiority and psychological distance also blinds us to the more universal human features of phenomena like FGM. For instance, we forget that FGM was occasionally practiced in Western Europe and the United States in the late nineteenth and early twentieth centuries—in some instances as late as the 1950s—to cure hysteria, masturbation, lesbianism, and other female "ailments."[90] More generally, there are important links between FGM, as a deeply entrenched cultural practice that in effect tells women that their bodies are "not O.K." without radical intervention, and Western cultural norms and practices, some of which, from breast augmentation to bulimia, also pose serious health threats. And we are all too familiar with the way social conventions can prompt people to harm themselves or others.

These considerations do not, however, justify the tendency for some African commentators to suggest that Westerners have no right to judge FGM or that the only real problem is Western arrogance.[91] This, too, can be a way of using other layers of judgment to avoid having to take a stand. Nor does it imply a moral equivalence between, for instance, a college-educated middle-aged woman's decision to get breast implants and a four-year-old child's subjection to FGM. But it is a useful reminder that we should try to approach the challenge of ending FGM with reflective humility, an appreciation of the limitations of our own perspective and effectiveness, and a spirit of solidarity with African women and men who, like us, struggle imperfectly to do the right thing for their families and communities.

(5) Judging appropriate and effective responses to FGM

How, then, in light of all of these layers of judgment, should we evaluate responses to FGM? While those who adopt a Manichean approach will be tempted to "send in the Marines," and those who lapse into moral equiocation are unwilling to take a stand, a layered approach to moral judgment provides a useful roadmap for weighing alternate strategies. If we affirm a moral imperative to work to end the practice but acknowledge its moral, social and cultural complexities, what strategies should we support? Over the past decade the anti-FGM movement, through the leadership of African nongovernmental organizations such as the IAC and Tostan, sometimes in partnership with Western or international organizations, has developed an array of creative strategies that, on a modest scale, have shown some success by recognizing the importance of a layered approach. These strategies build on certain key judgments:

1. Efforts to ban or criminalize FGM have consistently proven to be ineffective or even to evoke a backlash. Laws against FGM, like laws against footbinding or sati, will only be effective once there is a substantial social consensus against FGM. The key, therefore, is to change social attitudes.

2. Changing social attitudes toward FGM requires understanding the context of local power and enlisting the support of traditional opinion leaders such as village chiefs and Imams. Ultimately, as was the case in the successful effort to end foot binding in China, change has to be led and embraced from within a culture.

3. Changing attitudes requires disentangling the practice of FGM from people's commitments to uphold their religion and culture. Otherwise opposition to FGM is likely to evoke cultural animosity and backlash.

4. Efforts to abolish FGM will have to proceed hand in hand with other efforts to improve people's—and especially women's—access to education, hygiene, health care and economic opportunity.

One strategy that has proven to be effective at the village level has been the introduction of nonmutilating substitutes for FGM (such as "circumcision through words" or mild "pricking" rituals). These preserve a sense of cultural legitimacy and integrity, although they require continued engagement to prevent backsliding.

Anti-FGM activists often need to make complicated moral and practical judgments about the relative moral weight to place on preventing infection, preventing mutilation, and overcoming women's subordination. For instance, most activists oppose efforts to medicalize FGM by performing infibulation and clitoridectomy in hospitals and clinics, fearing that, while they may save girls from infection, they will prolong the use of FGM by rendering it legitimate in a modern medical context. But they favor nonmutilating forms of FGM that preserve, and even heighten, the "rite of passage" elements of the practice. They also argue vigorously over the value of human rights rhetoric, of general strategies of women's empowerment such as education and property rights reform, and of discussions of sexuality, to the movement to abolish FGM.

The complexities of judgment in this fifth layer take us back to the first, for the strategic choices faced by anti-FGM activists compel them to reconsider exactly why FGM is wrong. What is more crucial, health, autonomy, or equality? Is it better to free girls from the risk of infection at the price of legitimating mutilation? How "mild" must a milder form of FGM be for it to deserve support as an alternative?[92] To what extent must anti-FGM efforts embrace the cause of women's equality? These practical dilemmas reveal that, even among those who deem FGM wrong, there are important differences depending on the relative moral weight they give to the various harms inflicted by FGM.

Cultivating Moral Judgment, Conceptualizing Evil

I have tried to show how a layered approach to moral judgment enables us to combine the virtues of clarity and complexity in responding to deep cross-cultural disagreements. The dangerous shadow sides of clarity and complexity sketched so vividly by Yeats are, in both cases, the product of a failure to acknowledge and engage all of the layers. For while Manicheans have a tendency to move too quickly from evaluating practices to prescribing strategies, ignoring much of moral relevance both in those they condemn and in themselves, those who succumb to the opposite vice of relativism get so engrossed in the second, third, and fourth layers that they lose sight of the importance of where they stand and what is to be done. Taking all the layers seriously can help us grasp the moral stakes involved and to respond with both clarity and subtlety.

My case studies point to three other lessons we can draw about moral judgment and the problem of evil. First, judgments about evil are dependent on ground-level moral assumptions. The contrast between a commitment to noncombatant immunity and to *lex talionis* shows this clearly. Deliberately targeting noncombatants is a grave evil on the first account, since it is the crossing of a very strong moral boundary. But for some proponents of *lex talionis,* the same act will, in some cases, be an appropriate act of retributive justice. Similarly, if we value chastity over autonomy or health, we will come to very different judgments about FGM. All of these first-layer judgments will be rendered more nuanced by attentiveness to the four other layers, but this does not vitiate the importance of coming to a clear and defensible judgment about the practice itself.

Second, my discussion of FGM shows how the layers of judgment can serve not only to help us to answer the question "What should we do?" in a more nuanced way but also to reveal the complexities of judging a "practice." Debates over strategy among opponents of FGM reveal the extent to which FGM is a cluster of distinct harms, from infection to coercion to inequality. Hence the value of a layered model of judgment is not only to demonstrate ways of combining clarity and complexity but also to show how engaging with one layer can help inform and clarify another.

Finally, while terrorism, since it involves the intentional infliction of harm on enemies, is in some ways a paradigmatic kind of evil, FGM is an example of a large-scale evil committed without evil intent and even, in many cases, out of parental concern and love. It shows that, despite our tendency to see evil as involving malicious intent and aberrant behavior, it is possible for evil to become "normalized" in a cultural practice so that otherwise decent people contribute to the infliction of grave harm on a massive scale. In the case of FGM, this harm is linked to a deeply human impulse to reject, reshape, and improve upon our nature. Ironically, this very same impulse drives us to control our darkest tendencies to brutalize the defenseless. Only continuous efforts to cultivate moral judgment can help us tell the difference.

ACKNOWLEDGMENT

I am grateful to all of the contributors to this volume, and especially to our wonderful convenor Ruth Grant, for a stimulating series of discussions that have challenged and deepened my thinking about good, evil, and moral judgment. Particular thanks are owed to Jerome Levi, my thoughtful and generous commentator at the "Speak No Evil" conference in January 2005. Earlier versions of all or part of this chapter were presented to the University of Toronto's Legal Theory Workshop in March 2005 and at two public discussions on "Ethics and Terrorism" at Duke University in November 2004 and April 2005. I learned a great deal from audience questions and responses on all of these occasions and from five respondents at the Duke events: Peter Euben, Ruth Grant, Craig Kocher, Ebrahim Moosa, and David Wong. I have also benefited from additional conversations with Allen Buchanan, Joe Carens, Alex Downes, David Dyzenhaus, Peter Euben, Ruth Grant, Jeff Holzgrefe, Sandy Levinson, Cheryl Misak, Jenny Nedelsky, Noah Pickus, and Igor Primoratz. Finally, my thanks to Mohammed M. Hafez for providing me with a manuscript of his monograph, *Manufacturing Human Bombs*.

NOTES

1. Geoffrey Halt Harpham, *Shadows of Ethics: Criticism and the Just Society* (Durham, NC: Duke University Press, 1999), p. x.

2. William Butler Yeats, *The Poems*, Richard J. Finneran, ed. (New York: Macmillan, 1989), p. 187.

3. Mohammed M. Hafez, *Manufacturing Human Bombs: The Making of Palestinian Suicide Bombers* (Washington, DC: U.S. Institute of Peace Press, 2006), p. 4.

4. See pp. 5–6 in this volume.

5. In the aftermath of 9/11, Bill Maher, host of the television show *Politically Incorrect*, took issue with President Bush's characterization of the September 11 hijackers as "cowards," arguing that what they did was evil but that they exhibited courage in doing it. His remarks unleashed a firestorm of protest and may have contributed to the cancellation of his show. Yet Maher was clearly right. The incident vividly reveals the tendency of moral Manicheanism to elide and aggressively deny the distinctions among my five layers of judgment.

6. The "Joint NGO Statement on the Beslan Hostage Tragedy" issued on September 8, 2004, by eight human rights organizations is a good example. http://web.amnesty.org/library/print/ENGEUR460502004 (accessed on November 13, 2004).

7. James Reynolds, "Nobody is going to live forever" BBC News (July 16, 2004), at http://news.bb.co.uk/go/pr/fr/-/1/hi/world/middle_east/3899015.stm (accessed on November 11, 2004).

8. "Definitions of Terrorism," United Nations Office on Drugs and Crime. Available at http://www.unodc.org/unodc/terrorism_definitions.html (accessed on November 6, 2004).

9. Examples of state terrorism include Pol Pot's campaign against Cambodian civilians, the Japanese Rape of Nanking, the Allied firebombing of Dresden and other German cities during World War Two, and Argentina's "Dirty War."

10. This point is emphasized by David Rodin in "Terrorism without Intention," *Ethics* 114 (July 2004): 757–758.

11. Thomas Nagel points to such notions of fair play in discussing the distinction between "fighting clean and fighting dirty." Nagel, "War and Massacre" in *War and Moral Responsibility*, ed. Marshall Cohen, Thomas Nagel, and Thomas Scanlon (Princeton: Princeton University Press, 1974), p. 14. It is interesting to note that the passages in classical Muslim texts prohibiting the killing of women and children also condemn "cheating" and "treachery." John Kelsay, "Islam and the Distinction of Combatants and Non-Combatants" in *Cross, Crescent, and Sword: The Justification and Limitation of War in Western and Islamic Tradition,* ed. James Turner Johnson and John Kelsay (Westport, CT: Greenwood Press, 1990), pp. 198–199.

12. James Turner Johnson, "Maintaining the Protection of Non-Combatants," *Journal of Peace Research* 37, no. 4 (July 2000): 427–430.

13. *The Laws of Manu,* chapter 7, verse 92, cited in Henry Shue, *The Oxford Handbook of Practical Ethics* (New York: Oxford University Press, 2003), s.v. "war."

14. Hafez, *Manufacturing Human Bombs,* pp. 64–65. For a detailed and subtle discussion, see Kelsay, "Islam and the Distinction," pp. 197–220.

15. Jean-Paul Sartre cited in Walzer, *Just and Unjust Wars,* 3d ed. (New York: Basic Books, 2000), p. 204.

16. Hafez, *Manufacturing Human Bombs,* p. 4.

17. John C. Ford surveys these and other euphemisms in "The Morality of Obliteration Bombing," a 1944 essay reprinted in *War and Morality,* ed. Richard Wasserstrom (Belmont, CA: Wadsworth, 1970), esp. pp. 34–35.

18. Hafez, *Manufacturing Human Bombs,* pp. 57–61. Hafez notes that the Palestinian-Israeli conflict is particularly dangerous because many members of both communities fear, whether rightly or wrongly, that their community's very existence is at stake.

19. Hafez, *Manufacturing Human Bombs,* pp. 36–40.

20. Walzer, *Just and Unjust Wars,* pp. 255–263. See also Ford, "The Morality of Obliteration Bombing," pp. 35–38. Ford cites a particularly blunt example of this argument from a prewar 1932 speech in the House of Commons: "The only defense is offense which means you have to kill more women and children more quickly than the enemy can if you want to save yourselves" (p. 34).

21. "Full transcript of bin Laden's Speech" (October 30, 2004), at http://english.aljazeera.net/english/DialogBox/PrintPreview.aspx?NRORIGINALURL=% (accessed on November 11, 2004).

22. Hafez, *Manufacturing Human Bombs*, pp. 47–50.

23. Ford, "The Morality of Obliteration Bombing," pp. 33–34.

24. Virginia Held, "Terrorism, Rights, and Political Goals" in *Taking Sides: Clashing Views on Controversial Moral Issues*, ed. Stephen Satris, 4th ed. (Duskin: Guilford, 1994), p. 294.

25. Barry Buzan, "Who May We Bomb?" in *Worlds in Collision: Terror and the Future of the Global Order*, ed. Ken Booth and Tim Dunne (Basingstoke: Palgrave, 2002), pp. 85–94.

26. Sheikh Ahmed Yassin, *Al-Hayat*, May 22, 2002, cited in Hafez, "Manufacturing Human Bombs," p. 109, n. 43.

27. William James, "The Moral Equivalent of War" in *Morality and War*, ed. Richard Wasserstrom (Belmont, CA: Wadsworth, 1970), p. 5.

28. Ford, "The Morality of Obliteration Bombing," p. 19.

29. This argument is elaborated by Alison Dundes Renteln, *International Human Rights: Universalism versus Relativism* (Newbury Park, CA: Sage, 1990), pp. 88–137.

30. Thomas Nagel, "War and Massacre," pp. 23–24. Walzer, *Just and Unjust Wars*, pp. 251–268. Note that Walzer limited his discussion of "supreme emergency" to political communities, a point on which he is (rightly) criticized by C. A. J. Coady in "Terrorism, Morality, and Supreme Emergency," *Ethics* (July 2004): 782–787.

31. For a thoughtful qualified defense of Churchill's decision, see Walzer, *Just and Unjust Wars*, pp. 255–263.

32. According to Mohammad Hafez, suicide bombings have taken place in twenty countries since the 1980s, and suicide bombings have been on the rise even while terrorism in general has declined. Hafez, *Manufacturing Human Bombs*, p. 5.

33. The "torture memo" from Assistant Attorney General Jay S. Bybee, along with other documents on U.S. policy concerning interrogation methods, may be found at the National Security Archive Web site at http://www.gwu.edu/~nsarchiv/NSAEBB/NSAEBB127/ (accessed December 12, 2005).

34. Winston Churchill cited in Walzer, *Just and Unjust Wars*, p. 261. The Dresden attack killed an estimated 100,000 civilians.

35. Nagel, "War and Massacre," p. 6.

36. I want to thank Michaela Kerrissey for pushing me to confront this point.

37. Hafez, *Manufacturing Human Bombs*, p. 50.

38. Hafez, *Manufacturing Human Bombs*, pp. 29–30.

39. David Rodin, "Terrorism without Intention," *Ethics* 114 (July 2004): 752–771.

40. Marc Herold of the University of New Hampshire estimated that 3,800 Afghan civilians were killed between October 7 and December 7, 2001. BBC News, "Afghanistan's Civilian Deaths Mount," January 3, 2002, available at http://news.bbc.co.uk/1/hi/world/south_asia/1740538.stm. Others have claimed a somewhat lower figure, in the 1,000–1,500 range. Carl Conetta, "Operation Enduring Freedom: Why a Higher Rate of Civilian Bombing Casualties," Project on Defense Alternatives Briefing Report #11 (January 18, 2002, revised January 24, 2002), available at http://www.comw.org/ pda/0201oef.html.

41. Hafez, *Manufacturing Human Bombs*, p. 62.

42. Hafez, *Manufacturing Human Bombs*, p. 64.

43. Hafez, *Manufacturing Human Bombs*, pp. 59–60; see also chart no. 2, p. 77.

44. Onuma Yasuaki, "In Quest of Intercivilizational Human Rights: 'Universal' vs. 'Relative' Human Rights Viewed from an Asian Perspective," *Occasional Paper No. 2* (San Francisco: Asian Foundation, Center for Asian Pacific Affairs, 1996), pp. 1–16.

45. This point is elaborated by David Wong in his contribution to this volume.

46. Hafez, *Manufacturing Human Bombs*, p. 74–75.

47. Carl Connetta, "Operation Enduring Freedom."

48. U.S. military press release A041005b, "Marines make condolence payments in Najaf." (October 5, 2004). Available at the Civic Worldwide Web site (a nongovernmental organization dedicated to assisting "innocent victims in conflict") at http://www.civicworld-wide/compensation/compensation-marines-100504.htm.

49. Occupation Watch Center, Baghdad and National Association for the Defense of Human Rights in Iraq, *Joint Report on Civilian Casualties and Claims Related to U.S. Military Operations* (released January 2004) available at the Civic Worldwide Web site, http://www.civicworldwide.org/pdfs/compensationreport.pdf (accessed on October 10, 2005). See also Human Rights Watch, "Hearts and Minds: Post-war Civilian Deaths in Baghdad Caused by U.S. Forces," vol. 15, no. 9-E (October 2003), available at http://www.hrw.org. Sameer H. Yacoub, Sharon Crenson, and Richard Pyle, "Iraqi Civilian Death Tally at 3, 240," *USA Today* (June 10, 2003), available at http://www.usatoday.com/news/world/iraq/2003-6-11-iraqi-toll_x.htm (accessed on October 10, 2005).

50. Portions of this section were originally written for an expert witness report on FGM in a political asylum case. I am grateful for research assistance provided by Jessica Ballou, Megan Fotheringam, and Lauren Kernan.

51. Isabelle Gunning, "Arrogant Perception, World-Travelling and Multicultural Feminism: The Case of Female Genital Surgeries," *Columbia Human Rights Law Review* 23 (1991–1992): 189.

52. Rhoda E. Howard, "Human Rights and the Necessity for Cultural Change," *Focus on Law Studies* vol. 8, no. 1 (fall 1992): 4. Jack Donnelly develops his idea of "weak cultural relativism" in *Universal Human Rights in Theory and Practice* (Ithaca: Cornell University Press, 1989), chap. 6.

53. Renteln, *International Human Rights*, p. 58. Renteln's views have since changed, at least with respect to the issue of whether immigrants should be permitted to practice female genital mutilation in Western pluralistic societies. Renteln, *The Cultural Defense* (New York: Oxford University Press, 2004), p. 70.

54. World Health Organization, *Female Genital Mutilation: Report of a Technical Working Group* (Geneva: WHO, 1996), p. 9.

55. There are also isolated occurrences of FGM in some areas of Asia and the Middle East. World Health Organization, *Female Genital Mutilation: An Overview* (Geneva: WHO, 1998), p. 21.

56. Mary Knight, "Curing Cut or Ritual Mutilation?" *Isis* 92, no. 2 (June 2001): 317; Gerry Mackie, "Ending Footbinding and Infibulation: A Convention Account," *American Sociological Review* 61 (December 1996): 999–1017.

57. Population Reference Bureau, *Abandoning Female Genital Cutting: Prevalence, Attitudes, and Efforts to End the Practice* (Washington, DC: Population Reference Bureau, August 2001).

58. Susan Dillon, "Healing the Sacred Yoni in the Land of Isis: Female Genital Mutilation Is Banned (Again) in Egypt," *Houston Journal of International Law* 22 (winter 2000): 289ff.

59. Malik Stan Reaves, "Alternative Rite to Female Circumcision Spreading in Kenya," *Africa News Service* (November 19, 1997), available at http://allafrica.com/stories/200101080370.html.

60. Renteln, *International Human Rights*, p. 57. See also Alison T. Slack, "Female Circumcision: A Critical Appraisal," *Human Rights Quarterly* 10, no. 4 (1988): 445–450.

61. Jomo Kenyatta, *Facing Mount Kenya: The Tribal Life of the Gikuyu* (New York: Vintage Books, 1965), pp. 124–148.

62. Mamdouh Afifi, "Female Circumcision Ban Ignored by Egyptian Fundamentalists," *Agence France Presse* (January 5, 1998).

63. Corinne Packer, *Using Human Rights to Change Tradition*, (Antwerp: Intersentia, 2000). pp. 109, 125. The text of the Kigali Protocol is available at http://www.hrea.org/erc/Library/display.php?doc_id=806&%20category_id=31&category_type=3.

64. Rebecca Cook, Bernard Dickens, and Mahmoud Fathalla, *Reproductive Health and Human Rights* (New York: Oxford University Press, 2003), pp. 269–270.

65. United Nations General Assembly, "Declaration on the Elimination of Violence against Women" (A/RES/48/104), available at http://www.un.org/documents/ga/res/48/a48r104.htm (accessed 23 February 1994).

66. U.S. State Department, available at http://www.state.gov/g/wi/rls/rep/9273.html (accessed on November 10, 2003)

67. This point was made by Jerome Levi in "Relativism, Humanitarian Values, and the Limits of Tolerance," a comment on Elizabeth Kiss, "Making Clear and Complex Judgments," p. 13, presented at the conference "Speak No Evil: Moral Judgment in the Modern Age" held at Duke University on January 28, 2005.

68. For instance, Nahid Toubia, probably the world's leading expert on FGM, chose to title her book, coauthored with Anika Rahman, *Female Genital Mutilation: A Guide to Laws and Policies Worldwide*, although she uses the abbreviation FGM/FC throughout the book to acknowledge the widespread use of female circumcision as a less inflammatory or judgmental term.

69. For a fascinating look at both male and female circumcision, see George Denniston, Frederick Hodges and Marilyn Milos, *Understanding Circumcision: A Multi-Disciplinary Approach to a Multi-Dimensional Problem* (New York: Kluwer, 2001).

70. American Medical Association Council on Scientific Affairs, "Female Genital Mutilation," *Journal of the American Medical Association* 274, no. 21 (6 December 1995): 1714–1716; Cook, Dickens, and Fathalla, *Reproductive Health and Human Rights*, p. 266.

71. This is the standard invoked by Renteln to justify denying immigrant parents the right to mount a "cultural defense" to allow them to practice FGM on their daughters. Renteln, *Cultural Defense*, p. 79.

72. U.S. State Department at http://www.state.gov/g/wi/rls/rep/9273.html (accessed on November 10, 2003).

73. The WHO report calls for more research on this issue, arguing that it should be possible to establish a link between FGM and higher rates of infant mortality, though no rigorous research has yet been done. World Health Organization, *Female Genital Mutilation*, pp. 40–43.

74. Hanny Lightfoot-Klein, *Prisoners of Ritual: An Odyssey into Female Genital Mutilation* (Birmingham, NY: Haworth Press, 1989), pp. 22, 59, cited in Gerry Mackie, "Ending Footbinding and Infibulation: A Convention Account," *American Sociological Review* 61, no. 6 (December 1996): 1009.

75. U.S. State Department at http://www.state.gov/g/wi/rls/rep/9273.html (accessed on November 10, 2003).

76. *Alert Series Women: Female Genital Mutilation* (Washington, DC: INS Resource Information Center, 1994), p. 16.

77. For several examples, see Efua Dorkenoo and Scilla Elworthy, *Female Genital Mutilation: Proposals for Change*, 3d ed. (London: Minority Rights Group, 1992), pp. 24, 25, 29.

78. Karen Musalo, Jennifer Moore, and Richard Boswell, *Refugee Law and Policy: Cases and Materials*, (Durham, NC: Carolina Academic Press, 1997), pp. 677ff.

79. Marilyn Frye, *The Politics of Reality* (Trumansburg, NY: Crossing Press, 1983), p. 5.

80. Alison Slack makes a similar point in "Female Circumcision: A Critical Appraisal," p. 467.

81. Harpham, *Shadows of Ethics*, p. 261.

82. Gunning, "Arrogant Perception, World Travelling and Multicultural Feminism," pp. 237, 246.

83. See, for instance, Renteln, *International Human Rights: Universalism versus Relativism*, pp. 57–58.

84. Doriane Lambelet Coleman, "The Seattle Compromise: Multicultural Sensitivity and Americanization" *Duke Law Journal* 47 (1998): 717–783.

85. Who, given their participation in the documentary, are almost certainly not a representative sample.

86. An illustrative case is that of Fauziya Kasinga, who fled her native Togo as a sixteen-year-old to avoid forced marriage and mutilation and sought asylum in the United States, only to languish in jail for several years and have her claims summarily rejected by several courts before she finally succeeded on appeal. Musalo, Moore, and Boswell, *Refugee Law and Policy*, pp. 677ff.

87. The largest NGO devoted to the issue, the Inter-African Committee on Traditional Practices Affecting the Health of Women and Children (IAC), was founded in the 1980s and now has branches in 26 countries. Corinne Packer, *Using Human Rights to Change Tradition*, p. 9.

88. U.S. State Department at http://www.state.gov/g/wi/rls/rep/9273.html (accessed on November 10, 2003).

89. My thanks to Stephanie Amoako for this point.

90. Anika Rahman and Nahid Toubia, *Female Genital Mutilation: A Guide to Laws and Policies Worldwide* (New York: Zed Books, 2000), p. 7.

91. Seble Dawit and Salem Mekuria, "The West Just Doesn't Get It," *New York Times*, editorial page, December 7, 1993.

92. See Coleman, "The Seattle Compromise" for discussion of the furor that greeted a Seattle hospital's attempt to offer a mild, nonmutilating alternative to FGM to African immigrant clients.

Liberal Dilemmas and Moral Judgment

This book originated in a sense of urgency about moral judgment in U.S. public discourse on terrorism. The urgency is evident in my colleagues' essays, as it was in the deliberations in our seminars and in the closing conference. The general sense was that the capacity to reason about "evil" needs a quick reinforcement. The cynicism and relativism emerging from the left wing of the academy contrasts sharply with the self-righteousness and fanaticism of the U.S. government, but both combine to create the impression that we have lost our moral compass: something is fundamentally wrong with public moral reasoning. I do not share my colleagues' sense of moral urgency, but, when they rethought moral judgment in their essays, they did so in ways that seemed to me strangely familiar and congenial. Their thoughtfulness, nuance, and careful balancing represented a welcome alternative to the hysteria on the right and on the left, but the very familiarity of their discourse seemed to me to jar with their sense of a crisis. Why did an "unprecedented" crisis trigger such a traditional liberal response? As an intellectual historian and, like most of my colleagues, a liberal, I turned to the history of liberalism to see whether we might derive from it an explanation of the current sense of urgency as well as instruction for current efforts to shape moral judgment.

There is nothing in the public discourse on terrorism that seems to me unprecedented, politically or morally. The challenges it presents to liberal moral thinking are familiar, as are the dilemmas contemporary liberals face. Liberals urging the defense of liberty have often been anxious lest the public or government they sought to mobilize remain indifferent or, on the contrary, became fanatical, in either case putting liberty at risk. When my colleagues negotiate between conviction and indifference, bigotry and nihilism, commitment to universal values and cultural pluralism, they reflect the liberal experience of over two centuries and share its dilemmas. Politics provides the background for their moral deliberations, and properly so: moral judgment must weigh the political consequences of fanaticism and indifference, universalism and diversity. My colleagues have thus become part of a history of liberal dilemmas, with which we must live. Their carefully crafted responses will be negotiated anew when the next challenge comes. Consulting the history of liberalism, one gains distance from contemporary agitation and a measure of comfort in an "unprecedented crisis" rendered familiar. I am not anxious.

All the same, there is merit to presenting the agitated public with examples of sound liberal moral reasoning. Liberals are commonly portrayed as high-minded but naive idealists, or, conversely, as relativists, unable to recognize evil when they see it and unable to effectively mobilize against it. A history of failures to combat genocide, from Nazism in the 1930s to Rwanda in the 1990s, is used to support this criticism. I do not think that liberals are implicated in these failures any more than others. They share common human failings, chief among which is the limited ability to focus on faraway "people of whom we know nothing."[1] "In democratic ages," says Tocqueville, "the bond of human affections widens but loosens."[2]

But liberals do face dilemmas peculiar to liberalism as well. Liberal ambivalence about democracy, the hopes and anxieties that liberals have about democratic publics and governments, complicate moral judgment for good reasons and constrain liberals' ability to mobilize against evil. The history of liberalism shows, however, that the dilemmas did not paralyze judgment, and when they paralyzed action, the failure was one of persuasion. The public or government turned against the liberal agenda, and no political agent defended it. Designing institutions to minimize abuse has been the liberals' prime way of combating evil; assessing the risks of putting one's trust in the democratic public has become the art of liberal political judgment; and persuasion has become the art of mobilization in liberal political cultures. If I am to join my colleagues in vindicating liberal moral reasoning, I must show that liberals practiced these arts well often enough, and it is not their fault that history has often turned against them.

The charge of liberal relativism requires, however, a further response. Contemporary liberals seem to face more difficulties with moral judgment because of the discursive, or deliberative, turn of liberalism. Deliberation has always been central to liberal politics: liberals envisioned parliamentary debate as the preferred method for resolving political disagreements. But nineteenth-century liberals commonly supported deliberation with a foundationist vision of human nature. Nonfoundationist liberals (this author included) do not recognize moral judgment apart from critical deliberation and must give up on forming universal rules for recognizing evil. Tomorrow's deliberations may revise today's judgments. There is, however, no cause for despair. Provisional recognition of particular evils is sufficient for political persuasion and for educational and institutional work to protect against them. Deliberation sometimes fails miserably, but it has helped, on occasion, to mobilize democratic majorities to combat evils. Liberal democracy has known moments of great moral and political triumph. These provide liberals grounds for hope.

As nonfoundationist (or deliberative) liberalism would seem the one most susceptible to the charge of a morally incapacitating relativism, the first part of this paper explores the implications of the discursive turn for recognizing evil and mobilizing against it. The second part turns to the history of French liberalism and focuses on a series of episodes in which liberal intellectuals confronted the problem of mobilization against evil. It presents the dilemmas they faced and establishes a liberal historical pattern. Recognition of evil was never a major problem, but persuading a public to mobilize against it was. There is no reason to assume that the problems liberals face today are any different.

I

The only thing contemporaries seem to agree about concerning evil is that Hitler was evil. Liberals did not mobilize effectively against Hitler, and it is not coincidental that critiques of liberal deliberation first emerged in response to the failure to combat the rise of Nazism. The greatest fascist critic of liberalism, Carl Schmitt, insisted that belief in the efficacy of parliamentary discussion was the core of liberalism—and that it was wrong: endless public discussions failed to reach conclusion (hence parliamentary deals were cut behind the scenes). Liberalism was incapable of making the fundamental political distinction between friend and enemy, incapable of pronouncing both the Communists and the Nazis enemies of the State and outlawing them. It left the state defenseless. But it did worse. The friend-enemy distinction, thought

Schmitt, was arbitrary in character, hence political and not moral. Seeking to moralize political decisions, liberals introduced pseudouniversal standards, turning their rivals into enemies of humanity, an embodiment of evil. They made resolution of political conflicts impossible: they could not properly identify enemies, fight, or settle with them. The only way out was to recognize the fundamental incompatibility between liberal deliberation and democratic majority rule and overthrow liberal parliamentarism in favor of a plebiscitarian democracy that would entrust a popularly elected authoritarian president with fundamental decisions. A fascist state can stop the Nazis and the Communists.[3]

Leo Strauss responded that Schmitt misidentified the liberal problem and, indeed, remained part of it. Liberalism originated in the modern attempt, beginning with Hobbes, to envision a politics that sidestepped controversial moral issues and dedicated itself to goals shared by all, such as augmenting welfare and happiness. Schmitt's objections to liberal duplicity and incompetence made sense only as a moral critique of liberal frivolity, of the liberal failure to recognize that politics cannot avoid fundamental moral issues. Political decision is, at its most extreme, about good and evil. The liberal trust in deliberation reflected moral shallowness and creeping relativism, but Schmitt's own relativism only exacerbated the problem and, paradoxically, brought the modern liberal project of excluding moral judgment from politics to its conclusion.[4]

Schmitt and Strauss were both highly critical of liberal political culture and united in dismissing liberal deliberation as inadequate to the challenges of politics. Strauss had no greater confidence in democratic decision making, but Schmitt sought to separate majority rule from deliberation, democracy from liberalism, and opted for an illiberal plebiscitarian democracy. Liberal democrats responded by affirming both deliberation and majority rule and resisting the separation. Karl Popper's *The Open Society and Its Enemies,* written in the midst of World War Two, was an eloquent liberal defense of a deliberative democracy against totalitarianism. Popper created a unified vision of science, ethics, and politics and declared public discussion (or intersubjective criticism) the necessary and sufficient condition for the constitution of a scientific, moral, and political community.[5] In postwar years, Habermas's discourse ethic, relying on the deliberating public to sustain democratic decision making, retied the fortunes of democracy and liberalism (even if its intentions were not initially liberal).[6] Liberalism and democracy have had a long and tense relationship ever since liberalism emerged in the late eighteenth century. They seem less uncomfortable together today than they have been in most historical periods, as neither majorities nor plebiscitarian governments seem to place deliberation at serious risk in liberal democratic countries.

The theoretical challenge to deliberation remains, however. Historically, the major variants of liberalism have adhered to foundationist, rather than deliberative, moral visions (e.g., natural rights), but most have upheld deliberative politics. Liberals have all faced the problem of forming a consensus, the challenge of persuading a majority to, say, recognize evil and, once it is recognized, take action against it. Nonfoundationist liberals face an additional burden; the difficulty of showing evil to be evil without resort to foundational values. Schmitt's critique, especially as modified by Strauss, suggests that, whatever the moral grounding of deliberative politics, it encounters difficulties in forming clear judgments in the face of evil. Part 2 of this essay will discuss liberalism historically, and it will deal mostly with liberals whom we would consider today foundationist. Here I shall focus on nonfoundationist liberalism— the one that extends deliberation from politics to ethics and refuses to appeal beyond critical discourse for help in forming moral judgment. If the charge of inherent inability to form moral judgment sticks to liberalism, it should stick here.

Discourse (or deliberative) ethic, in the sense used here, assumes that only communicable and criticizable positions are ethical. It is procedural, not substantive in character: we cannot deduce synthetic moral principles (not even Kant's categorical imperative) from the mere idea of ethics. Discourse ethic sets the rules for the debate and leaves. It does assume that values are subject to criticism and argument and "we can learn in the realm of standards just as well as in the realm of facts,"[7] but it tells us nothing about these values. It does require a culture of debate to sustain it, but it cannot declare this culture, or social conditions, a moral (or political) requisite, and, indeed, it often subjects these very cultural and social conditions to criticism. Like deliberative democracy, discourse ethic implies equality and impartial truth: one must be willing to subject one's judgment to criticism and change it; other people have the right to be heard. But these values themselves are criticizable and indeed have been criticized, and they all seem mere tautologies of the definition of discourse ethic. Those who wish to take part in the debate are welcome without preconditions. Discourse ethic can do nothing about those who refuse. It cannot even declare those who wish to put an end to the debate morally reprehensible or evil without discussing their claims first. A day may come when they win the argument. It will be a sad day for liberals, but they cannot preclude the possibility and remain true to deliberation.

Critiques of discourse ethic have been legion. If some argue that it does too little, others suggest that it does too much: under the guise of tautology, it sneaks into the discussion rules a plethora of liberal values, which render presumably neutral procedures tracks for substantive decisions swayed in particular directions. Efforts to elaborate procedures and state the obligations of participants in the debate lend themselves to such charges. The more, it seems, the proponents of discourse ethic try to say, the less convincing their claims to impartiality appear.

The major problem of discourse ethic remains, however, the air of unreality surrounding it: the sense that neither individuals nor polities form judgments and make decisions this way. This was Schmitt's argument against liberal deliberation, and leftist critics of liberalism, especially Marxists, frequently echo Schmitt. Critical public discussion, it seems, remains a regulative ideal at best. This has led various writers, this author included, to suggest that we ought to think about how to construct the public sphere so that it facilitates critical debate. A fairly egalitarian socioeconomic structure may prove a prerequisite to an ideal speech situation (although debate under nonideal conditions is almost always preferable to no debate at all). This is a valid proposal for public debate, but trying to squeeze a social democratic order out of the ground rules for discourse ethic now seems to me a questionable enterprise. The political debate soon replaces the procedural one, and the impartial procedures become politically implicated. If discourse ethic (and deliberative democracy, too) is to be saved, we should not impose on it excessive political burdens.

We may need to change course in our thinking about discourse ethic and deliberative democracy by acknowledging that public debate may not be the major site where moral judgment and political decision are formed, although it remains the highest court. Discourse ethic need not insist that moral judgment is always a product of deliberation alone. Participants in debate rely on background knowledge, consisting of infinite judgments and decisions, which become a subject for public debate only when they seem to impinge on contentious problems on the agenda. This is neither to suggest that discourse ethic and deliberation have no role in settings such as family, religious community, and school nor, certainly, to suggest that we ought not to extend the reach of discourse ethic to political agencies removed from the public eye. It is to acknowledge that participants in public debate may arrive with their minds already made up and that we should marvel at the ability of such debate to occasionally change their opinions and regard such changes as a great triumph for liberal democracy.

This also means that anxieties about liberal indecision, even moral paralysis, are exaggerated. When faced with problem situations, both daily and extraordinary, moral agents fall back on traditions and institutions to guide their decisions and actions. Traditions and institutions are open to change, but they retain a degree of stability, which enables them to guide. Liberals may wish not to vest their entire fortune in seeking to elaborate ground rules for debate. Historically, liberal thinkers urged attention to family, school, religious community, and other voluntary associations as sites of moral and political formation. These may be the sites to which nonfoundationist liberals, too, should turn their attention. They may yet produce answers that will surprise Schmitt's fans, on the right and left alike.

II

The history of liberalism is instructive about the problems liberals have, and have not, encountered with moral judgment. Whatever the moral grounding of their politics, they seem to have had little trouble recognizing evil and calling it by its name (or equivalent names). Persuading the public to accept their view and, even more crucially, to recognize the urgency of taking decisive political action to combat evil is a different matter. There they ran into major difficulties, which reflect liberal dilemmas of democracy that do not admit of more than temporary solutions.

"Liberalism" entered political discourse in Restoration France, as a term describing a group of intellectuals around Benjamin Constant (1767–1830) and Germaine de Staël (1766–1817) who called for a representative government and opposed both royal absolutism and Jacobinism. In 1796–1797, De Staël and Constant—previous supporters of republican government—attempted to explain where the French Revolution had gone wrong. They recognized the Terror of 1793–1794, a historically unprecedented shocking event, as the great evil against the like of which republicans must guard. They were permeated with consciousness of the failure of the republican model of the democratic citizen, the independent peasant-soldier, and visited the Terror's sins on the ideal of an armed democratic citizenry, which, unsuitable for modern government in a commercial society, ended in a plebiscitary tyranny.[8] They began distinguishing themselves from republicans by asserting the primacy of constitutional guarantees over democratic participation and designating their own position "liberal."[9] They proposed to modify the democratic ideal, so that it did not endanger liberty and constitutionalism.

Representative government was their answer, an attempt to reconcile the democratic ideal of participation and self-determination with the modern nation-state and constitutional protection. The control of violence emanating from the state and the crowd alike, became their chief concern.

For three decades, they searched desperately for powerful social and political agents who would be able to control violence while enshrining a constitution guaranteeing individual liberties. They first trusted in Napoleon, then decried him from exile as a tyrant, then again sought a rapprochement, their inconsistency manifesting not so much opportunism as desperation in the face of an insoluble dilemma: How do you endow authority with a power sufficient to control violence, yet ensure that it does not unduly limit liberty? How do you encourage public participation without incurring the risks of "enthusiasm," "fanaticism," and the public turning into a mob? How does one mobilize a public to defend liberty and then assure that it does not abuse its power and endanger liberty? These dilemmas reflected no uncertainty as to the moral judgment of tyranny and terror but great difficulty in molding a public consensus favoring lawful liberty and translating this consensus into a constitution strong enough to withstand a military coup.

In his diatribe against Napoleon in 1813, "On the Spirit of Conquest and Usurpation," Constant opined that commercial society depended on liberty—above all, on freedom of opinion—thereby reversing the famous eighteenth-century *doux commerce* argument that represented liberty as a product of commerce.[10] No sooner, however, had he urged "modern liberty," constitutional safeguards, and private comforts against "ancient liberty," democratic participation, and martial virtues, than he was forced to reverse himself. The liberals constituted the left opposition to the restored Bourbon government, which instituted political arrangements reflecting both constitutional and authoritarian government but failed to find a stable coalition of elites to secure its rule. Confronting in 1819 the increasing danger of a Bourbon coup, Constant urged popular mobilization to defend the constitution.[11] Ancient and modern liberty, he now opined, must be joined. How did one join ancient and modern liberty, political participation and freedom to produce liberal results? How did one both mobilize a public and hold it in check?

Radicals claimed that this was a false dilemma. Liberals, they pointed out, denied political rights and economic welfare to parts of the populace they sought to mobilize. The Ultras' premier under the Restoration, Villèle, threatened liberals with introducing universal male suffrage that would produce, he said, a royal absolutist majority. For much of the nineteenth century, popular suffrage was both a socialist demand and a reactionary threat, liberal opposition to it a major obstacle to democratization. When Bismarck made good on the reactionary threat in 1870 by introducing universal male suffrage, he did so to weaken the liberal opposition. No wonder radicals regarded liberalism as the antidemocratic movement par excellence and thought revolutionary crowds rationally sought to secure legitimate demands for equal citizenship.

The totalitarian mobs of the twentieth century cast doubt on the radicals' notion that crowds commonly convey legitimate grievances about inequality and that liberal hostility toward them reflects social interest and cultural elitism. More importantly, the radical critics misdiagnosed liberal anxiety. It was rooted not in rejection of democracy but in ambivalence toward it. Often what made liberals antidemocrats in the present was their belief in a future orderly democracy. In the liberal utopia, liberty and democracy coexist in perfect harmony. Liberalism was born as a dilemma—commitment at one and the same time to universal citizenship and liberty, to public participation and orderly government, to public debate that threatened to degenerate into crowd violence. An in-between existence, constant negotiation of conflicting aims, volatile management of democracy, inability to commit to democracy or deny it are the historical trademarks of liberalism. When one either commits or denies, one is no longer a liberal.

Liberal moral judgment reflects these constant acts of rebalancing. It can form no useful universal standards for recognition of evil because it often seeks to deploy as remedy the very forces that had previously been declared a threat. Beyond abstract liberty, equality, and orderly rule, the threats and options are in constant flux, and the mobilization against evil a recurrent challenge. The freedom-loving crowd of yesterday may be the riotous mob of today but is potentially the deliberative public of tomorrow. The rebellious oppressed natives of yesterday may turn into the terrorists of today but may become the liberal democrats of the future. Under such conditions, moral judgment is of necessity provisional, but no less valid for it.

Alexis de Tocqueville (1805–1859) reveals the liberal dilemmas of the democratic public like no other. For his contemporaries, the Doctrinaires François Guizot and Augustin Thierry, democracy was a threat, and the same could be said for contemporary German liberals and the British Whigs. For Tocqueville, it was a both a danger and a prospect. Commentators note how untypical he is of French liberals. He is most untypical, however, in the depth of his ambivalence about democracy and in his espousal of civic humanist (or republican) values and discourse. Unlike most French liberals, he thought that democracy could work, and in the near future, and that republican ideals were vital. In *Democracy in America* (1835–1840), liberal dreams and nightmares about democracy interchange.[12] It is locus classicus for the liberal dilemmas of the democratic public.

"[I]n America, I saw more than America," said Tocqueville, "I searched for the image of democracy itself . . . that which we ought to hope or fear from her" (1: 12). His judgment was mixed. He admired the grassroots democracy of New England towns and marveled at the "great equality of conditions"—the absence of a ruling hereditary aristocracy setting social norms, the lack of permanent social distinctions, and the manner in which they seemed not to matter for the smooth functioning of government. But he was alive to the danger of new types of political oppression emerging from democracy. In volume 1, he spoke of the "tyranny of the majority." He identified it first with legislative tyranny—the concentration of all power in the legislature that could make incursions upon liberty without encountering resistance, "rendering the guarantees of representative government vain" (1: 258). Even worse was the tyranny of public opinion, communal pressure to conform that rendered formal liberties meaningless. Public opinion, which was the great bulwark against tyranny to eighteenth-century thinkers from Hume to Kant, now seemed a major threat. Legislative tyranny, thought Tocqueville, was mitigated through a variety of political mechanisms, above all decentralization, but the tyranny of public opinion was irresistible.

> I know no country where . . . there is less independence of mind and true freedom of discussion than in America. . . . [T]he majority has drawn a formidable circle around thought. . . . [W]oe to the writer who ventures beyond it. . . . Chains and executioners were tyranny's crude instruments in times past; nowadays civilization has been perfected into despotism itself. . . . The master . . . says: "You are free not to think as I do . . . but from this day you are a stranger among us." (1: 266–67)

The master, "the majority," was the liberal nightmare. The problem was, the majority looked identical in all but name to the public that the liberals wished to mobilize, on other occasions, against tyranny. This became clear in volume 2 of *Democracy*. There, the major danger to liberty was no longer the majority's zeal but its indifference, not communal pressure but inaction, "each citizen isolating himself from the mass of his fellows [*ses semblables*] and withdrawing into the background with his family and friends . . . gladly abandoning the larger society to itself"

(2: 105–106). Such isolation of individuals was conducive to despotism. In the most famous paragraph of *Democracy*, Tocqueville warned of a new tutelary despotism.

> I see an innumerable crowd of men, alike and equal, restlessly circling
> around to obtain petty and banal pleasures . . . each of them [acting] . . .
> as if he were a stranger to the fate of all the others. Over [them] stands an
> immense tutelary power . . . absolute, . . . orderly, provident, and gentle. . . .
> The citizens quit their state of dependence only momentarily to name their
> master . . . [a] compromise between administrative despotism and the sover-
> eignty of the people. . . . However important, this brief and infrequent per-
> formance [*usage*] of the free arbiter will not prevent them from gradually
> losing the faculty of thinking, feeling, and acting for themselves, and
> falling below the level of humanity. (2: 324–26)

And the solution? A return to the democratic public:

> [C]itizens bound to take part in public affairs necessarily separate from
> the milieu of their individual interests. . . . As soon as common affairs are
> treated in common, each man notices that he is not as independent of the
> likes of him as he first imagined and that to get their support he must often
> offer them his help. (2: 109)

How did one encourage such public participation without incurring the risks of the public turning into a crowd? How does one encourage a public to accumulate power, then not abuse it? Liberals have never been as good at answering this question as they have been at devising constitutional mechanisms to prevent excessive concentration of power (far from a foolproof method, of course). Their failure has always been one of persuasion, not of conviction. Tocqueville had a number of palliatives. Religion was one. Secularists, like Mill, put their trust in education. But the dilemma remained alive, unanswerable.

The period between the revolutions of 1848 and World War One saw the introduction of universal male suffrage throughout Western and Central Europe. The problems that emerged had been unforeseen by liberals and did not correspond to their nightmares. They had some grasp of the way the social question would become central once the masses entered the political process, but they did not foresee the emergence of ethnonationalism, that is, the ethnicization of political and cultural concepts of the nation, nor the forceful renewal of colonial expansion and imperial competition. When Fascism and Communism challenged liberal democracy in the interwar years, liberals, faced again with the challenge of mobilization against dictatorship, found it necessary to reach back beyond the age of imperialism and ethnonationalism to the liberals of the first half of the nineteenth century. What they recovered was not so much liberal values and principles as liberal dilemmas.

Raymond Aron (1905–1983) is not nowadays a household name, but among post–World War Two French intellectuals he was the undisputed leader of the liberal minority. He reintroduced Tocqueville as a major thinker in France, and his reading of Tocqueville provides a measure of the continuity of liberal dilemmas. Throughout his life, Aron confronted the problem of mobilization against dictatorship and changed his position about its role in liberal democracy. In the 1930s—a time when he was a heterodox socialist voting for the Popular Front but considering its policies suicidal—he witnessed how public mobilization on the left failed to measure up to the fascist threat. He urged that "when the totalitarian [i.e., Fascist] regimes threaten them, the democratic regimes must answer that they are capable of . . . the same virtues. The only difference, and it is an important one, is that in democracies, one must consent spontaneously to those necessities that are elsewhere imposed."[13] How one encourages spontaneous commitment to liberal democracy has remained a problem.

Returning from exile in England with De Gaulle after the War, Aron split with the French left, endorsing the military mobilization against Communism under U.S. leadership. By the mid-1960s, he felt that the West had measured up to the challenge. "Does the waning of ideology brought about by the partial success of the democratic-liberal synthesis foreshadow the death of the citizen?" he asked in his 1965 *An Essay on Freedom*?[14] He answered in the negative. Tocqueville's "tutelary despotism," he said, reflected exaggerated and misdirected fears: Twentieth-century totalitarianism was first and foremost "violent and ideocratic," and only secondarily "tutelary." "The concern for well-being," he added, "is general and, indeed, legitimate in an essentially secular and democratic society. . . . The indifference of 'similar and equal' individuals to everything that is outside of their milieu is . . . observed in periods of calm. . . . [P]hases of collective passion [are] more dangerous than those of egoistic withdrawal into the self."[15] A liberal polity may do well without "collective passion" as long as constitutional procedures and traditions governed it and a military (with a nuclear umbrella) stood ready to defend it.

The "period of calm" must have been all too calm. Fifteen years later, Aron no longer dismissed Tocqueville's anxieties but rearticulated them: "Europe must remember that, in a democracy, individuals are at once private persons and citizens. . . . If the morality of Westerners has become a morality of pleasure, of individual happiness, rather than of the virtue of the citizen, then survival is in doubt. If nothing remains of the citizen's duty, if Europeans no longer have the feeling that they must be capable of fighting to retain the opportunities for pleasure and happiness, then, we are, indeed, both brilliant and decadent."[16] But Aron had never developed a concept of citizenship or public mobilization that would seem persuasive. Unlike Tocqueville, who saw active citizenship as essential, Aron spoke of its virtues only in the context of combating totalitarianism. To him, a liberal French intellectual of Jewish origin, thankful to France for having emancipated the Jews and overcome Fascism, it was self-evident why liberal Europe should be defended, but, to the French citizen, qua citizen, he could offer little more than the right to vote and the duty to die. Once again, the liberal calls on the public he has held at arm's length to defend liberty and is surprised that the call goes unanswered.

At certain moments in his life, Aron thought he discerned in his society a lack of moral conviction not unlike the one that concerns my colleagues and gave rise to this volume. Aron was not sure how to cultivate commitment to liberalism. The threat of totalitarianism left postwar liberals with no means of forging a liberal public. They could no longer avail themselves of religion and education: They were apprehensive lest "education for democracy" turn into indoctrination, and, a mostly secular cohort (including many cosmopolitan Jews), they neither wished to cultivate established religions nor were sanguine about their beneficial effects, especially given their record in fascist Europe. Durkheim's "civic religion" they viewed with suspicion.[17] "Secular religion" (Marxism) was a subject of denunciation, not endorsement, a threat, not a solution. They were suspicious, to use Isaiah Berlin's terminology, of any "positive aim" of liberalism, any vision of ideal citizenship, any consensus beyond welfare.[18] Behind such visions lurked always the dogmatism and radicalism sustaining totalitarianism. Their pluralism was radical, and it had its costs: inability to articulate a vision for the formation of a liberal public. They became ever more aware of the unique conditions enabling liberal democracy in the West, ever more pessimistic about its prospect elsewhere.

Our situation today represents some improvement over postwar liberalism. If liberals remain skeptical about the prospect of liberal democracy in the developing world, they do not quite live on edge the same way, apprehensive about any sign of a weakening liberal consensus in Europe or the United States. If many are still apprehensive about education for democracy and disregard the contribution—actual and potential—of communal religious life to the making of the liberal public, they seem less anxious about much of it and no longer suspect voluntary associations quite the same way for being closed societies. Liberals should be able to see their way toward working on the formation of a liberal public more easily today than during the Cold War and most other periods in the history of liberalism.

III

This history of liberal dilemmas will put our project in perspective, I hope, and perhaps effect a revaluation of our task and modify our expectations. Neither now nor at any point in the history of liberalism has the formation of moral judgment encountered serious difficulties. Discourse ethic has articulated an alternative vision for the formation of judgment, and it may need to be adjusted to recognize multiple formative sites, not all subject to the same level of rational control. But there is no sign that discourse ethic has created special difficulties for liberals in making their judgments. Persuasion of the public of the need to mobilize against perceived evils seems to be less of a problem today than in most periods in the history of liberalism, and this includes liberal Europe, not only the United States. Ensuring that mobilization does not put liberty at risk is a real challenge. Government actions, dressed in a plebiscitarian democratic mantle, do represent a danger nowadays. But, dangerous as they are to the rights of ethnic minorities, aliens, and prisoners, we are not nearly in as much danger of democratic plebiscitarianism as Constant, De Staël, and Tocqueville were. And, I dare say, we went through equally, if not more difficult, times in this country with McCarthyism half a century ago, certainly insofar as the freedom of academic deliberation is concerned.

The calls to reexamine liberal moral judgment under these circumstances are understandable, and my colleagues' thoughtful contributions will represent an attractive subject for a future historian of liberalism. Whatever proposal we make for cultivating commitment and forging consensus, whatever balance we strike between moral conviction and intellectual openness, we should remain aware of the historical specificity of the proposal and the fragility of the balance. We are not likely to offer a universally applicable solution to the formation of moral judgment because today's solution will become tomorrow's problem. The roles liberal agents and policies play can quickly reverse themselves.

The peculiar dilemmas of liberalism defy universal resolution. We should be especially careful not to import the complexity of the present situation into procedural proposals for moral judgment, which would violate their universalism and improperly constrain both deliberation and the freedom of agency. Instead, we should seek to modify the conditions enabling moral judgment through religious, educational, and other voluntary organizations—the sites liberals have traditionally recommended. We should be fully cognizant that these proposals, too, may require changes within a short time. Anxious as some of us may be, we should not expect ethics to offer more than general guidance in the pursuit of political solutions. Above all, we should not contribute to the hysteria about an "unprecedented crisis." In times such as these, the history of liberalism dissuades us from overreacting by assuring us that we are not the first to face the challenges. It thereby brings us a measure of comfort.

ACKNOWLEDGMENT

My thanks to Frances Ferguson of the University of Chicago and to Ruth Grant of Duke University for helpful comments on the conference draft.

NOTES

1. Neville Chamberlain on the Czechs in 1938, in defense of the Munich agreement to cede the heavily fortified Czech Sudetenland to Hitler. "How horrible, fantastic, incredible it is that we should be digging trenches and trying on gas masks here because of a quarrel in a far-away country between people of whom we know nothing." *In Search of Peace* (New York: G. P. Putman's Sons, 1939), p. 393.

2. Alexis de Tocqueville, *De la démocratie en Amérique*, ed. J. P. Mayer, 2 vols., in *Oeuvres Complètes* (Paris: Gallimard, 1961), 2: 106.

3. Carl Schmitt, *The Concept of the Political*, trans. and intro. with notes by George Schwab, and with comments on Schmitt's essay by Leo Strauss (New Brunswick, NJ: Rutgers University Press, 1976). Nazi Germany was a Fascist regime, but Fascism is a more capacious category than Nazism, and German National Socialism was only the most extreme example of Fascism. Fascist and semi-Fascist regimes in Europe were among Hitler's first rivals and his first victims.

4. Strauss, "Notes on Carl Schmitt," in ibid., pp. 83–107.

5. Karl Popper, *The Open Society and Its Enemies,* 2 vols. (London: Routledge, 1945). For an elaborate account, see my *Karl Popper: The Formative Years, 1902–1945* (New York: Cambridge University Press, 2000).

6. Jürgen Habermas, *Moral Consciousness and Communicative Action,* trans. Christian Lenhardt and Shierry Weber Nicholsen (Boston: MIT Press, 1990). This is not the way Habermas and his students frame his project, but I regard Habermas as paradigmatic of the trajectory postwar Germany (at least the Federal Republic) took in negotiating its way to a liberal democratic political culture. The trajectory is replete with paradoxes.

7. Popper, *The Open Society,* vol. 2, addendum to the fourth edition, p. 386.

8. The language of civility and commerce precedes liberalism, of course, as does the defense of liberal values. *The Federalist Papers,* the English debates on parliamentary reform

in the wake of the Wilkes affair, and other prerevolutionary episodes foreshadow liberal dilemmas of democracy, as well as future liberal strategies of containment. But the dilemmas of democracy do not emerge full-blown until the Jacobin terror and Napoleonic plebiscitarianism, and the term "liberalism" enters political discourse to describe intellectuals confronting these dilemmas.

9. Anne-Louise-Germaine de Staël, *De l'influence des passions sur le bonheur des individus et des nations* (Lausanne: Mourer, 1796); Benjamin Constant, *Des réactions politiques* (Paris: Delaunay, 1797); K. Steven Vincent, "Benjamin Constant, the French Revolution, and the Origins of Modern Liberalism," *French Historical Studies* 23 (fall 2000): 607–638.

10. Benjamin Constant, "The Spirit of Conquest and Usurpation and Their Relation to European Civilization," in Biancamaria Fontana, ed. and trans., *Political Writings* (Cambridge: Cambridge University Press, 1988).

11. Constant, "The Liberty of the Ancients Compared with That of the Moderns," in ibid.

12. Tocqueville, *De la démocratie en Amérique*. I have consulted Mayer's English edition (trans. George Lawrence [Garden City, NY: Doubleday, 1969]), but have often modified the translation. Pagination in the text follows the French edition.

13. Raymond Aron, "États démocratiques et états totalitaires (juin 1939)," *Commentaire* 6, no. 24 (winter 1983–1984): 798.

14. Raymond Aron, *Essai sur les libertés* (Paris: Calmann-Lévy, 1965), p. 146 (translated as *An Essay on Liberty* by H. Weaver [Berkeley: University of California, 1966]).

15. Aron, *Essai*, pp. 143–144.

16. *Le Spectateur engagé* (Paris: Julliard, 1981), pp. 296, 295, respectively.

17. Emile Durkheim, "The Principles of 1789 and Sociology" and "Individualism and the Intellectuals," in *Emile Durkheim on Morality and Society*, ed. Robert Bellah (Chicago: University of Chicago, 1973); and Durkheim, *Professional Ethics and Civic Morals* (Glencoe, IL: Free Press, 1958).

18. Isaiah Berlin, "Two Concepts of Liberty" [1958], in his *Four Essays on Liberty* (New York: Oxford University Press, 1969).

Chapter 9

Thomas A. Spragens, Jr.

Between Bigotry and Nihilism

Moral Judgment in Pluralist Democracies

The exercise of good moral judgment is an important civic virtue for citizens in democratic societies. It is nonetheless a problematic virtue. To some extent, the problematic status of this virtue of moral judgment is one of its general features. Placing it into the context of pluralist democratic societies and considering it as a public and political virtue, however, has the effect of sharpening and deepening the moral tensions associated with it, because these societies require other virtues difficult to reconcile with it. Attempts to avoid these tensions by neglecting or submerging one of its core elements are, however well intended, illegitimate. Attempts to achieve some form of complete reconciliation of the conflicting norms are exercises in futility. The best we can do is to understand the legitimate moral grounds of the tensions surrounding the exercise of moral judgment, to give each of these grounds appropriate respect, and to pursue strategies that can help us negotiate the treacherous terrain between bigotry and a soft form of nihilism.

The Moral Ambivalence of Moral Judgment

My topic in this essay is the problematic status of moral judgment in pluralistic democratic societies. It is worth noting as a prolegomenon to this topic, however, that moral ambivalence attends the exercise of moral judgment in a more general way: it is not simply the demands and constraints of democratic pluralism that cause the problem. It is not necessary to canvass every extant or imaginable moral tradition in order to make this point. It is enough to observe how moral tension can surround the exercise of moral judgment without the values of democracy or the fact of pluralism ever entering the picture.

Those of us who received some exposure to the biblical tradition in our youth, for example, were acquainted early on with a certain ambivalence about moral judgment. On the one hand, it was clear that there were a lot of moral judgments being rendered in both the Old and New Testaments, to the apparent approval of those who reported them. Simply canvassing the headings in the books of the prophets in the New Revised Standard Version of the Bible gives ample testimony to the ubiquity of moral judgment being levied against varied categories of wrongdoing and wrongdoers: "The Wickedness of Judah," and "The Degenerate City," among others, in Isaiah; "Judgment on Egypt," "Judgment on the Philistines," "Judgment on Moab," and so on, in Jeremiah; "Relentless Judgment on Israel," in Hosea; "Judgment in the Valley of Jehoshaphat," in Joel; and so on. A whole lot of judgment going on.

The New Testament seems less judgmental. But Jesus pronounces woe on the scribes, the Pharisees, and hypocrites. He pronounces woe on the cities of Chorazin, Bethsaida, and Capernaum, telling them that "on the Day of Judgment it will be more tolerable for the land of Sodom than for you." He talks about things that "defile" people. He says that those who cause little children to sin would have been better off if a millstone were fastened around their neck and they were drowned in the depth of the sea. And of course he tells of the Last Judgment to come. So the message was pretty clear. There was good and there was evil. You needed to choose the one and avoid the other. To do that, you needed to exercise the requisite moral judgment to distinguish what was good and bad, right and wrong. And ultimately moral judgment would be pronounced on you. Better get it right.

If the exercise of good moral judgment seems to be a moral imperative, however, another well-known admonition from the Gospels warns of the moral perils occasioned by attempts to make such judgments. "Do not judge, so that you may not be judged. For with the judgment you make, you will be judged, and the measure you give will be the measure you get. Why do you see the speck in your neighbor's eye, but do not notice the log in your own eye? . . . You hypocrite, first take the log out of your own eye, and then you will see clearly to take the speck out of your neighbor's eye."[1] The virtue of having and making moral judgments, it seems, is not the same kind of virtue as those of, say, loving one's neighbor as yourself or honoring one's father and mother. These latter virtues are not attended by complications and complexities in their exercise. Of them, one could say, the more the better. Having good judgment in matters moral, on the other hand, is not a "maximizing" virtue. It comes with a warning label: handle with care, use with circumspection. When engaged in without restraint and without due regard for its context and its objects, this is a virtue that can turn into a vice.

Why the worries? Several reasons. The first of these is specifically a theological one. Ultimately, God is the only legitimate moral judge of the universe. Only His judgments are fully valid and just. Whenever we as finite creatures are so bold as to make moral judgments, we verge upon the blasphemy or self-idolatry of taking upon ourselves a role that belongs to God and God alone. We must make moral judgments to lead a good life, but whenever we do so it is fair to ask: who are you to judge? For anyone who believes in a moral universe governed by the Creator and Judge of all, moral judgments have to be made in fear and trembling.

The other principal worries about moral judgment expressed in the famous admonition "judge not" are not so expressly theological. The first of these is epistemic in nature. As finite and self-interested creatures, our moral perceptions are skewed and unreliable. We know our needs and situation in ways that we cannot know others' needs and situation, and we privilege our own. We suffer from systemic defects in our moral imagination, and our judgments are correspondingly flawed. That is why we see so keenly the minor sins of others and are often clueless about our own faults. The other worries represent moral concerns that bear upon social morality in general. The asymmetry of our moral perceptions leads to violations of the fundamental norm of reciprocity. And the mutual exaction of judgment, especially given the systemic asymmetry problem, disrupts the bonds of community and caritas.

Can these tensions, apparently intrinsic to the practice of moral judgment, be evaded? Several strategies suggest themselves in this context. How about separating moral discernment from moral condemnation, sequestering judgment from the penumbra of judgmentalism? How about hating the sin but loving the sinner? How about judging oneself and forswearing all moral assessments of others and their conduct? My sense is that each of these strategies helps lessen the strains created by the need to distinguish between good and evil, right and wrong, in conjunction with the warning about standing in judgment over other people. But problems remain, nonetheless.

The most useful precept to follow in the quest to honor these apparently conflicting obligations is to be diligent in morally appraising one's own behavior but to forswear invoking moral standards to criticize others. Leave the judgment of others to themselves, to God, perhaps to posterity. That way one can seek righteousness without becoming "self-righteous." But sometimes judgments of others are unavoidable, even obligatory. What if you are placed on a jury and have to decide whether certain actions of others were "heinous" or whether there were "mitigating circumstances"? Perhaps in some contexts it may even be deemed a service to others to convey to them your sense of moral disapprobation to alert them to problematic aspects of their behavior and possibly to help them avoid the potentially costly consequences of their arrogance, callousness, sloth, or other possible vices. John Stuart Mill, for one, thought so. "A person may so act as to compel us to judge him," Mill wrote, " and feel to him as a fool or as a being of an inferior order; and since this judgment and feeling are a fact which he would prefer to avoid it is doing him a service to warn him of it beforehand, as of any other disagreeable consequence to which he exposes himself. It would be well, indeed, if this good office were much more freely rendered than the common notions of politeness at present permit."[2]

It also is good advice to urge that we distinguish moral discernment from moralistic judgmentalism, practicing the former without veering into the latter. And it surely accords with the demands of caritas and the imperatives of forgiveness to say that we can and should "hate the sin but love the sinner." These distinctions, however, while clear enough in their verbal and abstract form, often prove hard to maintain when one seeks to apply them in concrete practice. If I "discern" that deed x is right or good to do and deed y is wrong or evil, and I say so, the implication is quite clear that I have judged person z who has done y to be a wrongdoer and, to that extent, morally suspect. However scrupulously I may forebear from manifesting scorn or opprobrium, that admirable attitudinal restraint cannot efface the moral reproach intrinsic to my cognitive attempt at moral discrimination.

Similarly, if you convey to me your judgment that I have behaved sinfully but you love me nonetheless, I can quite reasonably feel that you have put me down twice over: I am to know that I am not only a reprobate but I am in your debt for your charitable response to my malfeasance. It is, thus, unsurprising that those placed into the role of "sinners, but loved nonetheless" do not necessarily respond appreciatively to this kind of alleged benevolence.

Situating Moral Judgment: Democracy, Liberalism, and Pluralism

If the exercise of moral judgment is arguably an intrinsically problematic virtue—manifested inter alia by the conflicting admonitions regarding it within the biblical tradition—things become even more complicated in the context of today's pluralistic liberal democracies. The norms, practices, and brute empirical facts of these societies provide both added impetus and new constraints to our efforts to make, convey, and act upon our moral judgments.

Consider democracy first. Two of the core principles of democracy are popular sovereignty and political equality. The first of these core principles is expressed by the standard sayings that "here the people rule" and that legitimate government is based upon the "consent of the people." The second is captured by the standard of "one person, one vote," by the Constitutional mandate of the "equal protection of the laws" and by Jefferson's famous gloss on his declaration that we are all "created equal": "the mass of mankind has not been born with saddles on their backs, nor a favored few booted and spurred, ready to ride them legitimately by the grace of God."[3]

Each of these principles carries consequences for the exercise of moral judgment. To the extent that governance and the making of potential decisions involve elements of moral judgment, democracy universalizes among its citizenry the burdens and the rights of rendering such judgments. If the people are the source of political authority and ultimately govern themselves, the burdens of judgment cannot be delegated to a select few. We must all make judgments to carry out our political responsibilities, and we all labor pari passu under the obligation to attain the capacities needed to judge competently. And to the extent that we are political equals, our moral judgments must *ceteris paribus* carry equal weight. In short, the logic of democracy creates certain norms of civic virtue for its citizens, and it implies a radical diffusion of authority. Both of these logical implications have consequences for the way moral judgments are rendered and adjudicated.

Liberalism brings into the complex of norms governing most advanced contemporary societies the insistence that individual persons have rights whose institutionalization should protect them from the depredations of others. And liberalism also brings with it, partly as a practical corollary of the insistence upon individual rights, the idea of a principled distinction between public and private spheres. Each of these liberal principles also bears upon the ways that moral judgments may be involved in the political domain. The attribution of rights to individuals, together with the endorsement of personal autonomy as a good that informs the idea of rights, leads to what John Rawls has called "the liberal principle of legitimacy"—the stipulation that political power and legal coercion is fully proper only when exercised in conformity with principles that all citizens could "reasonably be expected to endorse in light of . . . their common human reason."[4] That principle complicates and constrains the kinds of moral judgments people can deploy when deciding upon institutions and policies with coercive implications. The establishment of a private sphere buffered from the exactions of public authority helps democratic societies deal with the same moral hazard Rawls's principle addresses by offering a mechanism for softening and evading political tensions and conflicts that can result from the presence of divergent moral judgments among the citizenry. You may judge aspects of my way of life to be immoral, but insofar as some of these practices are conducted within the private sphere of life, I am insulated from restrictions or corrections you might—as a consequence of your judgment—want to impose upon me.

Today's liberal democracies also tend to be—to varying degrees—"pluralistic" ones. They may—again to a greater or lesser extent—be composed of people of different races and ethnicities. But that sociological fact is not particularly relevant to the exercise of moral judgment in the society unless it is linked to, or results in the presence of, what is functionally significant in this context—namely, moral and religious pluralism. Moral and religious pluralism complicates and constrains the role of moral judgment in a society's public life because our moral judgments on specific cases and issues generally derive from fundamental moral intuitions, which in turn are justified and informed by these competing moral and religious conceptions of the good life. People can reach different moral judgments even within relatively homogeneous moral cultures. But they at least can deploy a common moral vocabulary to discuss and attempt to adjudicate their differences. Morally and religiously pluralistic societies, in contrast, have to cope with different and possibly incommensurable moral vocabularies that tend to frustrate and impede such discussions and attempts at adjudication. Hence, different modes of engagement may be required when divergent moral judgments are a function of the different moral cultures and their comprehensive doctrines.

Good Judgment as Democratic Imperative

Prior to the emergence of democratic regimes, good judgment could be said to have been an aristocratic political virtue. So long as government was by one or by the few, it was that one or those few who needed to possess and exercise the capacity for good judgment in order for their society to prosper. The many were political subjects who were neither called upon nor required to make judgments of political significance. One could say that their civic virtue was to obey the law and fulfill the responsibilities, whether military, economic, or familial, imposed upon them by their assigned role in society. Those who needed *phronesis* (the capacity for good judgment in matters relating to human action) and the virtues of intellect and character upon which *phronesis* depended were those who made the decisions. In the *Republic,* it was only the philosopher-kings who had to achieve knowledge of the Good. It sufficed for the auxiliaries to be valorous and for the workers to be productive. In medieval times, philosophers wrote books of advice for princes, not for the people. In the predemocratic or nondemocratic Enlightenment, in Voltaire and Comte, the philosophes sought the ear of despots to enlighten and savants were to set society's course for *industriels* to implement. The imperatives of judgment reach so far as the power to rule and no further.[5]

The democratic revolution resulted in a radical diffusion of political authority. Now the whole body of citizens, however defined, are the ultimate rulers. As a consequence, the imperatives of good judgment as a civic virtue undergo a corresponding radical expansion. If the people are to rule, the people must have sufficient capacities for judgment to exercise that power with at least a modicum of prudence and reasonableness, or disaster is likely. As Justice Holmes famously observed, in a democracy the people have the right to "go to hell in a hand basket." They also have the power to reach that destination, and absent an adequate capacity for judgment they will probably get there.

For a democracy to be a well-ordered society, then, the whole citizenry as an aggregate body must be able to exercise good political judgment. Good political judgment has several components, and some of these components clearly involve moral judgment. So although one can seek to distinguish political judgment from moral judgment, it would be quite mistaken to think that we could thereby identify a separate sphere of judgments that sufficed to cover political questions without having to trench upon the realm of moral judgment. All political judgments are not moral, and all moral judgments are not political. But many political judgments that have to be made are moral ones, just as many moral judgments have ineluctable political implications. In their capacity as members of the sovereign people, democratic citizens have to make judgments of several kinds. First, just as individuals have to make prudential calculations about what conduces to their self-interest and about what means are most likely to produce the desired outcomes, so as members of the body politic democratic citizens have to make judgments about what is advantageous to the society as a whole. Call these judgments of collective prudence.

Are we as a society likely as a whole to be better off with a completely unregulated free market economy, or is the public interest likely to be better served when some constraints are collectively imposed on the marketplace? How much gross national profit should be sacrificed for how much preservation or improvement of our natural environment? What levels of investment should we make in our local public schools at what cost in local property taxes? Will our city be better organized for the conduct of our lives, more habitable, if we have zoning laws; or should we let development and use patterns occur willy-nilly? And so on.

Now these judgments of collective prudence in part may be analogized to individual self-interested calculations of the sort modeled by "rational choice" theory. As Aristotle notes, there is a common "notion that it is the self-regarding man who is prudent."[6] But, as Aristotle also notes, both for individuals and for polities, prudential judgments cannot be reduced to purely technical calculations about the most efficient way to attain unproblematically predetermined ends. Instead, prudential judgments unavoidably invoke judgments about "the truth in things that are humanly good and bad."[7] Only delusional suppositions about the possibility of some morally neutral objective calculus of what is humanly desirable can obscure the truth that judgments about what is "advantageous" and in our "self-interest" are impossible apart from contestable judgments about the humanly good life. And these judgments about human flourishing and the human good are a species of moral judgment. Thus, in both the individual and the collective cases, deciding what is "prudent" unavoidably involves making judgments on questions such as "Is the good life one of maximum material accumulation, or should health, leisure, and play come first?" "Do communal interactions among citizens have value to the point that society should be structured to promote them, or are these inessential goods properly left to personal taste and unplanned contingencies?" Clearly, then, if judgments about what is humanly good are a species of moral judgment, moral judgments cannot be sidestepped when democratic citizens have to decide what is and is not collectively "advantageous" or prudent.

Democratic citizens also have to make judgments about the right as well as the good. In the first place, one could say that in order to be democratic citizens—in order to recognize themselves as such and to act accordingly—people must recognize and accept what Rawls and others have called the "formal constraints of the concept of right." Essentially, this means the recognition and acceptance of the norm of moral reciprocity, the understanding that one cannot expect to be a free rider exempt from the obligation to abide by universal rules. This is the fundamental principle of Kant's "kingdom of ends," of Rousseau's concept of law, and of the Constitutional mandate of "equal protection." Without accepting one's subjection to these formal principles of right, no one can accept his or her role and status as democratic citizen—that is, as an equal part of the sovereign democratic people—rather than remaining an "alien" who retains a determination to exercise a privileged sovereign status over others. Whether this acceptance of the rule of reciprocity is construed philosophically with the Scottish Enlightenment as part of our "moral sense" or with Kant as an intuition of pure practical reason, this entry requirement for democratic citizenship is itself one species of moral judgment about what is right and fair.

Beyond acquiescing in this entry-level moral judgment about fairness, democratic citizens as collectively sovereign are also compelled as a consequence of their association to make all sorts of judgments about the content of justice—both retributive and distributive. Some of the most salient and bitter issues in many recent elections at various levels have involved questions of retributive justice. Is the death penalty a morally appropriate punishment for certain especially terrible crimes? Is it fair to have divergent sentencing standards for cocaine and crack cocaine? Should abortion be criminalized? And so on. All sorts of issues are at bottom questions about distributive justice—about the fair terms of social cooperation. There are prudential issues surrounding tax policies: what kinds and levels of taxes will promote or discourage investment, encourage or discourage a prudent savings rate, lead to a robust economy? But questions of distributive justice are absolutely fundamental here, as well. What relative contributions to public purposes are appropriate for the wealthy, the poor, and the middle class? Is it wrong for people's estates to be taxed? Or is it conversely wrong for people to inherit tax-free while others have to pay taxes on earned income? Regarding health care, is it morally acceptable for children in a wealthy nation not to have access to health care? Is it fair for taxpayer-funded health care subsides to be distributed in a way that makes distinctions between maladies that are and are not caused by the patient's risky or self-destructive behavior? Regarding military security, is it morally acceptable to rely upon soldiers recruited by financial inducements, or does such a policy represent profoundly unjust class discrimination when it comes to allocating the risks of war? In social policy, are Medicare and Social Security appropriate ways to care for our elderly citizens and give them their just due for their years of work, or are the "greedy geezers" exploiting hard-pressed workers to fund their greens fees in a cushy retirement? In short, it is hard to conjure important political issues that carry no distributive consequences and are thereby devoid of questions about social justice. And that means that, whether thoughtfully or neglectfully, all those who make decisions bearing upon these issues—and that group ultimately encompasses the entire democratic electorate—are rendering moral judgments as they make their arguments and cast their votes.

The implicit explanatory "realism" of much political science—whether it be from garden-variety Machiavellianism, neo-Marxist assumptions about class interest, the group theory of politics, rational choice theory, or some combination of these—tends to blind us to this ubiquity of moral judgment in political judgment and political conflict. That blindness in turn tends to inhibit our understanding of patterns of political behavior and affiliation that seem to be based on "anomalous" intrusions of "values questions" into the "normal" logic of political self-interest. But there is a reason for the hoary admonition to avoid discussions of politics or religion on social occasions: it is because politics and religion both involve a heavy admixture of moral judgments, and these are the kinds of judgments that are most passionately contested and most incapable of adjudication. Discussions of political matters would be much less contentious and hence not such a danger to wary hostesses intent on enforcing conviviality if they turned simply around matters of clear self-interest. The political battles over conflicts of interest might be vicious, but the discussion of them would not be all that volatile. Participants would only be "declaring their interest" in the manner of British members of Parliament, and none would have grounds for taking offense from the declarations of the others—which would be both straightforward and on a clear logical par with their own. It is the moral stuff that in one sense makes us better people but, at the same time, raises the ante and causes the trouble.

The imperatives of moral judgment in politics and the diffusion of its relevant exercise among the entire adult citizenry in a democratic regime have always led the advocates of more democratic governance to emphasize the importance of an educated populace. However much they may have opposed the elitist conclusions Plato drew from his analogy of the ship in his *Republic,* they knew he had a valid point—one that presented one of democracy's greatest challenges. If the people in charge of steering the ship of state are clueless about the relevant facts or lack the capacity to make the necessary judgments, the chances of a safe voyage are rather dim. That is why people like Condorcet, Mill, Jefferson, Jane Addams, and Horace Mann all emphasized in their different ways the great need for education. Democratic governance requires its citizens to have the knowledge base and the intellectual capacities to make informed and competent judgments about political matters. No regime can survive an ignorant and foolish sovereign; so no democracy can expect success with an uneducated populace.

One final observation on the topic of the imperatives of judgment in a democracy: the role and extent of these imperatives will vary somewhat depending upon the specific conception of democracy serving as the normative reference point. This observation can perhaps best be made by considering illustrative examples from opposing ends of the relevant spectrum of possibilities. If your underlying model of democratic governance is deliberative, participatory, and civic republican, then your responsible citizens will carry extensive burdens of political and moral judgment. The public sphere will be a significant one, so the scope of public judgment will be correspondingly large. In participatory regimes, people have to engage more fully and directly in political decision making and accordingly must render the judgments that determine these decisions and the attendant actions. And when they are participants in the democratic dialogue within deliberative forums, people are called upon to make arguments that are species of phronetic reasoning and that contain the practical judgments about the human good intrinsic to that kind of reasoning. They must, moreover, stand in constant judgment over the multiple and conflicting arguments presented for their consideration by their fellow citizens.

At the other end of the spectrum, the citizens of libertarian regimes, modus vivendi regimes, and regimes run in accord with Burkean norms of representation would carry lesser burdens of political and moral judgment. Burkean citizens would effectively offload much of their responsibility for judgment by delegating it to their representatives, who in turn make the judgments on their behalf as their trustees. To the extent that a democratic regime is understood to be a set of institutions designed simply to effect a modus vivendi among self-interested citizens—a straightforward pact of convenience to allow people to live together in relative peace—the relationships among the citizens are in a sense "de-moralized." Not being tied together by moral bonds, the collective decisions they might have to make lose much of the moral content of decisions made in democratic regimes that construe themselves as moral associations. These "decisions" are instead simply bargains, and bargains require only calculations of personal advantage and not moral judgments. The same minimizing of the scope of relevant moral judgment by citizens would occur within a libertarian polity—of the sort, say, sketched by a

Robert Nozick or a Milton Friedman.[8] For in such regimes, citizens relate to each other as participants in a free market—hence as mutually disinterested bargainers—whose moral relations with each other consist in the nontransgression of boundaries set by libertarian conceptions of individual rights.

The need for democratic citizens to make moral judgments cannot, however, be wholly evaded even within these elitist (Burkean) or minimalist (modus vivendi, libertarian) forms of government. The Burkean masses, for example, would have to use their judgment to decide to consent to trusteeship norms of representation. That is, they would have to stand in judgment over the merits of Burke's argument to the electors of the city of Bristol in which he made his pitch for these norms. Moreover, these commoners in a Burkean regime would still have to choose their representatives and, in so choosing, make the relevant judgments of character—which are themselves an important species of moral judgment. And citizens of democratic regimes with a minimal public domain and where people relate purely as bargainers are, by acquiescing in these modes of governance, implicitly also making very important moral judgments. They are making judgments about where the line between public and private should be, about what we as citizens do and do not owe each other, about whether social justice is a "mirage," as Friedrich von Hayek claims, or whether taxation for redistributive purposes is tantamount to theft or not, about whether social peace rather than justice is the first virtue of political institutions, and so on. In short, with popular sovereignty comes an inescapable burden of making judgments with uneliminable moral dimensions that democratic citizens have to carry.

Constraints on Moral Judgment in Pluralist Liberal Democracies

A car drove by me the other day bearing a bumper sticker that read: "Non-Judgment Day Is Near." Needless to say, it did not come with an appended moral or political argument; but it provided wry testimony to the fact that in pluralistic societies important democratic and liberal principles are in play that impose constraints upon the making of moral judgments. If democratic citizens are burdened with obligations to render moral judgments in their collective capacity as political sovereign, they also face limitations on their actions in this area that are themselves ultimately moral in origin.

The fact of pluralism provides the backdrop for these constraints and their logic. Pluralism here refers to the presence within the society of multiple comprehensive moral persuasions. These moral persuasions may be a function of different religions, or they may be a function of not specifically religious or even doctrinal moral cultures or ways of life. The crucial thing is that they produce a lack of unanimity within the society about the defining features and moral requirements of the humanly good life. Morally homogeneous polities such as the Amana community, Islamic theocracies, or Jewish kibbutzim may well have conflicts of interest among their members, but their internal moral contests are, absent apostates, limited to what we could call differences about the proper application of commonly held moral principles. In morally and culturally pluralistic societies, in contrast, conflicts over proper human goods and behavior cut more deeply, often emanating from disagreements over fundamental principles.

In the context of this deeper form of social pluralism, basic democratic and liberal norms generate imperatives of nonjudgment in matters moral. This happens because an insistence upon imposing your own moral judgments upon fellow citizens who do not subscribe to or accept them is a form of coercion. And such coercive impositions by one segment of society over others conflict with liberal and democratic principles mandating consent to authority, political equality, and individual autonomy.

Both democracy and liberalism entail a theory of political obligation that derives the legitimacy of governance from the consent of the governed. The measure of that consent has variously been conceived as empirical, rational, and/or reasonable. Empirical consent refers to the expressed consent by words or deeds of the actual people in question. Rational consent derivations of political obligation are based on "rational choice" calculations about what free, equal, and knowledgeable individuals would consent to in order to maximize their self-interest within the limits of possibility. (Hobbes's account of the social contract as the solution to an n-person prisoners' dilemma is a classic example.) Reasonable consent metrics are basically accounts of political obligation based upon the moral principle of reciprocity or fair play. (Kant's account of the republic of ends and Rawls's account of the fair terms of social cooperation provide examples here.) All of these accounts have in common the moral intuition that it is prima facie morally improper to force people to do things when the coercive measures in question cannot be justified to them within a moral vocabulary they are willing to accept. Hence, if I seek to impose measures upon you on the basis of moral judgments of mine that cannot be adequately translated into your own moral vocabulary, then under the liberal/democratic principle of legitimacy

I am morally constrained to forebear from this imposition insofar as that is possible.[9]

The moral logic of democratic equality similarly leads to obligatory constraints on moral judgment. Begin here with the fundamental premise that "all are created equal": all citizens in a democratic regime are presumed to have equal moral and political status. Their wishes and goals have equal worth. They should be accorded equal respect. That moral premise leads to the juridical principle of the equal protection of the laws. These moral imperatives, taken in concert with the fact of pluralism, then generate a principle of institutional moral constraint and forbearance on the part of the democratic state. That is, given that all citizens are to be given equal respect and treated equally, and given that they subscribe to different conceptions of the human good, the state must as far as possible adopt a stance of neutrality vis-à-vis these different conceptions of the good.

Finally, liberal moral premises contribute the principle of personal autonomy. All human persons are entitled as moral beings to live in accord with principles and goals of their own choosing. It is a violation of their moral integrity and their right of self-determination to require them to be mere functionaries within a plan of life scripted in accord with someone else's moral judgments or desires. Robert Nozick's provision in his thought experiment about liberal utopia captures this imperative in his stipulation of the absolute right of his utopia's citizens to emigrate from any particular association they may join. And Mill's disparagement of a life not lived in accord with self-determined principles as "apelike" rather than truly human expresses this same fundamental moral intuition regarding the value of personal autonomy and its incompatibility with subjection to someone else's judgments about the good life.

This complex of principled constraints against imposing one's moral judgments on others provides the moral foundation for the ethos and practice of toleration.[10] It turns out, however, that the meaning and requirements of the related moral imperatives of respect, toleration, and the relinquishment of the inclination to force others to live in accord with your moral judgments can take different forms. These differences, moreover, can be quite important in their implications for the ways we might try to navigate our way between the obligations to exercise and to constrain our moral judgments. For the sake of both political relevance and simplicity, let me focus upon two of the most pertinent of these competing accounts of the political implications of the morality of nonjudgmentalism. These accounts turn around contrasting understandings of what it means to respect and to tolerate one's fellow citizens.

The first account is the more traditional and familiar. Its main strands appear in Locke's *Letter concerning Toleration* and Mill's *On Liberty*. Its paradigm case is religious conflict or what today might be generically characterized as the presence of multiple and at least somewhat incompatible comprehensive moral or religious doctrines. Its central claim is that institutionalized disengagement (e.g., separation of church and state) and mutual forbearance are not only prudentially beneficial (by lessening social conflict) but also are practices grounded in moral principles endemic to democratic liberalism. The basic democratic/civic republican principle of moral and political equality among citizens and the basic liberal value of autonomy both constitute moral warrants for a mandate of mutual respect. I respect someone both by acknowledging their equal status and also by according them a right to self-determination: I am precluded morally from either dominating or oppressing them. The mandate of respect brings the mandate of toleration as its corollary when it is situated within what might be called, with apologies to Hume, "the circumstances of tolerance": namely, moral and religious pluralism. I may consider your belief system to be delusionary and its attendant moral code improper. I may make you aware of that judgment and try to persuade you to adopt my own views regarding the good life. But out of respect for you as a political equal and a moral (free) subject, I must prescind from my natural impulse to force upon you a code of conduct or plan of life predicated on my moral convictions about the human good.

This account of principled toleration need not and usually does not forswear a "cognitivist" conception of moral truth. There may be a "right" or "correct" doctrine of the human good, a valid account of the "one true path" to salvation or moral probity. But this account insists that it is both unavailing and improper for me to attempt to compel you to affirm and act upon that truth for the reasons aforementioned. Generally, on the basis of either or both hard experience (e.g., the Wars of Religion) and epistemological reflections (e.g., Locke's *Essay concerning Human Understanding*) this account of respect and toleration is associated with and bolstered by a recognition of the fallibility of our cognitive capacities in their attempts to ascertain moral truth—an acknowledgment that we "see through a glass darkly" in these matters. Or, as another recently seen bumper sticker admonished, "I don't know and you don't either." (This was probably a rejoinder to yet another entrant in the bumper sticker wars: "God said it, I believe it, and that's that.")

Another account of these matters has appeared in recent years that offers a different interpretation of the meaning of "respect" and "toleration." This interpretation imposes a more stringent account of obligations and constraints required by these norms. And in so doing it raises the bar when it comes to the moral imperatives of nonjudgmentalism, which in turn results in a very different depiction of the tension between the obligation to be morally discriminating on the one hand and to be forbearing toward our fellow citizens on the other.

This newer account of the imperatives of nonjudgmentalism takes leave in part from observations and interpretations of changes in the political sociology of democratic societies. The idea here is that the traditional account of the meaning and demands of toleration was based on its paradigm case of religious conflict. But we no longer live in Locke's time, the argument goes, and the grounds and axes of social pluralism are now quite different from what they were. The principles of free exercise and nonestablishment of religion, together with the lesser salience and intensity of sectarian doctrinal wars, have in effect regularized and institutionalized religious toleration and made it widely accepted—albeit not universally so—within contemporary liberal democracies. The kind of social and moral pluralism now generating most social conflict, the argument continues, is a product of group affiliations and social identities that bring with them alternative, and sometimes conflicting, patterns of behavior or ways of life.

In this changed context, the argument continues, the traditional account of respect and toleration is no longer appropriate or useful. Traditionally conceived, toleration was grudging and minimal. It assumed and legitimated moral disapproval, requiring only that people not act upon it aggressively to oppress people with different conceptions of the good life. The traditional account of respect was likewise too abstract and formalistic. It involved juridical protection of the political rights of all people, but these protections were compatible with hostility to particular ways of life and to the groups endorsing them.

In this newer understanding of the meaning and demands of respect and tolerance, this moment of begrudgment and animosity is itself delegitimated. Members of well-ordered democratic societies should not be praised for merely holding their moral disapproval and animosity toward alternative ways of life in check. They are instead obligated to recognize their censoriousness and animus as itself morally improper and to abandon it altogether. Rather like God loving those who do not simply give, but do so with good cheer, so those who endorse this account of democratic civic virtue would require that respect and toleration of others be a form of positive recognition and affirmation rather than reluctant resignation and acceptance.[11] Perhaps, indeed, as some on both sides of this discussion have observed, the use of "toleration" as the relevant norm here should be abandoned outright as misleading and obsolescent. Insofar as the notion of being tolerant incorporates and permits a moment of principled disapproval of those tolerated, it is not adequate to convey what this viewpoint construes as the standard of appropriate attitude and behavior.

This account, one that in effect radicalizes the demands of respect and toleration, would clearly have an important impact upon the way that we understand the respective domains and proper balance between the exercise of moral judgment and the principled constraints upon it. For on this account, one could say, having and expressing moral disapprobation of other social identities or conceptions of the good is ipso facto improper and destructive, whether or not it eventuates in active persecution. Certainly it would seem that in this view Mill's claim, noted earlier, that it constitutes a "good office" and "doing him a service" to "warn" someone that you "judge him" to be "a fool or a being of an inferior order" is seriously in error.[12] Indeed, it would seem that in this account anyone entertaining the kinds of judgments Mill describes here would have to be seen as a moral bigot, and the honest expression of such judgments, so far from being a service or good office, would have to be seen as, to some degree or another, a form of hate speech.

Constructions of Moral Judgment and the Problem of Bigotry

Where then does all this leave us in terms of the role of moral judgment in pluralist liberal democracies? Not in very good shape, I fear. It leaves us with options at the extremes that are morally and politically problematic, but there also is no clear middle ground that does not have difficulties of its own. The polar positions can each be clearly specified, but they produce different forms of what can be styled from some moral perspective as bigotry and its attendant exclusions, which in turn generate political conflict. The middle ground between these polar alternatives holds the promise of at least mitigating the problems of exclusion and conflict; but its own criteria and boundaries are not fully determinate, and attempts to specify and enforce them will themselves remain inescapably subject to contestation at both the philosophical and the political level.

At one extreme stands the familiar moral absolutism of those who insist upon the validity of a particular conception of the good and who push toward its implementation. For these deeply committed adherents of a comprehensive moral and/or religious doctrine, there is good and there is evil, right and wrong, and the only proper course of action is to organize human life in accord with what is good and right. For these partisans of a particular conception of the good, the imperatives of moral judgment are clear, the imperatives of nonjudgmentalism only tactical or a sop to the feelings of the morally obtuse. The component of grudging in any toleration they practice is very high, always threatening to overwhelm forbearance altogether. The opposing polar position is the radicalized account of respect and toleration championed by those who insist upon the affirmation and recognition of all moral identities as incumbent on both the democratic state and democratic citizens. Here, one could say, the imperative of nonjudgmentalism exerts complete moral hegemony over any putative imperatives of moral judgment. Indeed, not even complete forbearance is enough: it must be replaced by the generous accreditation of all the different ways of life within our pluralistic society.

The element of moral bigotry and the resultant urge to repress alleged miscreants is pretty obvious in its traditional form, the one grounded in a dogmatic insistence upon the veridicality of a particular conception of the good: the Ten Commandments should be graven on large tablets in courthouses, sodomy and abortion should be criminalized, moral or religious apostates should be kept out of public offices, suspect texts should be purged from public libraries, and so on. What is less obvious is that the opposite extreme comes with its own form of bigotry and exclusion.

On the surface, this latter claim seems logically inconceivable and almost oxymoronic. How can a stance of pan-nonjudgmentalism, inspired by a generous aspiration to embrace and affirm the worth of all people and their different ways of life, contain any admixture of bigotry or any exclusionary implications? If all conceptions of the good are affirmed, how can any be subject to disapprobation or exclusion?

The answer to this conundrum is that the pan-nonjudgmentalism of the "affirmation and recognition" mandate is in fact utterly nondogmatic in theory and antidogmatic in practice when it comes to conceptions of the human good; but it is predicated upon a metalevel dogmatism, which generates its own kinds of discriminators and exclusions. The "toleration as recognition" persuasion may affirm all conceptions of the good, but it can be so totally nondiscriminating at this level only by a dogmatic insistence upon a contestable metaconception of the human good. Or, to put it another way, this account is wholly neutral about *conceptions* of the good but "it has a very distinct *conceptualization* of what it means to have a conception of the good."[13] Actually, this position might be consistent at the metalevel with somewhat different "conceptualizations of conceptions of the good": it could construe conceptions of the good as products of ontologically unconstrained existential choice, as manifestations of aesthetic tastes, or as sets of desires and preferences generated by the accidental concatenation of historical contingencies. However, this is a moral and political doctrine that is not compatible with metaconceptions ("conceptualizations") of the good which are cognitivist or morally objectivist in any significant way. That is, it cannot be rendered consistent with philosophies that construe the content of the human good as something ascertainable by the mind and/or grounded in a teleological nature or in a divinely created human *eidos*. This is an account of moral judgment seamlessly at home in a Weberian, Derridean, or Rortyan universe; but it is inconsistent with a Christian or Judaic or Islamic or Aristotelian understanding of what it means to have a conception of the good.

This somewhat abstruse philosophical point has its real-world political consequences. A civic morality of panjudgmentalism says to adherents of what might be characterized as "onto-theological" beliefs:[14] you are free to hold your beliefs and to have them "affirmed and recognized" but only insofar and to the extent that you are willing to have these beliefs understood for all practical purposes as tantamount to contingent and idiosyncratic preferences or desires you happen to have. One consequence of this understanding of the imperatives of nonjudgment and its attendant civic morality, then, is that some members of society wind up being treated in a somewhat patronizing and marginalizing fashion. They are told in effect that their moral identity is "affirmed and recognized" but only in a manner that de facto logically depicts it as being delusionary. Simply to put it that way, of course, demonstrates an unfortunate but inexorable consequence of the metalevel dogmatism regarding the status of conceptions of the good informing this account of the public role of moral judgment: it demonstrates that, however well-intentioned, this account cannot avoid incoherence and hypocrisy when it is put into practice in a morally pluralistic society some of whose members are moral cognitivists / realists. Were we all to become what Rorty calls "ironists"—people who see their deepest commitments as purely contingent facts about ourselves—and to adopt his attitude of "light-hearted" self-distancing from those commitments, this problem would disappear. But in the meantime (and this is a meantime that will likely never end) this de facto "bigotry" of enforced pan-nonjudgmentalism represents a genuine problem. This is, if you will, a "softer" form of bigotry, one much less likely to lead to killing or oppression and hence one much to be preferred to the old-fashioned kind. It remains a genuine pitfall of this kind of superficial level hypertolerance, however, and one that has occasioned understandable misgivings.[15]

Finally, the "do not judge others but recognize and affirm all ways of living" stance, when carried out to its logical conclusion, arrives at a destination that should be disquieting to anyone who believes in the value of good moral judgment. For it seems a corollary of this position that, strictly speaking, there is no such thing. To engage in moral judgment is to discriminate among modes of human behavior, designating some as better or nobler or more humanly fulfilling or more praiseworthy than alternatives. But you cannot so discriminate and simultaneously accord full and equal "affirmation" to every way of living. Where blanket affirmations are sincerely conferred, there can be no moral judgment. It is also important to insist here that, contrary to what seems to be the tacit assumption made by many who champion this position, judgments about justice cannot be protected against this undermining dynamic of pan-nonjudgmentalism. That is a consoling delusion likely induced by an uncritical assimilation of the dubious premises of deontological liberalism. The fact is that beliefs about the right are judgments that can be reduced to matters of idiosyncratic taste in the same way as judgments about the human good.[16]

Negotiating the Contested Terrain between Manicheanism and Hypertoleration

It is one of the purposes of Kant's moral philosophy to provide an explanation of why it is that we as human beings are uniquely creatures who have to live in the moral tension between what is and what should be. His answer is that we are uniquely subject to this moral tension because we uniquely are both animal and rational. We live in both the phenomenal and noumenal worlds. Beasts have sensations but not reason; hence they obey their brute impulses without compunction. Divine beings are wholly free and are not dragged down by animal impulse. We are torn between both worlds and experience the opposing tugs of duty and desire in pangs of conscience.

Kant's metaphysical explanation may be flawed, but the tension he references is quite real. And a similar tension is played out in human life between the moral imperatives of judgment and the imperatives to constrain our judgment of others. Beasts would never think to judge. The judgments of a perfect and omniscient God will always be true and just.

But we, as moral beings, must render moral judgments; and we, as contingent and timebound social animals who must live with others and whose judgments are not perfect, must temper and constrain our judgments. This latter tension, in addition, takes on a heightened form in the conflicting demands placed upon democratic citizens of pluralistic societies. As members of the sovereign, it is incumbent upon us to make judgments—regarding the good and the right—about the purposes, policies, and procedures of our society. As citizens who must live with fellow citizens of different moral cultures and persuasions, we must forbear from forcing our moral views upon others—not alone for reasons of social peace but also out of respect for their personal autonomy and equal standing. It has been a principal purpose of this essay to explain the sources and dynamics that give rise to this moral tension surrounding the imperatives of judgment and forbearance and to explain why it is such a visible feature in the political life and conflicts within contemporary pluralist democracies. It is a corollary of my argument that no legitimate way exists to obviate or evade the tension, because the conflicting imperatives that produce it both have legitimate moral grounds and practical considerations on their side.

It has also been my purpose to argue that the legitimate imperatives on each side of the tension create pressures that threaten to cannibalize those coming from the other direction. Whenever those pressures have their way, we encounter perils both political and moral. These perils are reflected in what I have characterized as alternative forms of bigotry: a hard and traditional bigotry that would force all to knuckle under one dominant conception of the human good (or, arguably, to one conception of social justice); and a softer form of metalevel bigotry that would exclude and marginalize those who insist upon a different conceptualization of what it means to have a conception of the human good. It was, in fact, a tacit recognition of these dual dangers that provided the impetus for this volume as a whole: to wit, these dangers seemed manifest in polar forms of response and judgment to the terrible events of 9/11. On the one hand were those who invoked a Manichean language of an "axis of evil" and a campaign of "infinite justice" to combat the evil. On the other hand were those whose worries about this kind of moral absolutism and whose principled inhibitions against moral judgment seemed to strike them dumb and leave them bereft of any capacity for moral outrage in the face of atrocity. In some quarters this nonjudgmentalism took the form of a thoroughgoing perspectivism, as in, "One person's terrorist is another's freedom fighter."

When I began this project, I was anticipating that my inquiry into the problem of moral judgment in pluralist democracies would eventuate into one of those Goldilocks arguments: one extreme is too hard, the other too soft, and in the middle we can find a position that is just right. I have come to realize, however, that any expectation of finding a clearly specifiable golden mean here is a vain hope. I retain the conviction that the polar positions are unjustified and unwise. An insistence on levying unqualified moral judgments flouts what all who consider the matter seriously recognize as the partial and fallible status of all attempts to ascertain what is good and just in human life; and a blanket refusal to entertain any conviction that some forms of behavior and social institutions are better or fairer than others runs counter to both evidence and personal experience. I now have the chastened view, however, that the middle territory betwixt these untenable absolutions contains no point devoid of costs and reasonable complaints. We cannot ever fully resolve the tensions between our quest for moral discernment, with all its frailty, and our aspirations to be inclusive and respectful of all our fellow citizens. And, of course, the more pluralistic the society—in both the breadth and depth of the differences of culture and moral or religious doctrines it encompasses—the less resolvable the tensions. The best we can do in this setting is to engage in the kind of perpetual balancing act made famous by the Supreme Court whenever it confronts in particular cases an opposition between important principles, neither of which it is willing to abandon. Attempts to strike the right balance represent a high form of moral casuistry—in the good and legitimate sense of that term. Those who seek to do so have no choice other than to attend carefully to the particular circumstances they face. And they can lament their fate and simultaneously console themselves with the currently popular mantra of tragic recognition: nothing without loss.

Realizing that the moral tension we have been wrestling with here is not fully resolvable no doubt constitutes a result that is disappointing theoretically and frustrating practically. Perhaps, however, I can somewhat lessen this disappointment and frustration (my own and not merely my readers'—I still hanker for that unattainable "just right" outcome) by offering a few concluding reflections that might provide some modest guidance for our attempts to negotiate the troubled via media between dogmatic judgmentalism and a blanket default of moral discernment. First, I want to note two important issues that need the thoughtful attention of those seeking the best balance between the extremes of dogmatism and what some have called "nihilism with a happy face." And second, I shall suggest in closing as aspiration that should serve as our ultimate, albeit systematically elusive, goal in this endeavor.

The two important issues warranting our attention turn out upon examination to be theoretical loose strings left dangling by John Stuart Mill in his essay *On Liberty*. Mill did not give these issues the attention they logically deserve, I think, because he lived within a society more morally homogeneous than our own; and it is the effects of moral pluralism that bring those into relief. In short, Mill could leave these loose strings unattended to because they presented less of a practical problem for him than they do for us today.

The first of these issues can be put in the form of a question: where is the boundary between variations of human life and behavior worthy of celebration under the rubric of "diversity" and variations of human life and behavior that are distinguishable on some kind of moral metric? Mill clearly assumed that there was such a boundary between morally relevant differences and morally indifferent ones. But he gave precious little attention to specifying the location of that boundary. The clear burden of his argument in the famed chapter 3, "Of Individuality," is that more differences among human beings than generally believed should be seen as morally indifferent and socially valuable. Following the lead of the German idealist Wilhelm von Humboldt, Mill praised "individual vigor and manifold diversity." He wrote that "no one's idea of excellence in conduct is that people should do absolutely nothing but copy each other." It is diversity that brings a "greater fullness of life" to society and that makes human beings "noble and beautiful objects of contemplation." And he says that it is "their remarkable diversity of character and culture" that "has made the European family of nations an improving instead of a stationary portion of mankind."[17]

If Mill is insistent on the value of diversity and the goodness of a multiplicity of forms of life, however, he nonetheless clearly believes—as indeed the word "improving" in the last quotation indicates—that there are qualitative moral differences. That was, in fact, the crux of his complaint against his mentor, Bentham, who put all human pleasures on a moral par. For Mill, the very measure of what he called "utility in the largest sense" was the mental and moral improvement of humankind. Some differences among human traits and forms of life, therefore, are not morally indifferent but distinctions between better and worse, degrees of virtue and vice. There are such things, Mill tells us, as "moral vices" which "constitute a bad and odious moral character." Seriatim, these vices include such traits as rashness, obstinacy, self-conceit, envy, duplicity, selfishness, cruelty, drunkenness, incontinence, idleness, pleonexia, extravagance, and bigotry.[18]

So there are human differences to celebrate as sources of richness and fullness of life; and there are human differences to deplore as sources of social disruption and personal deterioration. But Mill tells us very little about how to go about deciding which are which. And today, in the context of deeper and wider cultural pluralism, we are arguably not much better off in this regard. We still have with us champions of "one true way" who see all departures from their ontotheological norm as moral error. At the other extreme, we have the acolytes of "difference" who see all evaluative distinctions as illegitimate and arbitrary "binaries" begging for deconstruction and dismissal.

To the extent that philosophical reflection and analysis can be expected to make any useful contribution to the task of tiptoeing through the treacherous middle ground between excessive and insufficient invocation of moral judgment, the problem Mill left dangling begs attention. I certainly am not suggesting that political and moral philosophers will ever reach consensus about the boundary between morally freighted and morally irrelevant human differences. Setting that boundary, in fact, arguably represents the ultimate metamoral judgment, and as such it is permanently contestable. I do, however, entertain the hope that careful consideration of many pertinent particular differences of character traits and behavioral patterns—as contrasted with purely abstract claims about diversity and moral metrics—might generate a reasonably constrained spectrum of intelligible intermediate accounts of this fundamental issue. And these accounts, in their turn, could offer practically valuable illumination for us as we struggle to decide where to affirm moral judgments and where to refrain from them.

The second and related issue Mill leaves dangling in *On Liberty* regards a fuller specification of the norms of what he calls "the real morality of public discussion."[19] In Mill's brief account, its key elements are an avoidance of "vituperative language" and argument ad hominem, together with an attempt to present one's case as fairly and objectively as possible. At a somewhat deeper level, however, it appears that the key problem here is how to determine the right balance between norms of candor and norms of civility in public discourse—discourse whose heat, of course, often stems from contested moral judgments. Mill gestures toward this central question but does not go very far toward solving it. He only tells us that participants in public discourse deserve condemnation whenever "in [their] mode of advocacy either want of candor, or malignity, bigotry, or intolerance of feeling manifest themselves."[20]

The difficulty here is that both candor and civility come with very strong moral warrants and practical considerations on their side, but in practice they are not easy to combine. The virtue and imperative of candor as a norm of democratic discourse goes back a very long way. Sara Monoson provides us with a very useful account of the importance to Athenian democracy of an "ethic of frank speaking" (*parrhēsia*), which was held "to be a necessary precondition for the smooth functioning of democratic deliberative and decision-making institutions." *Parrhēsia* was "consistently and closely associated with two things: criticism and truthtelling." To speak frankly thus involved confronting, opposing, and finding fault with others, implying "a claim on the part of the speaker to be capable of assessing a situation and pronouncing judgment upon it."[21] This norm of candid judgment represented, in effect, the Habermasian norm of sincerity as a demand of communicative competence. And it was valued not only on that basis but for its important functional role in "illuminating what is right and best."[22]

The expression of candid moral judgment, as the Athenians recognized, is seemingly essential for morally serious democratic deliberation—discussion that seeks "what is right / and best." But, as the Athenians also realized, demanding candid expression of citizens' moral judgments "has a dangerous underside in the potential for harmful speech."[23] Thus that demand needs to be balanced or constrained not only by legal prohibitions against slander but also by norms and expectations of civility in discourse. And these norms, as Mark Kingswell notes, require "self-restraint and tact." Such civility in democratic discourse, Kingswell argues, is sufficiently important to be incorporated into norms of communicative competence, which could then "no longer be conceived as the unforced force of the better argument, but instead would involve the civil phrasing of arguments and concerns for the interests of other interlocutors."[24]

The difficulty here, of course, as Kingswell effectively recognizes, is that so reconstructing the norms of communicative competence introduces into them a significant degree of internal tension, for civility "encourages, and even demands, a kind of insincerity."[25] And what this tension effects in its turn, here in the context of deliberative norms, is the very moral tension between the imperatives of judgment and restraint of judgment that has been our central concern. So one concrete and practically pertinent way to gain additional purchase on the best way or ways to negotiate this tension is for us to try to work out how we can be both civil and candid in our civic discourse. As the many controversies that have arisen over whether this or that utterance constitutes "hate speech" gives evidence, this also will not be an enterprise that will likely produce definitive criteria or full consensus. But carefully thinking through this issue and specific cases that embody it may help us reach a better understanding about how to situate moral judgment within the politics of democratic pluralism.

As for the aspiration that should serve as our ultimate goal as we seek to achieve good moral judgment without inappropriate judgmentalism, another hint from ancient moral philosophy may be useful. As Ronald Beiner pertinently reminds us, Aristotle's account of phronesis includes the idea that we "must be able to experience fellow-feeling or empathy in order to come to terms with a matter of concrete practical decision."[26] Good moral judgments must always be communal to a certain extent—not only in the sense of being dependent upon the sharing of perspectives but also in being dependent upon sympathy and mutual understanding. That claim is inscribed within Greek terms for judgment and sympathy in a way missing in the English counterparts. The Greek word *suggnome*—translated as forgiveness, pardon, or sympathetic understanding—incorporates the idea of *gnome*, judgment or good sense. The Greek etymology thus suggests an important idea not suggested by the English: namely, that arriving at good moral judgments, however controversial and contestable they may be, requires nonetheless a process of cooperative attentiveness to others. Kant to the contrary, in the real world practical reason can be neither "pure" nor monological. It is not noumenal minds that reach good moral judgments but social animals. Good judgment, we might even say, depends to some extent upon a measure of friendship. Since we have no Archimedean point from which we can promulgate our judgments, moral judgments with any real claim to credibility must be a form of "judgment with" and not simply "judgment of."

Given its inescapable contingency, attaining good judgment in matters moral and political is a systematically elusive enterprise. People will—especially with the impetus and bias of their conflicting interests pushing them in divergent directions—always wind up in different places, always have to deal with moral disagreement. But the insight about moral judgment embedded in the notion of *suggnome* can at the least lead us to the hopeful recognition that human plurality is not simply an obstacle to moral judgment but also a dialectical resource for achieving it.[27]

NOTES

1. Matthew 7:1–5 (New Revised Standard Version of the Bible).

2. John Stuart Mill, *On Liberty* [1859] (Indianapolis: Bobbs-Merrill Co., 1956), p. 94.

3. Thomas Jefferson, "Letter to Roger C. Weightman," June 24, 1826, in *Political Thought in America*, ed. Michael B. Levy, 2d ed. (Prospect Heights, IL: Waveland Press, 1992), p. 84.

4. John Rawls, *Political Liberalism* (New York: Columbia University Press, 1993), p. 137.

5. Peter Euben provides a thoughtful confrontation with and assessment of these kinds of assumptions regarding the bearing of one's social role and class status on the obligation to exercise moral judgment in his essay in this volume.

6. Aristotle, *Nicomachean Ethics*, book 8, chapter 8.

7. Aristotle, *Ethics*, op. cit.

8. See, for example, Robert Nozick, *Anarchy, State and Utopia* (New York: Basic Books, 1974); and Milton Friedman, *Capitalism and Freedom* (Chicago: University of Chicago Press, 1962).

9. Of course it may also be morally improper to constrain or coerce people on grounds that are part of their own moral vocabulary, albeit for different reasons.

10. Counsels of political tolerance are grounded in a prudential calculus, as well. The basic prudential reasoning is that social conflict—hence one's personal safety and chances for commodious living—can be greatly attenuated by policies of mutual moral forbearance. Live and let live is smart policy in this context, irrespective of any moral considerations that might come into play. I note and acknowledge the importance of prudential considerations here but will largely subordinate them in what fellows in order to focus upon the moral conundrums involved.

11. The standard of "affirmation and recognition" of all groups in society is the moral touchstone of the "egalitarian politics of difference" that Iris Young defines as the substance of social justice. See, for example, her claim that "groups cannot be socially equal unless their specific experience, culture, and social contributions are publicly affirmed and recognized." *Justice and the Politics of Difference* (Princeton, NJ: Princeton University Press, 1990), p. 173. A recent book-length application of this standard to the norms of toleration is Anna Galeotti, *Toleration as Recognition* (Cambridge: Cambridge University Press, 2002).

12. Mill, *On Liberty*, p. 94.

13. Patrick Neal, *Liberalism and Its Discontents* (New York: New York University Press, 1997) p. 38.

14. William Connolly, *Identity\Difference* (Ithaca: Cornell University Press, 1991). Connolly appropriates this term from Heidegger and uses it in a way that I believe fits here.

15. See, for example, John Tomasi, *Liberalism beyond Justice: Citizens, Society, and the Boundaries of Political Theory* (Princeton, NJ: Princeton University Press, 2001); and Nomi Stolzenberg, "He Drew a Circle That Shut Me Out: Assimilation, Indoctrination, and the Paradox of a Liberal Education," *Harvard Law Review* 106 (1993): 581–667.

16. Those who think otherwise should ponder works such as Hans Kelsen, *What Is Justice?* (Berkeley: University of California Press, 1957); and Stuart Hampshire, *Justice Is Conflict* (Princeton, NJ: Princeton University Press, 2000).

17. Mill, *On Liberty*, pp. 70, 76, 88.

18. Mill, *On Liberty*, pp. 96, 95, 98, 99, 102.

19. Mill, *On Liberty*, p. 67.

20. Mill, *On Liberty*, p. 66.

21. S. Sara Monoson, *Plato's Democratic Entanglements: Athenian Politics and the Practice of Philosophy* (Princeton, NJ: Princeton University Press, 2000), pp. 52–53.

22. Monoson, *Plato's Democratic Entanglements*, p. 53.

23. Monoson, *Plato's Democratic Entanglements*, p. 52.

24. Mark Kingswell, *A Civil Tongue: Justice, Dialogue, and the Politics of Pluralism* (University Park: Pennsylvania State University Press, 1995), p. 203.

25. Kingswell, *Civil Tongue*, p. 218.

26. Ronald Beiner, *Political Judgment* (Chicago: University of Chicago Press, 1983), pp. 75–76. Adam Smith's account of the origins of the "moral sentiments" incorporates a similar claim.

27. In very thoughtful comments delivered at a conference on the issues addressed in this volume, Georgia Warnke argues that the way in which reasonable people address

hermeneutic problems may offer us a good model here—one that helps to mitigate my concerns. Often, she argues, "the problem posed by pluralism is not that we do not share moral principles or a moral vocabulary but that we can understand the principles we share in different, equally compelling ways." Where that is the case (and "as Americans we all take seriously principles of life, liberty, equality and diversity"), "looking to interpretation"—where "we do not insist in a bigoted way that our own interpretation of a test is the only possible one"—can "provide a way of articulating the dialectical resources that Spragens suggests pluralism may provide."

There is, I believe, much to be said for this suggestion. Indeed, in a recent book in which I argued on behalf of what I called "persuasive definitions" of the "essentially contested concepts" of liberty, equality, and fraternity (*Civil Liberalism: Reflections on Our Democratic Ideals* [Lanham, MD: Rowman and Littlefield, 1999]), I was engaged in exactly the kind of hermeneutic conversation she commends to us. It is also possible that, as Amy Gutmann and Dennis Thompson have argued, such "hermeneutic" dialogue can have the added benefit of enabling those who have conflicting moral positions on public matters to recognize that their opponents are principled people. See *Why Deliberative Democracy?* (Princeton, NJ: Princeton University Press, 2004), pp. 79–81, 151–56.

It is, however, necessary to remember that moral disagreements that bear upon political outcomes are not merely theoretical and academic. As a consequence, these forms of hermeneutic dialogue in the quest for communal moral judgment have their practical limits. They can, especially within the context of sometimes deeply divergent moral vocabularies, only soften and help us navigate the political and moral dilemmas created by the imperatives and frailties of moral judgment.

Bibliography

"700 Club" telecast, September 13, 2001. Available at http://www.truthorfiction.com/rumors/f/falwell-robertson-wtc.htm (accessed July 18, 2004).

Afifi, Mamdouh. "Female Circumcision Ban Ignored by Egyptian Fundamentalists." *Agence France Presse* (January 5, 1998).

American Medical Association Council on Scientific Affairs. "Female Genital Mutilation." *Journal of the American Medical Association* 274 ,no. 21 (December 6, 1995): 1714–1716.

Amnesty International. *Joint NGO Statement on the Beslan Hostage Tragedy,* September 8, 2004. Available at http://web.amnesty.org/library/print/ENGEUR460502004.

Antoun, Richard T. *Understanding Fundamentalism: Christian, Islamic, and Jewish Movements.* Walnut Creek, CA: Altamira Press, 2001.

Arendt, Hannah. "The Crisis in Culture." In *Between Past and Future.* New York: Penguin, 1993.

———. *"Thinking," Life of the Mind.* Vol. 1. London: Sacker and Warburg, 1971.

———. *On Revolution.* London: Penguin Books, 1963, 1965.

———. *Eichmann in Jerusalem: A Report on the Banality of Evil.* New York: Penguin, 1963, second edition 1964.

Aristotle, *Nichomachean Ethics.* Translated by Martin Ostwald. New York: Macmillan, 1962.

Aron, Raymond. *Essai sur les libertés.* Paris: Calmann-Lévy, 1965. Berkeley: University of California: trans. H. Weaver, 1966.

———. *Le Spectateur engagé.* Paris: Julliard, 1981.

———. "États démocratiques et états totalitaires" [June 1939]. In *Commentaire* 6, no. 24 (winter 1983–84): 701–9.

Augustine. *Confessions.* Translated with an introduction by R. S. Pine-Coffin. Baltimore: Penguin Books, 1961.

——. *Confessions and Enchiridion.* Translated and edited by Albert Oulter. Philadelphia: Westminster Press, 1955.

——. *The City of God.* Translated by Henry Bettenson. Harmondsworth: Penguin, 1977.

Barth, Karl. *Church Dogmatics, IV/1.* Translated by G. W. Bromiley. New York: Scribner's Son, 1956.

BBC News. "Afghanistan's Civilian Deaths Mount," January 3, 2002. Available at http://news.bbc.co.uk/1/hi/world/south-asia/1740538.stm.

Becker, Ernest. *The Structure of Evil.* New York: George Braziller, 1968.

Beiner, Ronald. *Political Judgment.* Chicago: University of Chicago Press, 1983.

Bell, David A. "Why Books Caused a Revolution: A reading of Robert Darnton." In *The Darnton Debate: Books and Revolution in the Eighteenth Century.* Edited by Haydn T. Mason. Oxford: Voltaire Foundation, 1998.

Berlin, Isaiah. "Two Concepts of Liberty." In *Liberty: Incorporating Four Essays on Liberty.* Oxford: Oxford University Press, 2002.

——. "Two Concepts of Liberty." In *The Proper Study of Mankind.* New York: Farrar, Straus, and Giroux, 1997.

——. "Two Concepts of Liberty." In *Four Essays on Liberty.* New York: Oxford University Press, 1969.

Bernstein, Richard J. *Radical Evil: A Philosophical Interrogation.* Cambridge: Polity Press, 2002.

Bin Laden, Osama. Speech, October 30, 2004. Available at http://english.aljazeera.net/english/DialogBox/PrintPreview.aspx?NRORIGINALURL=% (accessed November 11, 2004).

Blum, Carol. *Rousseau and the Republic of Virtue: The Language of Politics in the French Revolution.* Ithaca: Cornell University Press, 1986.

Bonhoeffer, Dietrich. *Creation and Fall: A Theological Interpretation of Genesis 1–3.* London: SCM Press, 1962.

Bouroumand, Ladan, and Roya Bouroumand. "Terror, Islam, and Democracy." *Journal of Democracy* 13 (2002): 17–18.

Boyd, Richard. "Pity's Pathologies Portrayed: Rousseau and the Limits of Democratic Compassion." *Political Theory* 32, no. 4 (August 2004): 519–546.

Browning, Christopher R. *Ordinary Men.* New York: HarperCollins, 1992.

Burke, Edmund. *Reflections on the Revolution in France.* Indianapolis: Bobbs-Merrill, 1955.

Bush, George W. State of the Union Address, February 2, 2005. Available at http://www.whitehouse.gov/stateofunion/2005/ (accessed May 11, 2005).

——. Address to Joint Session of Congress and the American People, September 20, 2001. Available at http://www.whitehouse.gov/news/releases/2001/09/20010920-8.html (accessed July 20, 2004).

——. Remarks on Operation Iraqi Freedom and Operation Enduring Freedom, March 19, 2004. Available at http://www.whitehouse.gov/news/releases/2004/03/20040319-3.html (accessed July 7, 2004).

Buzan, Barry. "Who May We Bomb?" In *Worlds in Collision: Terror and the Future of the Global Order.* Edited by Ken Booth and Tim Dunne, pp. 85–94 (Basingstoke: Palgrave, 2002).

Bybee, J. S., U.S. Justice Department memo, August 2002. Available at National Security Archive Web site, http://www.gwu.edu/~nsarchiv/NSAEBB/NSAEBB127/.

Card, Claudia. *The Atrocity Paradigm: A Theory of Evil.* Oxford: Oxford University Press, 2002.

Carey, Benedict. "For the Worst of Us, the Diagnosis May Be 'Evil.'" *New York Times.* February 8, 2005.

Cassirer, Ernst. *The Question of Jean-Jacques Rousseau.* Translated by Peter Gay. New York: Columbia University Press, 1954.

CBS/New York Times Poll, March 7–9, 2003. Available at http://www.cbsnews.com/htdocs/CBSNews_polls/iraq_back310.pdf.

Chamberlain, Neville. *In Search of Peace* New York: G. P. Putman's Sons, 1939.

Coady, C. A. J. "Terrorism, Morality, and Supreme Emergency." *Ethics* (July 2004): 772–789.

Coleman, Doriane Lambelet. "The Seattle Compromise: Multicultural Sensitivity and Americanization." *Duke Law Journal* 47 (1998): 717–783.

Connetta, Carl. "Operation Enduring Freedom: Why a Higher Rate of Civilian Bombing Casualties." *Project on Defense Alternatives Briefing Report,* 11 (January 18, 2002), revised January 24, 2002. Available at http://www.comw.org/pda/020loef.html.

Connolly, William. *Identity / Difference.* Ithaca: Cornell University Press, 1991.

Constant, Benjamin. *Political Writings.* Edited by Biancamaria Fontana. Cambridge: Cambridge University Press, 1988.

———. *Des reactions politiques.* Paris: Delaunay, 1797.

Cook, Rebecca, Bernard Dickens, and Mahmoud Fathalla. *Reproductive Health and Human Rights.* New York: Oxford University Press, 2003.

Cooper, Laurence, D. *Rousseau, Nature and the Problem of the Good Life.* University Park: Pennsylvania State University Press, 1999.

Costanzo, Philip. "Morals, Mothers, and Memories: The Social Context of Developing Social Cognition." In *Context and Development.* Edited by R. Cohen and A. W. Siegal. Hillsdale, NJ: Erlbaum, 1991.

Dallaire, Romeo. *Shake Hands with the Devil: The Failure of Humanity in Rwanda.* New York: Carroll and Graf, 2004.

Darnton, Robert. *Forbidden Best-Sellers of Pre-Revolutionary France.* New York: W. W. Norton and Co., 1995.

Dawit, Seble, and Salem Mekuria. "The West Just Doesn't Get It." *New York Times,* December 7, 1993.

De Staël, Anne-Louise-Germaine. *De l'influence des passions sur le bonheur des individus et des nations.* Lausanne: Mourer, 1796.

De Tocqueville, Alexis. *Democracy in America.* Introduction by Sanford Kessler, translated by Stephen D. Grant. Indianapolis: Hackett. 2000.

———. *De la démocratie en Amérique,* edited by J. P. Mayer. In *Oeuvres Complétes.* Paris: Gallimard, 1961.

Delbanco, Andrew. *The Death of Satan: How Americans Have Lost the Sense of Evil.* New York: Farrar, Strauss and Giroux, 1995.

Denniston, George, Frederick Hodges, and Marilyn Milos. *Understanding Circumcision: A Multi-Disciplinary Approach to a Multi-Dimensional Problem.* New York: Kluwer, 2001.

Devine, Patricia G. "Prejudice and Out-Group Perception." In *Advanced Social Psychology.* Edited by Abraham Tesser. New York: McGraw-Hill, 1995.

Dillon, Susan. "Healing the Sacred Yoni in the Land of Isis: Female Genital Mutilation Is Banned (Again) in Egypt." *Houston Journal of International Law* 22 (winter, 2000): 289ff.

Donnelly, Jack. *Universal Human Rights in Theory and Practice.* Ithaca: Cornell University Press, 1989.

Dorkenoo, Efua and Elworthy, Scilla. *Female Genital Mutilation: Proposals for Change.* 3d ed. London: Minority Rights Group, 1992.

Durkheim, Emile. *Emile Durkheim on Morality and Society.* Edited by Robert Bellah. Chicago: University of Chicago, 1973.

———. *Professional Ethics and Civic Morals.* Glencoe, IL: Free Press, 1958.

Eagleton, Terry. *After Theory.* New York: Basic Books, 2003.

Edwards, James. *The Plain Sense of Things: The Fate of Religion in an Age of Normal Nihilism.* University Park: Pennsylvania State University Press, 1997.

Esposito, John L. *Unholy War: Terror in the Name of Islam.* Oxford: Oxford University Press, 2002.

Evans, G. R. *Augustine on Evil.* Cambridge: Cambridge University Press, 1994.

Euben, Roxanne. *Journeys to the Other Shore: Travel, Theory and the Search for Knowledge.* Princeton: Princeton University Press, forthcoming.

Feuerbach, Ludwig. *The Essence of Christianity.* Translated by George Eliot. New York: Harper & Row, 1957.

Fogelin, Robert. *Walking the Tightrope of Reason: The Precarious Life of a Rational Animal.* New York: Oxford University Press, 2003.

Ford, John C. "The Morality of Obliteration Bombing," *War and Morality.* Edited by Richard Wasserstrom. Belmont, CA: Wadsworth, 1970.

Friedman, Milton. *Capitalism and Freedom.* Chicago: University of Chicago Press, 1962.

Frum, David, and Richard Perle. *An End to Evil: How to Win the War on Terror.* New York: Balantine Books, 2004.

Furet, François. "Rousseau and the French Revolution." In *The Legacy of Rousseau.* Edited by Clifford Orwin and Nathan Tarcov. Chicago: University of Chicago Press, 1997.

Furet, François, and Mona Ozouf, eds. *A Critical Dictionary of the French Revolution.* Translated by Arthur Goldhammer. Cambridge, MA: Belknap Press, 1989.

Frye, Marilyn. *The Politics of Reality.* Trumansburg, NY: Crossing Press, 1983.

Galeotti, Anna. *Toleration as Recognition.* Cambridge: Cambridge University Press, 2002.

Giddens, Anthony. *The Consequences of Modernity.* Stanford, CA: Stanford University Press, 1990.

Gordon, Avery. *Ghostly Matters: Haunting and the Sociological Imagination.* Minneapolis: University of Minnesota Press, 1996.

Grant, Ruth W. "Political Theory, Political Science and Politics," *Political Theory* 30, no. 4 (2002): 577–595.

———. *Hypocrisy and Integrity: Machiavelli, Rousseau and the Ethics of Politics.* Chicago: University of Chicago Press, 1997.

Griswold, Charles L., Jr. *Adam Smith and the Virtues of the Enlightenment.* Cambridge: Cambridge University Press, 1999.

Gunning, Isabelle. "Arrogant Perception, World-Traveling and Multicultural Feminism: The Case of Female Genital Surgeries." *Columbia Human Rights Law Review* 23 (1991–92): 189–248.

Gutmann, Amy, and Dennis Thompson. *Why Deliberative Democracy?*. Princeton: Princeton University Press, 2004.

Habermas, Jürgen. *Moral Consciousness and Communicative Action.* Translated by Christian Lenhardt and Shierry Weber. Boston: MIT Press, 1990.

Hacohen, Malachi. *Karl Popper: The Formative Years, 1902–1945.* New York: Cambridge University Press, 2000.

Hafez, Mohammed M. *Manufacturing Human Bombs: The Making of Palestinian Suicide Bombers.* Washington, DC: U.S. Institute of Peace Press, 2006.

Haidt, Jonathan, and Craig Joseph. "Intuitive Ethics." *Daedalus* 135 (fall 2004): 55–67.

Hamilton, Alexander, James Madison, and John Jay. *The Federalist Papers.* New York: New American Library, 1961.

Hampshire, Stuart. *Justice Is Conflict.* Princeton: Princeton University Press, 2000.

Hanby, Michael. *Augustine and Modernity.* London: Routledge, 2003.

Haney, Craig, Curtis Banks, and Philip Zimbardo. "Interpersonal Dynamics in a Simulated Prison." *International Journal of Criminology and Penology* 1 (1973): 69–97.

Harpham, Geoffrey Halt. *Shadows of Ethics: Criticism and the Just Society.* Durham, NC: Duke University Press, 2002.

Hauerwas, Stanley. *Naming the Silences.* Grand Rapids, MI: Eardmans, 1990.

———. *With the Grain of the Universe: The Church's Witness and Natural Theology.* Grand Rapids, MI: Brazos Press, 2001.

———. "Why Time Cannot and Should Not Heal the Wounds of History, But Time Has Been and Can be Redeemed." In *A Better Hope: Resources for a Church Confronting Capitalism, Democracy, and Postmodernity.* Grand Rapids, MI: Brazos Press, 2000.

———. "Remembering as a Moral Task: The Challenge of the Holocaust." In *Against the Nations: War and Survival in a Liberal Society.* Notre Dame: University of Notre Dame Press, 1992.

———. "From System to Story: An Alternative Pattern for Rationality in Ethics." In *Truthfulness and Tragedy: Further Investigations into Christian Ethics.* Notre Dame: University of Notre Dame Press, 1977.

Haybrun, Daniel M. "Moral Monsters and Saints." *Monist* 85, no. 2 (April 2002): 276–80.

Hedman, Carl G. "Rousseau on Self-Interest, Compassion and Moral Progress." *Trent Rousseau Papers.* Edited by Jim MacAdam et al. Ottawa: University of Ottawa Press, 1980.

Held, Virginia. "Terrorism, Rights, and Political Goals." *Taking Sides: Clashing Views on Controversial Moral Issues.* Edited by Stephen Satris. 4th ed. Duskin: Guilford, 1994.

Hesse, Carla. "Precedent and Invention: The Problem of the Past in Revolutionary Politics," unpublished paper delivered at the National Humanities Center, Research Triangle Park, NC, November 1, 2002.

Holmes, Stephen. "The Permanent Structure of Antiliberal Thought." In *Liberalism and the Moral Life.* Edited by Nancy L. Rosenblum. Cambridge, MA: Harvard University Press, 1989.

Howard, Rhoda E. "Human Rights and the Necessity for Cultural Change." *Focus on Law Studies* 8, no. 1. (fall 1992).

Human Rights Watch. "Hearts and Minds: Post-war Civilian Deaths in Baghdad Caused by U.S. Forces." Vol. 1 No. 9 (E): October 2003.

INS Resource Information Center. *Alert Series Women: Female Genital Mutilation* AL/NGA/94.001.

Ignatieff, Michael. "The Terrorist as Auteur." *New York Times Magazine,* November 14, 2004, 51.

Ishiguro, Kazuo. *The Remains of the Day.* New York: Vantage, 1988.

James, William "The Moral Equivalent of War." In *Morality and War.* Edited by Richard Wasserstrom. Belmont, CA: Wadsworth, 1970.

Jenson, Robert. "Nihilism: Sin, Death, and the Devil." *Newsletter: Report from the Center for Catholic and Evangelical Theology* (summer 1998).

Johnson, James Turner. "Maintaining the Protection of Non-Combatants." *Journal of Peace Research* 37, no. 4. (July 2000): 427–430.

Kant, Immanuel. *Perpetual Peace and Other Essays.* Translated by Ted Humphrey. Indianapolis: Hackett Publishing, 1983.

———. *Religion within the Limits of Reason Alone.* Translated by Theodore Green and Hoyt Hudson. New York: Harper and Brothers, 1960.

Kateb, George. "The Adequacy of the Canon." *Political Theory* 30, no. 4 (2002): 482–505.

———. *Hannah Arendt: Politics, Conscience, Evil.* Totowa, NJ: Rowman and Allanheld, 1984.

Kelly, George Armstrong. "A General Overview," *The Cambridge Companion to Rousseau.* Edited by Patrick Riley. Cambridge: Cambridge University Press 2001.

Kelsay, John. "Islam and the Distinction of Combatants and Non-Combatants." *Cross, Crescent, and Sword: The Justification and Limitation of War in Western and Islamic Tradition.* Edited by James Turner Johnson and John Kelsay. Westport, CT: Greenwood Press, 1990.

Kelsen, Hans. *What Is Justice?* Berkeley: University of California Press, 1957.

Kenyatta, Jomo. *Facing Mount Kenya: The Tribal Life of the Gikuyu.* New York: Vintage Books, 1965.

Keohane, Nannerl. O. "'But for her sex . . .': The Domestication of Sophie." In *Trent Rousseau Papers.* Edited by Jim MacAdam et al. Ottawa: University of Ottawa Press, 1980.

———. "'The Masterpiece of Policy in Our Century': Rousseau on the Morality of the Enlightenment." *Political Theory* 6, no. 4 (November 1978): 457–484.

Kershaw, Ian. *Making Friends with Hitler: Londonderry, the Nazis and the Road to World War II.* New York: Penguin, 2004.

Kingswell, Mark. *A Civil Tongue: Justice, Dialogue, and the Politics of Pluralism.* University Park: Pennsylvania State University Press, 1995.

Knight, Mary. "Curing Cut or Ritual Mutilation?" *Isis* 92, no. 2 (June 2001): 317–338.

Koestler, Arthur. *Darkness at Noon.* Translated by Daphne Hardy. New York: Modern Library, 1941.

Koonz, Claudia. *The Nazi Conscience.* Cambridge, MA: Harvard University Press, 2003.

Konstan, David. *Pity Tranformed.* London: Duckworth, 2001.

Lakoff, Sanford. *Equality in Political Philosophy.* Cambridge, MA: Harvard University Press, 1964.

Laqueur, Thomas. "Four Pfennige per Track km." *London Review of Books.* 4 November 2004, 7.

Lear, Jonathan. *Happiness, Death and the Remainder of Life.* Cambridge, MA: Harvard University Press, 2000.

Levy, Michael B. *Political Thought in America.* 2d ed. Prospect Heights, Illinois: Waveland Press, 1992.

Lightfoot-Klein, Hanny. *Prisoners of Ritual: An Odyssey into Female Genital Mutilation.* Birmingham, NY: Haworth Press, 1989.

Locke, John. *Of the Conduct of the Understanding.* In *Some Thoughts Concerning Education and Of the Conduct of the Understanding.* Edited by Ruth W. Grant and Nathan Tarcov. Indianapolis: Hackett, 1996.

Machiavelli, Niccolo. *The Prince and the Discourses.* Introduction by Max Lerner. New York: Modern Library, 1950.

MacIntyre, Alasdair. *Whose Justice? Which Rationality?* Notre Dame: University of Notre Dame Press, 1988.

Mackie, Gerry. "Ending Footbinding and Infibulation: A Convention Account." *American Sociological Review* 61 (December 1996): 999–1017.

Marks, Jonathan. "The Savage Pattern: The Unity of Rousseau's Thought Revisited." *Polity* 31, no. 1 (fall 1998): 75–106.

Marshall, David. *The Surprising Effects of Sympathy: Marivaux, Diderot, Rousseau and Mary Shelley.* Chicago: University of Chicago Press, 1988.

Mason, John Hope. *The Indispensable Rousseau.* London: Quartet Books, 1979.

Masters, Roger. *The Political Philosophy of Rousseau.* Princeton: Princeton University Press, 1968.

Mathewes, Charles. *Evil and the Augustinian Tradition.* Cambridge: Cambridge University Press, 2001.

McCabe, Herbert. "Evil." In *God Matters.* Springfield, IL: Templegate Press, 1991.

Melzer, Arthur M. "Rousseau and the Modern Cult of Sincerity." In *The Legacy of Rousseau.* Edited by Clifford Orwin and Nathan Tarcov. Chicago: University of Chicago Press, 1997.

———. *The Natural Goodness of Man: On the System of Rousseau's Thought.* Chicago: University of Chicago Press, 1990.

Menand, Louis. *The Metaphysical Club: A Story of Ideas in America.* New York: Farrar, Straus, and Giroux, 2001.

Milbank, John. *Theology and Social Theory: Beyond Secular Reason (Signposts in Theology).* Oxford: Blackwell, 1990, 1993.

Milgram, Stanley. *Obedience to Authority: an Experimental View.* New York: Perennial, 1974.

Mill, John Stuart. *On Liberty.* Indianapolis: Bobbs-Merrill Co., 1956.

Mitchell, Richard P. *The Society of the Muslim Brothers.* New York: Oxford University Press, 1993.

———. "The Islamic Movement: Its Current Condition and Future Prospects." *The Islamic Impulse.* Edited by Barbara Freyer Stowasser. London: Croom Helm, 1987.

Monoson, S. Sara. *Plato's Democratic Entanglements: Athenian Politics and the Practice of Philosophy*. Princeton: Princeton University Press, 2000.

Moore, Jr., Barrington. *Moral Purity and Persecution in History*. Princeton: Princeton University Press, 2000.

Moscovici, Serge. *Social Influence and Social Change*. London: Academic Press, 1976.

Moussalli, Ahmad S. *Moderate and Radical Islamic Fundamentalism: The Quest for Modernity, Legitimacy, and the Islamic State*. Gainesville: University Press of Florida, 1999.

Musalo, Karen, Jennifer Moore, and Richard Boswell. *Refugee Law and Policy: Cases and Materials*. Durham, NC: Carolina Academic Press, 1997.

Nagel, Thomas. "War and Massacre." In *War and Moral Responsibility*. Edited by Marshall Cohen, Thomas Nagel, and Thomas Scanlon. Princeton: Princeton University Press, 1974.

Neal, Patrick. *Liberalism and Its Discontents*. New York: New York University Press, 1997.

Neiman, Susan. *Evil in Modern Thought: An Alternative History of Philosophy*. Princeton: Princeton University Press, 2002.

Nietzsche, Friedrich. *The Gay Science with a Prelude in Rhymes and an Appendix of Songs*. Translated by Walter Kaufmann. New York: Random House, 1974.

Nozick, Robert. *Anarchy, State and Utopia*. New York: Basic Books, 1974.

Occupation Watch Center, Baghdad and National Association for the Defense of Human Rights in Iraq. *Joint Report on Civilian Casualties and Claims Related to U.S. Military Operations* (January 2004). Available at http://www.civicworldwide.org/pdfs/compensationreport.pdf.

Okin, Susan Moller. *Women in Western Political Thought*. Princeton: Princeton University Press, 1979.

Orwell, George. "Reflections on Gandhi." In *A Collection of Essays*. Garden City, NY: Doubleday and Co., 1954.

Packer, Corinne. *Using Human Rights to Change Tradition*. Antwerp: Intersentia, 2002.

Phillips, Adam. *The Beast in the Nursery*. New York: Pantheon, 1998.

Popkin, Jeremy D. "Robert Darnton's Alternative (to the) Enlightenment." In *The Darnton Debate: Books and Revolution in the Eighteenth Century*. Edited by Haydn T. Mason. Oxford: Voltaire Foundation, 1998.

Popper, Karl. *The Open Society and Its Enemies*. 2 vols. London: Routledge, 1945.

Population Reference Bureau. *Abandoning Female Genital Cutting: Prevalence, Attitudes, and Efforts to End the Practice*. Washington, DC: Population Reference Bureau, August 2001.

Power, Samantha. *A Problem from Hell: America and the Age of Genocide*. New York: Basic Books, 2002.

Protocol to the African Charter on Human and Peoples' Rights on the Rights of Women in Africa. September 13, 2000. Available at http://www.hrea.org/erc/library/display.php?doc_id=806&%20category_id=31&category_type=3.

Qutb, Sayyid. *Milestones*. Chicago: Kazi Publications, 1993.

———. *Social Justice in Islam*. Translated by John B. Hardie. Oneonta, New York: Islamic Publications International, 1953.

Rahman, Anika and Toubia, Nahid. *Female Genital Mutilation: A Guide to Laws and Policies Worldwide.* New York: Zed Books, 2000.

Rawls, John. *Political Liberalism.* New York: Columbia University Press, 1993.

———. *A Theory of Justice.* Cambridge, MA: Belknap Press of Harvard University, 1971.

Raz, Joseph. "Multiculturalism: A Liberal Perspective." *Dissent* 41 (1994): 67–79.

Reaves, Malik Stan. "Alternative Rite to Female Circumcision Spreading in Kenya." Africa News Service (November 19, 1997), Available at http://allafrica.com/stories/200101080370.html.

Reisert, Joseph. *Jean-Jacques Rousseau: A Friend of Virtue.* Ithaca: Cornell University Press, 2003.

Renteln, Alison Dundes. *The Cultural Defense.* New York: Oxford University Press, 2004.

———. *International Human Rights: Universalism versus Relativism.* Newbury Park, CA: Sage, 1990.

Reynolds, James "Nobody is going to live forever." *BBC News,* July 16, 2004. Available at http://news.bbc.co.uk/go/pr/fr/-/1/hi/world/middle_east/3899015.stm.

Riley, Patrick, ed. *The Cambridge Companion to Rousseau.* Cambridge: Cambridge University Press, 2001.

Rodin, David. "Terrorism without Intention." *Ethics* 114 (July 2004): 752–772.

Rosenbaum, Ron. *Hitler: The Search for the Origins of His Evil.* New York: HarperCollins, 1999.

Rousseau, Jean-Jacques. *The Discourses and Other Early Political Writings.* Edited by Victor Gourevitch. Cambridge: Cambridge University Press, 1997

———. *The Confessions and Correspondence Including the Letters to Malesherbes.* Translated by Christopher Kelly, edited by Christopher Kelly, Roger D. Masters, and Peter G. Stillman. Hanover, NH: University Press of New England, 1995.

———. *Collected Writings of Rousseau.* Translated by Judith R. Bush, Christopher Kelly, and Roger D. Master. Hanover, NH: University Press of New England, 1990.

———. *Emile.* Translated by Allan Bloom. New York: Basic Books, 1979.

———. *The Government of Poland.* Translated by Willmoore Kendall. Indianapolis: Bobbs-Merrill Co., 1972.

———. *The First and Second Discourses.* Edited by Roger D. Masters. Translated by Roger D. and Judith R. Masters. New York: St. Martin's Press, 1964.

———. *Oeuvres Complètes.* Edited by Bernard Gagnebin and Marcel Raymond. Paris: Gallimard, 1964.

Schaar, John H. "Equality of Opportunity and Beyond." In *Legitimacy and the Modern State.* New Brunswick, NJ: Transaction Books, 1980.

Schmitt, Carl. *The Concept of the Political.* Translated by George Schwab. New Brunswick, NJ: Rutgers University Press, 1976.

Schumpeter, Joseph. *Capitalism, Socialism, and Democracy.* London: Harper and Brothers, 1943.

Scott, John T. "The Theodicy of the *Second Discourse*: The 'Pure State of Nature.'" *American Political Science Review* 86, no. 3 (September 1992): 696–711.

Shklar, Judith. *The Faces of Injustice.* New Haven: Yale University Press, 1990. Reprint edition, 1992.

——. "Jean-Jacques Rousseau and Equality." Reprinted in *Rousseau's Political Writings*. Edited by Alex Ritter and Julia Conaway Bondanella. New York: Norton and Co., 1988.

——. *Ordinary Vices*. Cambridge, MA: Harvard University Press, 1984. Reprint edition 1985.

Shue, Henry. "War." *The Oxford Handbook of Practical Ethics*. New York: Oxford University Press, 2003.

Slack, Alison T. "Female Circumcision: A Critical Appraisal." *Human Rights Quarterly* 10, no. 4 (1988): 445–450.

Smith, Melancton. *The Anti-Federalist*. Edited by Herbert J. Storing. Chicago: University of Chicago Press, 1981, 1985.

Spragens Jr., Thomas. *Civil Liberalism: Reflections on our Democratic Ideals*. Lanham, MD: Rowman and Littlefield, 1999.

Staub, Ervin. *The Psychology of Good and Evil: Why Children, Adults, and Groups Help and Harm Others*. Cambridge: Cambridge University Press, 2003.

Stolzenberg, Nomi. "He Drew a Circle That Shut Me Out: Assimilation, Indoctrination, and the Paradox of a Liberal Education." *Harvard Law Review* 106 (1993): 581–667.

Surin, Kenneth. *Theology and the Problem of Evil*. Oxford: Basil Blackwell, 1986.

Tilley, Terrence. *The Evils of Theodicy*. Washington, DC: Georgetown University Press, 1991.

Tomasi, John. *Liberalism beyond Justice: Citizens, Society, and the Boundaries of Political Theory*. Princeton: Princeton University Press, 2001.

United Nations General Assembly. "Declaration on the Elimination of Violence Against Women." Resolution A/RES/48/104. Available at http://www.un.org/ documents/ga/res/48/a48r104.htm (accessed February 23, 1994).

United Nations Office on Drugs and Crime. "Definitions of Terrorism." Available at http://www.unodc.org/unodc/terrorism_definitions.html.

U.S. State Department. Available at http://www.state.gov/g/wi/rls/rep/9273.html (accessed November 10, 2003).

U.S. Military. Press Release A041005b, "Marines make condolence payments in Najaf," October 5, 2004. Available at http://civicworldwide/compensation/compensation-marines-100504.htm.

Vincent, Steven K. "Benjamin Constant, the French Revolution, and the Origins of Modern Liberalism." *French Historical Studies* 23 (October, 2000): 607–637.

Voltaire. *Candide and Related Writings*. Translated with an introduction by David Wootton. Indianapolis: Hackett, 2000.

Waldron, Jeremy. "Does 'Equal Moral Status' Add Anything to Right Reason?" Paper presented to the American Political Science Association, September 2004.

Waltz, Kenneth N. *Man, the State and War: A Theoretical Analysis*. New York: Columbia University Press, 1954, 1959.

Walzer, Michael. *Just and Unjust Wars.*, 3d ed. New York: Basic Books, 2000.

——. "World War II: Why Was This War Different?" *Philosophy and Public Affairs* 1 (1971): 18–19.

Washington Post poll, August 7–11, 2003. Available at http://washingtonpost.com/
      wp-srv/politics/polls/vault/stories/data082303.htm (accessed July 25, 2004).

Weber, Max. "Politics as a Vocation." In *From Max Weber: Essays in Sociology.* Translated
      and edited by H. H. Gerth and C. Wright Mills. New York: Oxford University
      Press, 1958.

Wetzel, James. *Augustine and the Limits of Virtue.* Cambridge: Cambridge University
      Press, 1992.

Williams, Bernard. *Shame and Necessity.* Berkeley: University of California Press, 1993,
      1994.

Williams, Rowan. "Politics and the Soul: A Reading of the 'City of God.'" *Milltown
      Studies* 19/20 (1987): 55–72.

Wolin, Sheldon. *Politics and Vision,* rev. ed.. Princeton: Princeton University Press, 2004.

World Health Organization. *Female Genital Mutilation: Report of a Technical Working Group.*
      Geneva: WHO, 1996.

———. *Female Genital Mutilation: An Overview.* Geneva: WHO, 1998.

Yacoub, Sameer H., Bassem Mroue, Charles Hanley, Ellen Knickmeyer, Tina Tran,
      Louis Meixler, Sharon Crenson, and Richard Pyle. "Iraqi Civilian Death Tally at
      3,240." *USA Today* (June 10, 2003). Available at
      http://usatoday.com/news/world/iraq/2003-06-11-iraqi-toll_x.htm (accessed on
      October 10, 2005).

Yassin, Sheikh Ahmed. *Al-Hayat.* May 22, 2002.

Yasuaki, Onuma. "In Quest of Intercivilizational Human Rights: 'Universal' vs.
      'Relative' Human Rights Viewed from an Asian Perspective." In *Occasional Paper No.
      2.* San Francisco: Asian Foundation, Center for Asian Pacific Affairs, 1996.

Yeats, William Butler. *The Poems.* Edited by Richard J. Finneran. New York:
      Macmillan, 1989.

Young, Iris. *Justice and the Politics of Difference.* Princeton: Princeton University
      Press, 1990.

Zimbardo, Philip G. "A Situationist Perspective on the Psychology of Evil:
      Understanding How Good People Are Transformed into Perpetrators." In *The Social
      Psychology of Good and Evil: Understanding Our Capacity for Kindness and Cruelty.* Edited
      by Arthur Miller. New York: Guilford, 2004.

Zimbardo, Philip G., Craig Haney, and Christina Maslach. *Obedience to Authority: Current
      Perspectives on the Milgram Paradigm.* Mahwah, NJ: Lawrence Erlbaum
      Associates, 2000.

Name Index